John Templeton Award for Theological Promise

"A stellar contribution. Doyle exposes in masterful fashion how Christian hope, operating on the concupiscent passions and the will and basing itself on faith in a reality 'beyond' the scope of natural reason, can alone sustain the enterprise of bringing God's providential plan for the full development of his creation to completion, because only Christian hope is prepared ahead of time to accept the setbacks, disappointments, and frustrations of a world hemmed in with limitations and sin, by living out this dedication in the cruciform pattern of its Master." —*Heythrop Journal*

The Promise of Christian Humanism

Thomas Aquinas on Hope

DOMINIC DOYLE

A Herder & Herder Book
The Crossroad Publishing Company

The Crossroad Publishing Company
www.CrossroadPublishing.com

© 2011 by Dominic Doyle

All rights reserved. No part of this book may be reproduced, stored in a retrieval system, or transmitted, in any form or by any means, electronic, mechanical, photocopying, recording, or otherwise, without the written permission of The Crossroad Publishing Company.

The stylized crossed letter C logo is a registered trademark of The Crossroad Publishing Company.

In continuation of our 200-year tradition of independent publishing, The Crossroad Publishing Company proudly offers a variety of books with strong, original voices and diverse perspectives. The viewpoints expressed in our books are not necessarily those of The Crossroad Publishing Company, any of its imprints or of its employees. No claims are made or responsibility assumed for any health or other benefit.

Printed in the United States of America.

The text of this book is set in Sabon.

Cataloging-in-Publication Data is available from the Library of Congress

Books published by The Crossroad Publishing Company may be purchased at special quantity discount rates for classes and institutional use. For information, please e-mail info@CrossroadPublishing.com

ISBN 13: 978-0-8245-24692

2 3 4 5 6 7 8 9 10   14 13 12

Table of Contents

Introduction   HOPE AND CHRISTIAN HUMANISM   1
- The Question and an Overview of the Argument
- Method
- The Meaning of "Christian Humanism"

Chapter One   THE RENEWAL OF CHRISTIAN HUMANISM: CHARLES TAYLOR AND NICHOLAS BOYLE   6
- The Christian Humanist Project in the Twentieth Century
  - Christian Humanisms: Past, Present, and Future Orientations
  - Jacques Maritain and the Quest for Synthesis
- Charles Taylor and Nicholas Boyle
  - Taylor's and Boyle's Christian Humanisms
  - Taylor's and Boyle's Christian Humanist Interpretations of Modern Identity
- Conclusion

Chapter Two   THE SOURCES OF CHRISTIAN HUMANISM: THE PROBLEM AND A PROPOSAL   24
- The Limitations of the Contemporary Renewal of Christian Humanism
  - The Limitations of Boyle's Christian Humanism
  - The Limitations of Taylor's Christian Humanism
- A Partial Solution: Jacques Maritain and John Courtney Murray on Faith in the Incarnation
  - Jacques Maritain
  - John Courtney Murray
- A Proposal: Thomistic Hope as Theological Source for Christian Humanism
- Clarification by Contrast: Rowan Greer's *via media*
- Objections to the Proposal
  - Gordon Kaufman
  - Jürgen Moltmann
  - Nicholas Wolterstorff
- Conclusion

Chapter Three **PRESUPPOSITIONS OF AQUINAS'S DOCTRINE OF HOPE** 49

- The Creator-Creation Relationship as Non-competing
  - Creation's Participation in the Creator as the Origin of Its Being
  - Creation's Return to God as the Ultimate Good
- The Natural Desire for God
  - The Intellect's Desire for the Vision of God
  - The Will's Desire for the Absolute Good
  - The "Need" for Grace
- Grace Perfects Nature
  - Grace Moves Human Nature to Its End
  - Grace as Participation in God's Nature
- Conclusion

Chapter Four **AQUINAS ON HOPE** 72

- From Grace to Virtue
- The Passion of Hope
- Hope as an Infused, Theological Virtue
- Hope Distinguished from Faith and Charity
  - Specification
  - Faith
  - Hope
  - Charity
- Hope Related to Faith and Charity
- Conclusion

Chapter Five **HOPE AND RELIGIOUS TRANSCENDENCE** 96

- From Religious Transcendence to Theological Hope
- Faith, Hope, and Charity as the Potency, Motion, and Act of Christian Humanism
  - The Meaning of Hope as *motus*
  - Hope's Motion as the Process of Actualizing the Humanistic Potency of Faith
  - Charity as the Act, or Culmination, of Christian Humanism
  - Benefits of Understanding Faith, Hope, Charity as the Potency, Motion, Act of Christian Humanism
- The Existential Significance of Specifying Transcendence as Hope
  - The Way of Transcendence as Cruciform
  - The Goal of Transcendence as Eschatological
- Conclusion

Chapter Six   **HOPE AND THE PRESENT HUMAN GOOD**   **119**
- Eschatological Hope Protects and Sustains Secular Hopes
  - Eschatological Hope Protects Secular Hopes
  - Eschatological Hope Sustains Secular Hopes
  - Despair Reveals Hope as the Underlying Modality of Secular Action
- Secular Hopes Participate in Eschatological Hope as the Means of Its Realization
  - Clarification by Contrast: *Spe salvi* on the Relationship between Eschatological and Secular Hopes
  - Eschatological Hope Orders Secular Hopes to Their Transcendent Goal
  - Secular Hopes Constitute the Means of Eschatological Hope's Realization
- How Secular Hopes Prepare the Person for God: Two Examples
  - The Fourth Commandment
  - The Fourth and Fifth Beatitudes
- Hope in the World: Not Resignation but Re-Creation
  - Not Resignation …
  - … but Re-Creation
- Conclusion

Conclusion   **THE HUMANISM OF HOPE**   **145**
- Addressing the Conflict of Interpretation over Vatican II
- Fundamentalism: Substituting Security for Hope

Select Bibliography   154

Notes   163

Index   226

Endcards   232

Abbreviations

Comp. theol.	*Compendium theologiae*
De pot.	*Quaestiones disputatae De potentia*
De spe	*Quaestiones disputatae De virtutibus, quaestio 4*
De ver.	*Quaestiones disputatae De veritate*
In ad I Tim.	*Super I Epistolam ad Timotheum*
In ad Eph.	*Super Epistolam ad Ephesios*
In Post. Anal.	*Expositio libri Posteriorum Analyticorum*
In III Sent.	*Scriptum super Libros Sententiarum III*
SCG	*Summa contra gentiles*
ST	*Summa theologiae*

For my parents,
John and Geraldine Doyle,
with love and gratitude

Permissions

The Scripture quotations contained herein, with the exception of the epigraph, are from the New Revised Standard Version Bible, copyright © 1989 by the Division of Christian Education of the National Council of the Churches of Christ in the U.S.A., and are used by permission. All rights reserved.

Parts of chapter six draw upon material in my article "*Spe salvi* on Eschatological and Secular Hope: A Thomistic Critique of an Augustinian Encyclical," *Theological Studies* 71/2 (June 2010), 350–79. Copyright © Theological Studies, Inc., 2010.

Parts of chapter one and parts of the conclusion draw upon material in my article "Retrieving the Hope of Christian Humanism: A Thomistic Reflection on the Thought of Charles Taylor and Nicholas Boyle," *Gregorianum* 90/4 (2009), 699–722. © 2009 Gregorian & Biblical Press, Roma.

The quotation from Emily Dickinson on page 18 is reprinted by permission of the publishers and the Trustees of Amherst College from THE POEMS OF EMILY DICKINSON: VARIORUM EDITION, edited by Ralph W. Franklin, Cambridge, Mass.: The Belknap Press of Harvard University Press, Copyright © 1988 by the President and Fellows of Harvard College. Copyright © 1951, 1955, 1979, 1983 by the President and Fellows of Harvard College.

Acknowledgements

Writing this book taught me a lot about hope. Now that it is finished, I want to thank those who helped me along the way. Michael Buckley, S.J., directed the earlier dissertation version with such rigorous attention and kind encouragement that I consider myself most fortunate to have come under his guidance. I cannot thank him enough for his support and friendship. The readers, Stephen Pope and Stephen Brown, gave invaluable feedback, both during and after the dissertation stage. I am grateful to the Department of Theology and to the Graduate School of Arts and Sciences at Boston College for their financial assistance while a doctoral student, including the award of a Fortin Grant. I am also grateful to the following members of the theology faculty: Lisa Cahill, Charles Hefling, David Hollenbach, S.J., Frederick Lawrence, and especially Michael Himes for his friendship and wise advice.

The following people gave helpful feedback on parts of the book: John Bowlin, Romanus Cessario, O.P., Grant Kaplan, James Keenan, S.J., Benjamin King, Philip McCosker, John Moffat, S.J., Anna Moreland, John O'Malley, S.J., Charles Matthewes, Howard Rhodes, Michael Rota, John R. Sachs, S.J., Stephen Schloesser, S.J., Denys Turner, and Jeremy Wilkins. Matthew Levering went beyond the call of duty to read the whole manuscript. I am especially grateful to Nicholas Boyle and Charles Taylor for their comments on my representation of their work. I am also grateful to Eamon Duffy and Sarah Coakley, my mentors at Cambridge and Harvard respectively, for their support and advice over the years, and to John Jones, my editor at Crossroad, for soliciting this work and shepherding it to completion with grace and humour. Thanks are due, too, to the members of the Catherine LaCugna Award Committee of the Catholic Theological Society of the America for selecting an earlier draft of chapter 1 as the winner of the 2008 award, and to the evaluators of the John Templeton Award for Theological Promise for selecting this book as one of the 2010 awardees.

I must also thank my colleagues at the theologate formerly known as Weston Jesuit School of Theology, now incorporated into the School of Theology and Ministry at Boston College. They are a model of support and encouragement for junior faculty beginning a career in teaching and research. It is a great honor to work alongside them in the intellectual apostolate of the Church. I am grateful, too, for the granting of a sabbatical to complete this project.

I owe a huge debt to the following three friends: Andrew Stead, Howard Rhodes, and Ben King. I doubt that I would have completed this project without them. I am also immensely grateful to Jill Macdonald and to Christopher Jamison, O.S.B., as well as to the Benedictine community of Worth Abbey, who have welcomed me on numerous occasions, and the Jesuit community at Campion Hall, Oxford, who housed me during the final push. Thanks are also due to the following friends for their conversation and company over the years: Shekhar Aiyar, Gareth Evans, John Hardt, Brian Hughes, Niamh Lynch, Madhavi Menon, Rich Miller, Michael and Anna Moreland, Matt Petillo, Chris Ross, Shmoo Swaroop and, last but not least, Tracy Wanner, who is living proof for me of Aquinas's argument that hope can blossom into love.

Finally, I want to give thanks for the uncountable blessings of having such a close family and for learning there something about what unconditional love means. My siblings—Edmund, Patrick, Catherine, and John—have been wondering for some time what I have been up to in the States all these years. I hope the following gives them some idea. For reasons that will be obvious in my discussion of Aquinas's reflections on the fourth commandment, I dedicate this book to my parents, John and Geraldine Doyle.

Introduction

HOPE AND CHRISTIAN HUMANISM

The Question and an Overview of the Argument

There is nothing modest or timid about the hope that Christians bear in their hearts. It seeks nothing less than happiness that will last for eternity and that cannot be broken or taken away by any more suffering or injustice. It therefore endures difficulty as it supports believers through those events they wish had not happened. But this same hope also rejoices, finding in present but passing joys a foretaste of future and unending happiness. It expects, however opaquely, to pass through death to a lasting vision and enjoyment of God.

Because the ultimate goal of Christian hope is radically transcendent and thus impossible to attain by human means, it inevitably raises questions as to its relationship with ordinary life here and now. These questions become criticisms when such hope deflects attention from redressing injustice and counsels passive resignation instead. In these circumstances, Christian hope is often condemned for undermining commitment to the needs of this world. Indeed, at the heart of modern atheistic humanism lies the assumption that belief in God harms humanity: Hope for God acts as a powerful solvent on the demands and joys of the present. Divine action and human freedom compete in a zero-sum game. More of one means less of the other. Thus, to aspire to any sort of humanism, to advocate the dignity and freedom of the human person, one must reject Christianity.[1]

Christian humanism argues the exact opposite. It claims that the more one comes to understand and love what is authentically human, the more one will resonate with the good news proclaimed by Christianity. Conversely, the deeper one enters into Christian discipleship through prayer and good works, the more one fulfills the natural human desire to understand and to love. Why? Because the gospel presents God as a lover of humanity (Titus 3:4) who did not create the world in vain, but so that it might be lived in (Isa. 45:18), and that its inhabitants might have abundant life (John 10:10). Indeed, Christian humanism believes Jesus Christ embodies this love so perfectly that in him God and humanity are intimately united. Christian faith in the Incarnation therefore entails a relationship of direct, not inverse, proportion between the divine and the human. More of one does not mean less of the other. Divine love does not compete with human longing, but completes it. On the basis of these convictions, Vatican II's "Pastoral Constitution on the Church in the Modern World," *Gaudium et spes*, asserts that "nothing that is genuinely human fails to find an echo in the hearts ["of the followers of Christ"],"[2] and that "it is only in the mystery of the Word made flesh that the mystery of humanity truly becomes clear."[3]

So runs, in bare outline, the nineteenth- and twentieth-century dispute between atheistic and Christian humanism. At the heart of this disagreement lies the following question: Does belief in a transcendent God help or hinder human flourishing in the world? The goal of this book is to explore how contemporary Christian humanism is responding to this question as it enters the twenty-first century, and to develop adequate theological sources for that response.

For the idea of Christian humanism has been powerfully retrieved in our day by two of the most widely respected Catholic intellectuals, Charles Taylor and Nicholas Boyle. Their penetrating analyses of two far-reaching and critical developments—secularization and globalization—offer new ways to understand Christian identity in the modern West. Relying more on Hegel than on Aquinas, their work marks a significant development in the Christian humanist project from more Thomistically inspired, mid-twentieth-century authors, such as Jacques Maritain and John Courtney Murray (chapter 1). Writing as cultural critics and philosophers, however, they understandably do not say everything that could be said about the theological sources of a renewed Christian humanism. Crucially, the connection between the desire for religious transcendence and the commitment to the present human good requires development. To articulate that connection, I propose that the classical grounds of Christian humanism—namely, faith in the doctrine of the Incarnation, which Maritain and Murray articulated so clearly—be broadened to include the theological virtue of hope, understood by Thomas Aquinas as the desire for the future, difficult, yet possible, good of eternal happiness with God. This hypothesis, however, is not without problems, since important contemporary theologians, such as Jürgen Moltmann and Nicholas Wolterstorff, judge Aquinas's doctrine of hope to be irrelevant to any substantial Christian account of human flourishing now (chapter 2).

To counter these objections, I present three basic Thomistic presuppositions that convey the humanistic spirit pervading Aquinas's theology: first, the broad metaphysical vision of the non-competitive, participation relationship of creation to Creator; second, the specific philosophical claim of a natural human desire for God; third, the classic Thomistic theological axiom that God's grace perfects human nature. In general terms, these presuppositions undercut the objections to using Aquinas's notion of hope in support of Christian humanism (chapter 3). But whether in fact Thomistic hope, specifically, provides theological support requires a detailed examination of this virtue. I therefore offer an exegesis of Aquinas's understanding of Christian hope. And since hope forms but a part of the triad of the three theological virtues, I situate it amidst its flanking virtues of faith and charity in order to give a more complete account of its meaning and function within Aquinas's theological system (chapter 4).

In the last two chapters, I apply Aquinas's understanding of hope to the problem of contemporary Christian humanism. I argue that hope gives theological depth and substance to the transcendence Christian humanism would promote, not least by specifying that transcendence as cruciform and eschatological (chapter 5). But precisely because of the realistic and radical nature of that transcendence, hope can sustain the concern for the temporal human good. Furthermore, it incorporates those secular longings into the comprehensive movement to God as the very means whereby the believer attains the goal of eternal happiness (chapter 6).

By uniting the desire for religious transcendence with a commitment to the present human good, hope securely grounds the contemporary renewal of Christian humanism. It deepens the theological resources upon which Christian humanism can draw, moving from a doctrinal appeal to the Incarnation to a personal appropriation of the cross. It therefore awakens the promise of Christian humanism to transform the difficulties and sufferings of this world by opening us to love in the way that Christ loved, which, when all is said and done, is the best witness to his resurrection.

Method

The six chapters of this book divide into three parts. The first part (chapters 1 and 2) introduces the contemporary renewal of Christian humanism, identifies the problematic nature of its theological sources, and advances a hypothesis to address that limitation. The second part (chapters 3 and 4) provides a general and then a specific exegesis of Aquinas's thought as it relates to the hypothesis and as it meets the objections that others have posed. The third part (chapters 5 and 6) applies Aquinas's understanding of hope to the question of contemporary Christian humanism's theological sources. In bringing an urgent question of today to a great text of the past, this inquiry is less an exegesis (despite comprising exegetical parts) and more what Hans-Georg Gadamer calls a "fusion of horizons," in which a classic text sheds light on a current debate, even while our understanding of that text may itself undergo development as it is submitted to questions previously unasked.[4] This study may therefore be called, following W. Norris Clarke, a "creative appropriation" of Aquinas.[5] It is based on, but not limited to, an exegesis. And while some of my developments of Aquinas are not found explicitly in his text—for the questions posed by a contemporary Christian humanism are not necessarily his—I nonetheless believe they are continuous with his thought.

This book is therefore not a comprehensive and genetic study of all Aquinas's writings on hope.[6] Instead, it focuses on his most thorough and mature exploration—questions 17–22 of the *secunda secundae* in the *Summa theologiae*—and that section's place within the treatise on the theological virtues. While some of his earlier discussions will be mentioned for support or clarification by contrast, it is assumed that the *Summa theologiae* provides Aquinas's most considered and developed understanding of hope.

Finally, it should be noted that Aquinas's views, despite their ecclesiastically sanctioned prominence within the Catholic tradition, are not the single, authoritative Catholic account of hope. That tradition exhibits a pluralism of understanding, from which one could have selected other distinctive and influential treatments beyond Thomas and his commentators. For example, John of the Cross and Karl Rahner offer significant reformulations of Aquinas's understanding of hope, which (in another study) could be explored for their convergence and contrast with Thomas's views.[7] But in order to set manageable limits, this inquiry focuses on Aquinas's text. It is his understanding of hope that provides the guiding hypothesis of this study and, I will argue, gives critical theological support to the contemporary renewal of Christian humanism.

The Meaning of "Christian Humanism"

Before beginning this investigation, a semantic distinction must be drawn between two meanings of the term "Christian humanism": historical and systematic. In historical terms, humanism is most commonly associated with the intellectual and pedagogical movement of the Renaissance that, originating with Petrarch in the fourteenth century, focused upon classical literature.[8] That return *ad fontes* sought to unite rhetorical eloquence with practical wisdom, and so inculcate a sense of political service dedicated to the common good. In theological settings of that time, it was often contrasted with scholasticism, owing to its literary-critical reading of scriptural sources and its distaste for the abstractions and technicalities of Aristotelian logic and dialectics, fostering instead the internalization of religious sentiments and ideals.[9] This ethos is vividly present in one of the most famous humanists of the age, Erasmus of Rotterdam. Although obviously a powerful stimulus to Reformation ideals, the movement cut across confessional divides, influencing figures as diverse as Thomas More, Philipp Melanchthon, and John Calvin. Some interpreters extend the meaning of the term to include the formation of a humane spirit that leads students to appreciate the greatness of human achievements and, in doing so, allows them to realize more fully their own dignity.[10]

In this book, I focus not on the historical meaning of the term "humanism" in the Renaissance and Reformation, but on its ideational use in systematic theology. This systematic use, while retaining the concerns for practical wisdom, personal appropriation of faith, and the common good, has acquired various and complex meanings throughout the history of theological reflection. The basic idea, however, derives from the claim in the Hebrew scriptures that the human person is created in God's image, "a little lower than God, crowned ... with glory and honor" (Ps. 8:5). This dignity accorded to the human person is magnified through the Christian belief in the Incarnation, the claim that God became human in Jesus Christ out of love for the world. These basic convictions have found theological expression in various ways across the centuries. Perhaps the most famous is Irenaeus's oft-quoted claim of the incarnational grounds of deification, paraphrased thus: "Christ became human so that humans might become what he is himself."[11] From this central appreciation of the Incarnation flows his strikingly positive assessment of the theological significance of the *humanum*: "The glory of God is a living human person."[12] What is less well known—but critically important for any genuinely Christian humanism—is that Irenaeus immediately goes on to claim that "the life of the human person, however, is the vision of God."[13] In medieval theology, the Christian humanist impulse appropriated Aristotle's philosophical account of human friendship to describe the person's union with God.[14] Thomas Aquinas himself provides one of the central axioms of Christian humanist thought: "Grace does not destroy nature, but perfects it."[15] Consequently, the Christian humanist enterprise aspires to some form of synthesis: intellectually, between faith and reason; and socially, between church and culture. In modern theological reflection, it resists the atheistic humanist claim that belief in God harms the human. This ideational, systematic use of the term "Christian humanism" reflects its primary meaning in this book.

Chapter One

THE RENEWAL OF CHRISTIAN HUMANISM: CHARLES TAYLOR AND NICHOLAS BOYLE

The Christian Humanist Project in the Twentieth Century

From some quarters, it may look as though the conversation about Christian humanism has run its course. It no longer provides a widely chosen medium to express and advance theological ideas, as it did in the preconciliar heyday of Christopher Dawson, Jacques Maritain, and John Courtney Murray. Its signature document, *Gaudium et spes*, has been charged with naïve optimism.[16] Other movements, such as liberation theology and radical orthodoxy, have since captured the theological imagination. More challengingly, the ever-greater use of cultural studies in theology undercuts any talk of "the human" as some timeless, universal essence. Aware of the manifold expressions of Christian belief across time and space, theologians can no longer straightforwardly appeal to the pleasing generalities of Christian humanism.

Nonetheless, two leading Catholic intellectuals, Charles Taylor and Nicholas Boyle, frame their powerful critiques of modernity in the terms of Christian humanism. That theological choice raises some interesting questions. Do they genuinely retrieve, and not merely repeat, earlier versions? Do they rework the idea such that it offers a distinctive contribution to contemporary theological reflection?

Christian Humanisms: Past, Present, and Future Orientations

The newness of Taylor's and Boyle's Christian humanism can be gauged by the following broad comparisons with two previous influential Christian humanists, Christopher Dawson and John Courtney Murray. These comparisons reveal significant differences in the temporal foci of their work—that is, the times to which these thinkers look for the adequate social expression of Christian belief. For Dawson, it was the past achievement of Christendom; for Murray, it was the (then) present coherence, intellectual and social, of the Catholic community in the post–World War II United States; for Boyle and Taylor, it is the new identities that may emerge from, respectively, the transition to a worldwide economic system and Christianity's encounter with a deeply engrained secularism.[17] Although these thinkers are far too complex to be neatly pigeonholed, these characterizations nonetheless capture something of how they understand the task of Christian humanism as either recreating what is past, manifesting what is present, or realizing what is to come.

For Christopher Dawson, the temporal focus was the past. Although by no means a restorationist, he repeatedly contrasted the spiritual depth and social cohesion of medieval Christian culture with the divisions of modern nationalism and the dehumanization of mass society. Drawing on premodern humanistic and Christian influences (for example, Greek philosophy, the life of St. Francis, the thought of Aquinas, and the art of Dante), he advocated a Christian humanism that alone does justice to the unity and spiritual dignity of humanity.[18] His Gifford lectures of 1948–49, *Religion and the Rise of Western Culture*, charted the emergence and flourishing of the Christian Middle Ages out of the barbaric "Dark Ages." Written shortly after another period of barbarism, they concluded with the question, "What have we done with this inheritance [of a "Christian culture ... the common inheritance of Western man"]?" The answer: "At least we have *had* it."[19] And since we have had it, we should not give up hope that we may have it again. Thus, ten years later, as Europeans sought to repair the damage of two world wars, Dawson entitled the final chapter of his *Understanding Europe* "The Problem of the Future: Total Secularization or a Return to Christian Culture." This chapter concludes a section of the book called "The Present Crisis of Western Civilization."[20] When the present is in crisis and the future is a problem, then the past understandably becomes more attractive and its faults can be charitably overlooked.[21]

If Dawson's temporal focus was the past, John Courtney Murray's was the present, as befits a figure caught up in the triumphalism of mid-twentieth-century American Catholicism. His scholastic training had already taught him that the purpose of theology was to mount "a triumphantly argumentative defense of the faith against error."[22] Coupled with Murray's exceptional rhetorical gifts, his confidence in Catholic thought captured, even heightened, the "Catholic moment" in the post–World War II U.S. In 1951, he asserted that

> the present task of Catholics is to work toward the purification of the liberal tradition ... and of the democratic form of state in which it finds expression, by restoring both the idea and institutions of democracy to their proper Christian foundations.[23]

American Catholics thus stand ready to assume "guardianship of the original American consensus."[24] Interpret the First Amendment to subordinate church to state, Murray warned, and you will create "immediately in this country some 35,000,000 dissenters, the Catholic community."[25] They are ready to dissent because they know that

> the principles of Catholic faith and morality stand superior to, and in control of, the whole order of civil life. The question is sometimes raised, whether Catholicism is compatible with American democracy. The question is invalid as well as impertinent; for the manner of its position inverts the order of values. It must of course be turned round to read, whether American democracy is compatible with Catholicism.[26]

To paraphrase Murray: Ask not how your church conforms to your country, but how your country shapes up to the church.

The coherence of the mid-twentieth-century U.S. Catholic church, however, owed more to sociological factors than to scholastic logic, as Mark Massa and others have shown.[27] Emerging from a tightly knit immigrant subculture, it had been protected from the social and intellectual forces that had split American Protestantism decades earlier. For a brief moment it combined the cohesion of its origins in the ghetto with the stature of its emergence into the mainstream. But that moment, to which Murray gave such brilliant expression, passed. Catholics discovered that they too were not immune from the "acids of modernity." Only a decade after Murray's confident pronouncements, millions of Catholic dissenters were created—not by secularist readings of the constitution, but by a papal encyclical on contraception. (And as for those educational institutions that facilitated their social elevation, U.S. Catholics cannot even agree on which of them are *really* Catholic.) For better or worse, the present is not what it used to be.

If Murray's temporal focus was the present, then Boyle's and Taylor's is the future. They give sweeping historical accounts of two major transitions—to the global economy (Boyle) and to widespread secularism (Taylor)—that preoccupy contemporary attempts to understand Western identity. Their accounts are not motivated by a desire to remake the past—as if there were some pristine time before these changes to which we might unproblematically return—but to understand the present, in all its complexity and contradiction. The goal of this understanding is to create the conditions for an intelligent and decisive Christian contribution to the ongoing construction of the common good.

Boyle thus writes as a "liberal Catholic humanist," meaning "'liberal' in a political sense, to refer to one who thinks change is inevitable and often for the better."[28] Whatever meaningful identity we have now, in the midst of the dislocations of globalization, derives in large part from the identity we envisage for the future, by which we hope to see the transition to a global economy managed equitably. We therefore need educational institutions whose "concern is not with society as it is at present but with its future, with the standards and ideals by which it will seek to change into something better and with its very capacity for change at all."[29] We can only articulate who we are now if we have some vision of who we want to become.[30] The theological consequences of this sensibility are seen in the concluding pages of his essay "After History: Faith in the Future" (conceived in part as a reply to Francis Fukuyama's "The End of History"), which rejects the return to "some past golden age—in the Christianity of the catacombs, or the Middle Ages, or the recusant period,"[31] and instead seeks to discern a future Christian identity in the midst of current economic realities and social aspirations.

Taylor's thought shares a similar accent on the future. He rejects nostalgic appeals to Christendom[32] and uncovers deep "cross pressures" in contemporary belief that destabilize triumphant calls for Christianity to restore a civilization of the past or defend democracy in the present. But because contemporary unbelief faces analogous dilemmas, new forms of belief may emerge and challenge the "immanent frame" of secular modernity. Thus, Taylor advocates "new and unprecedented itineraries" for faith,[33] which "refuse paradigmatic status to … one historically-embedded order of Christian life."[34]

By their openness to the future, Boyle and Taylor eschew restorationism (which comes with an accent on the past) and triumphalism (which comes with an accent on the present). Thus, they stand closer to Maritain than to Dawson or Murray, by seeking to move Christian self-understanding and social expression towards something as yet unrealized.[35] They are heirs to Maritain's *Integral Humanism*, which sought to articulate a new, post-Christendom social vision explicitly in terms of Christian humanism. In a crucial section of that classic book, "Statement of the Problem: Medieval Christendom and a New Christendom," Maritain asserted the "radical irreversibility of historical movement."[36] The fact of new cultural conditions emerging in history, coupled with the belief in providence working in and through time, bars any attempt to "immobilize in a past form … the ideal of a culture worthy to be the end of our action."[37] In a word, "medieval civilization … has borne its fruit,"[38] and it is time to elaborate "a Christian historical ideal capable of existing and inviting existence under a new historical sky."[39]

To understand Maritain's presentation of that ideal requires a brief account of the social context in which it was developed. This closer examination in turn sets the stage for exploring the very different social context that shapes the expression of Christian humanism today.

Jacques Maritain and the Quest for Synthesis

The Christian humanist vision, as noted in the introduction, has markedly synthetic aspirations, seeking to reconcile faith with reason and church with culture. In Thomas Aquinas, Maritain believed he had found the intellectual source for nothing less than the "task of universal integration."[40] No recondite scholastic, he sought to give social expression to this synthetic vision. He even conceived his popular 1930 book on Aquinas as "a kind of Thomist manifesto, especially directed to the French Catholic public."[41] Happily, the cultural needs of many in that public resonated with these synthetic ideals. Stephen Schloesser's brilliant study of the post–World War I French Catholic revival, *Jazz Age Catholicism*, situates Maritain within that movement's attempt to go beyond the nineteenth-century opposition between Catholicism and the modern world (exemplified in Pius IX's 1864 *Syllabus of Errors* and the Modernist crisis at the turn of the century).[42] The oppositional spirit of Ultramontanism emphasized the dualisms of unchanging eternity versus temporal progress, church versus republic, religion versus science, metaphysics versus reductive materialism, and so on. Many post–World War I French Catholics, on other hand, were susceptible to the attempt to reconcile Catholicism and modernity. For not only had church and state reconciled in the face of a common enemy during the First World War, but the trauma of conflict itself created the need for what Schloesser calls a "mystic realism"[43]—that is, a "realism" that would squarely face the enormity of loss and reject the previous generation's myth of a "liberal rationalism" that was believed to have caused it; but also a *"mystic realism"* that, unlike nineteenth century positivism, allowed for the spiritual dimensions in which the 1914 generation could mourn for, and find meaning in, seemingly meaningless events. As part of the postwar Catholic revival, Maritain's integral humanism was received into a French Catholic culture seeking the synthesis he provided.

Schloesser traces how Maritain's synthetic genius voiced the needs of this post–World War I generation primarily in the realm of aesthetics, especially in his 1920 *Art and Scholasticism*, which combined traditional metaphysics with avant-garde formalist (nonmimetic) art. These new and strange artistic forms, Maritain argued, could be accepted by Catholics on the grounds of the very traditional scholastic theory of hylomorphism. For it is precisely the transcendence of "eternal forms ... [that] allowed for [their] universal incarnation in different matter"—or different times. By thus connecting the stability of the ancient Catholic tradition with the artistic groping towards new forms that could do justice to the trauma of wartime experience, the cultural synthesis of the Catholic revival enabled the mourning of the 1914 generation.

Maritain continued and expanded this synthetic impulse into the realm of social philosophy, especially in his 1936 *Integral Humanism*. Maritain proposed not a return to past Christendom, but a construction of a new Christendom, characterized by integral humanism, which retained the eternal truths of Christian faith but poured them into the new wineskin of democratic, pluralist politics. "The supernatural idea of this humanism would no longer be that of God's *sacred empire* over all things, but the idea of *holy freedom* of the creature whom grace unites to God."[44] This new style of Christian civilization articulates a very different political theology from the *Sacrum Imperium* of medieval Christendom. Instead of a unity imposed from above for the construction of a holy empire, there is instead a minimal, organic unity of orientation that proceeds from a shared aspiration for a "common life that is best in accord with the supratemporal interests of the person."[45] If the Christian monarch was the agent of unity in yesterday's city, argued Maritain, today that task falls to the most politically aware and spiritually devout Christian citizens, who do not constrain their fellows by force of law, but influence them by moral example. Furthermore, because it is *integral* Christian humanism, it remains firmly attached to its theological origins when honoring the claims of justice. It therefore promotes what Maritain called a "new style of sanctity" that intends the "socio-temporal realization" of the gospel. And so, as with the aesthetic synthesis, Maritain attempted to bring the enduring ideas that once animated traditional Catholic social forms (such as the transcendent dignity of the human person) into the democratic, pluralist social forms of modernity.

Maritain's aesthetic synthesis, however, differs significantly from this social synthesis. The primary function of the aesthetic synthesis was to give a measure of cultural ratification to a social reality in France: namely, the rapprochement of the traditionalism of the Catholic Church with the modernism of the post–World War I generation. The goal of his social synthesis, on the other hand, was to give philosophical guidance amidst political fragmentation across Europe. For while the aesthetic synthesis in the early 1920s gave meaning to what had just happened, the social synthesis arose from the need to avoid what, after the success of German fascism in 1933, looked increasingly likely to happen. Its goal was not to heal a culture war lingering in France, but to prevent a real war looming over Europe.

To address these more demanding exigencies, Maritain extended the range of his synthetic method. His *Integral Humanism*, written while the Spanish civil war was being fought, strove to incorporate the socialist emphasis on the common good of justice with the liberal emphasis on the natural right of the individual. After World War II and the ensuing cold war, his 1951 *Man and State* expressed that personalist vision in terms of a *via media* between the communist collectivism of the East and the capitalist individualism of the West. Throughout these endeavors, Maritain strove to present a vision of social life that synthesized elements often opposed, most notably, the recognition of the person's eternal destiny with the demand for his or her material improvement:

> The dualism of the preceding age is at an end. For the Christian, separatism and dualism have had their day.... An important process of integration is taking place in our time, by a return to a wisdom at once theological and philosophical, a return to a vital synthesis.[46]

At the heart of this synthetic vision for the reconstruction of society lay Maritain's Christian humanist insistence on the transcendent dignity of the person, vouchsafed by God's participation through Christ in the common lot of human flesh. It fell to others, such as the Christian democrats in Europe and especially Latin America, to try and realize this vision in political bodies so obviously and destructively divided.[47]

Today, over seventy years after the publication of *Integral Humanism*, enormous political and social changes set a very different context for this Christian vision of the human person. Two of the most significant of those changes are the deepening of secularization and the emergence of the global market. Taylor and Boyle offer interpretations of these major transitions of modern identity and, in their theological reflection upon those changes, bring the Christian humanist project into the twenty-first century.

Charles Taylor and Nicholas Boyle

Before examining Taylor's and Boyle's understanding of Christian humanism, it is important to register the influence of their readings of modern identity. Even those who do not share their faith cannot fail to be impressed by the intelligence of their interpretation of modern Western culture and by the sensitivity with which they describe its joys and hopes, its griefs and anxieties. As a result, each author commands widespread respect. Richard Rorty has dubbed Taylor "among the dozen most important philosophers writing today, anywhere in the world."[48] His early work established his reputation as a leading Hegelian scholar, while his subsequent reflections on modern identity have been so influential that Alan Wolfe has claimed that "for sociologists, there is no more important philosopher writing in the world today than Charles Taylor."[49] His latest work, *A Secular Age*, is, according to David Martin, "a towering achievement ... [that] transforms the secularization debate."[50]

A similarly formidable Catholic Hegelian, as well as a leading scholar of modern German literature, Boyle has written an acclaimed multivolume biography of Goethe.[51] His own reading of modern identity, *Who Are We Now? Christian Humanism and the Global Market from Hegel to Heaney*, presents an erudite and fiercely persuasive defense of Christian humanism. It was Eamon Duffy's choice for book of the year because of its "profound reflection on the crisis of post-modernism and the options for Christian action within it."[52] This prominent historian went on to say that "no cultural theorist since Christopher Dawson seems to me to have Boyle's instinct for the shape and sweep of history, or his unblinking realism." Nicholas Lash has described *Who Are We Now?* as a "marvelously lucid, learned and pugnacious study."[53] Capturing the spirit of these tributes, Fergus Kerr draws the following parallel: "*Who Are We Now?* could do for us today what Maritain's *Humanisme Intégral* did for many Catholics decades ago."[54]

Moreover, the praise does not originate exclusively from Catholic quarters. Rowan Williams considers this "brilliant collection of essays"[55] "one of the most intellectually nourishing books on the Christian social vision for many years,"[56] a judgment shared by John Milbank.[57] Hilary Putnam, of Harvard's secular philosophy department, discusses the book and its author in glowing terms,[58] while Stanley Hauerwas admires this "extraordinary book" in an article more or less in full agreement.[59] When the archbishop of Canterbury, a Jewish pragmatist, and a fiery Texan Methodist concur on the excellence of a book advocating Catholic humanism, the reader may be curious as to its content.[60]

In spite of these impressive recommendations, however, sustained theological reflection on Taylor's and Boyle's powerful retrievals of Christian humanism has been slow to appear.[61] That the authors are significant Catholic intellectuals working outside of professional theological circles invites a response from systematic theologians, who currently pay little attention to the concept.[62]

Taylor's and Boyle's Christian Humanisms

What, then, are the key aspects of Taylor's and Boyle's Christian humanisms? Taylor defines humanism as "a doctrine, a view, or an attitude, which ... understands the nature of man on a model [*Vorbild*] and tries to ground a practical philosophy on that model."[63] As with Renaissance humanism, Taylor's definition combines a philosophical understanding of the person alongside a practical embodiment of that understanding. He rejects the claims of an "exclusive humanism—that is, one based exclusively on a notion of human flourishing, which recognizes no valid aim beyond this."[64] In fact, he identifies himself as one "who feels a connection with some form of Christian humanism"[65] as he rejects both secular humanism[66] and reactionary Christian "anti-humanism,"[67] and forwards instead the notion of the divine "affirmation of human."[68] An early article, "Humanismus und moderne Identität,"[69] discusses themes that became central to *Sources of the Self* and *A Secular Age* explicitly in terms of humanism. There, Taylor presents two theological responses to a modern, secular humanism that overemphasizes the autonomy of human capabilities by dismissing their dependence upon God. The first theological response holds that the emphasis on the human undermines religious belief because it "tends essentially, with regard to its ... inner logic, toward its atheistic variety, [and thus is] unable to find a place for God."[70] The second response, from Christian philosophers such as Jacques Maritain, argues that modern humanism is "an essentially Christian doctrine ... which has been distorted atheistically and requires purification."[71] The difference between these two responses is "one of the focal points of the controversy."[72] Siding with the latter response, Taylor asks whether the wholesale refusal of modern humanism could really be authentically Christian, if we see the world and human existence as good and therefore able to share in God's love. "Men can only love themselves through participation in the love that God pours over them."[73] This striking confession leaves no doubt that the term "Christian humanist" accurately captures Taylor's theological sensibilities.

In this Christian humanist spirit, Taylor recognizes in "Judeo-Christian theism ... its central promise of a divine affirmation of the human, more total than humans can ever attain unaided."[74] That affirmation brings one into contact with

> a love or compassion that is unconditional ... as based on what you are most profoundly, a being in the image of God ... standing among others in the stream of [God's trinitarian] love. [This way of life is possible] only to the extent that we open ourselves to God, which means, in fact, overstepping the limits set in theory by exclusive humanisms. If one does believe that, then one has something very important to say to modern times.[75]

That "overstepping" is a form of transcendence, "a radical decentering of the self in relation to God,"[76] which entails "being called to a change in identity."[77] This authentic connection with the deepest moral source can then sustain the most demanding moral commitments in the world, the commitments to benevolence and justice, because it gives and elicits unconditional love.[78] Taylor's Christian humanism, then, possesses two fundamental and related components: a concern for the human good and an insistence on religious transcendence.

Nicholas Boyle's collection of essays, *Who Are We Now?*, also exhibits the same twofold concern. He explicitly locates his work within the "tradition of Catholic humanism" that is "inspired by the belief that all areas of human life must be reached by the good news and can be bearers of it, and that that is in the nature of the good news itself."[79] It is precisely in this concern for the common human good that we can discover our religious transcendence, because secularity, understood theologically as the radical appropriation of, and engagement with, the world, is

> the process by which the divinity of our human world—our human social and institutional world—is at last consciously grasped: the divine is no longer relegated to special churchy institutions or special churchy parts of life, but our whole life, personal, social, and political, is understood as the product of the divine spirit which breathes through our own free actions.[80]

Like Taylor's, Boyle's Christian humanism registers two fundamental, inseparable claims: a concern for the common human good and a desire for religious transcendence. In fact, for Boyle, the study of the various disciplines that are required to speak intelligently about the common good cannot be divorced from theology. As he ranges across economics, politics, philosophy, and literature in his attempt to understand modern identity, he is "sustained by the belief that these different branches of humane study grow, in the end, from the same theological stem."[81]

Christian humanism, then, is a central and integrating concept for both thinkers: central, because it captures their sense of belonging to the Christian enterprise and provides the lens through which they read the world about them; and integrating, because it aspires to understand that world as a unified whole in which religious conviction permeates all aspects of ethical life. Whereas earlier thinkers sought integration through metaphysics (for example, in a synoptic vision of the "one and the many"), these authors, following the spirit of the age, use cultural studies to seek the intelligible unity across diverse fields of inquiry into human meaning.[82] For both, their Christian humanism aspires to a comprehensive understanding of our contemporary situation—and not unreasonably so, for one cannot talk of God's grace without some understanding of the human order that is to be graced. How, then, do they understand that order?

Taylor's and Boyle's Christian Humanist Interpretations of Modern Identity

The most basic feature of their accounts is that modern identity must be understood historically, as the titles of their relevant works suggest: *Sources* of the Self: The Making of Modern Identity, A Secular Age,* and *Who Are We Now? Christian Humanism and the Global Market from Hegel to Heaney*. Those titles convey none of the ahistoricism of Reinhold Niebuhr's (modestly entitled) *The Nature and Destiny of Man*; nor the restorationism of Aiden Nichols's *Christendom Awake*,[83] nor the purportedly timeless claims of less sophisticated versions of the natural law. For both Taylor and Boyle, identities change. To understand who we are now, we must understand who we were then, and give some account of what brought us from "then" to "now," whether it be from an era of widespread belief in God to a "secular age," or from the reign of imperial nation states to a global economy. We need historical narrative, Taylor observes, because "our past is sedimented in our present, and we are doomed to misidentify ourselves, as long as we can't do justice to where we come from."[84]

This historically sensitive Christian humanist interpretation of modern identity is best seen in concrete discussions. What follows is one example from each thinker that gives specific content to his Christian humanist reading of modern identity. From Taylor, I have selected his theme of "the affirmation of ordinary life"; from Boyle, his reflections on our differing experience of time as consumers and as producers. Each example offers a historically aware interpretation of one feature of modern identity that attempts to hold together both aspects of the Christian humanist enterprise: concern for the human good and promotion of religious transcendence.

Taylor

The example I select from Taylor comes from one of the three sources (as he sees it) of our[85] modern identity: the affirmation of ordinary life.[86] Taylor describes this key aspect of modern selfhood as follows:

> The cultural revolution of the early modern period, which dethroned the supposedly higher activities of contemplation and the citizen life, put the center of gravity of goodness in ordinary living, production, and the family. It belongs to this spiritual outlook [of the affirmation of ordinary life] that our first concern ought to be to increase life, relieve suffering, and foster prosperity.[87]

Although prominent in the Reformation and the Enlightenment, this theme of affirming ordinary life, Taylor argues, was "one of the most fundamental insights of the Jewish-Christian-Islamic religious tradition, that God as creator himself affirms life and being."[88] From this conception of modern identity flow the many benefits of its "ethic of authenticity" (the title of Taylor's shorter rendition of *Sources of the Self*).[89] Among those advances are the ideals of universal benevolence and their political expression in universal human rights.[90] But as in this abridged presentation, originally entitled *The Malaise of Modernity*, Taylor's longer work is no uncritical plug for modernity.[91]

Clearly, as a humanist, Taylor supports the modern affirmation of ordinary human life. But as a Christian, he asks whether this ideal can survive the rise of secularism that also emerges in modernity. For Taylor, that process of secularization, understood negatively as the rejection of religious belief, takes place in the broader context of "disenchantment." Metaphysical horizons that once gave objective frameworks for moral sentiments, he argues, have receded or collapsed.[92] Modern naturalist consciousness has eroded those encompassing ontological claims, such that "we no longer see human beings as playing a role in a larger cosmic order or divine history."[93] "What Weber called 'disenchantment,' the dissipation of our sense of the cosmos as a meaningful order, has allegedly destroyed the horizons in which people previously lived their spiritual lives."[94] The erasure of this "background picture" calls into question the moral and spiritual intuitions that it once sustained. Any coherent discussion of them becomes fraught with difficulty.[95] We therefore live in an age characterized by the "inarticulacy of the good."

Since our identity—our "understanding of who we are, of our fundamental defining characteristics as human beings"[96]—is inseparable from our notion of the good, we find ourselves in the midst of a crisis of identity. A person totally without a fundamental framework, with only a "view from Dover Beach,"[97] would "fall into a life which is spiritually senseless."[98] "He wouldn't know where he stood on issues of fundamental importance, would have no orientation in these issues whatever, wouldn't be able to answer for himself on them."[99] So while our ancestors feared condemnation for failing to conform to a credible and commonly held moral ontology, we sense a pervasive meaninglessness in its absence.[100]

In theological terms, the crucial shortcoming of modern conceptions of identity is the pervasive secularism that denies or suppresses religious experience. By secularization, Taylor means the denial of belief in God and the corresponding desire "to push farther the process of making religion irrelevant in the public sphere."[101] This process of secularization entails a severe narrowing of range in our understanding of the good and a fundamental loss in our corresponding sense of identity. And since "high [moral] standards need strong sources," we cannot reject the strongest Source and still aspire to the best life.[102]

The inadequacies of secularism are contrasted with Taylor's crucially important "hunch" that the "significance of human life" cannot be vindicated in a "non-theistic, non-cosmic, purely immanent-human fashion."[103]

> Secular humanism ... has its roots in Judaeo-Christian faith; it arises from a mutation out of a form of that faith. The question

can be put, whether this is more than a matter of historical origin, whether it doesn't also reflect a continuing dependence.... My belief, baldly stated here, is that it does.

Credible, authentic "moral sources ... seem to me to involve a God. All this remains to be argued out."[104]

I will return to evaluate Taylor's arguments for this assertion, but for now it is enough to note that this line of thinking leads him to qualify his support for one of the key features of modern identity, the affirmation of ordinary life. Rejecting what he calls the "spiritual lobotomy" of secular humanism, he makes a reserved wager at the end of *Sources of the Self* on a theistic position that banks on "a hope I see implicit in Judaeo-Christian theism ... and in its central promise of a divine affirmation of the human, more total than humans can ever attain unaided."[105] With this *divine* affirmation of human life comes an "overstepping [of] the limits set ... by exclusive humanism,"[106] a movement of religious transcendence that challenges some commonly held positions of a contemporary secular culture. For example, the religious conviction that "life isn't the whole story,"[107] that "suffering and death [are] not merely negation," that, as Emily Dickinson puts it, "this world is not conclusion"—this belief contradicts the "widespread inability to give any meaning to suffering and death, other than as dangers to be avoided or combated."[108] Thus, while the affirmation of ordinary life and its concern to relieve suffering are praiseworthy aspects of modern identity, there remains a deep-seated "inability to be content simply with an affirmation of life."[109] Whether it be the experience of beauty in art, the need for reconciliation in politics, or the draw of transcendence in limit situations, something is glimpsed beyond the "immanent frame" that would enclose a secular culture.[110] Indeed, a crucial aim of *A Secular Age* is to show how "our modern culture is restless at the barriers of the human sphere."[111] Authentic human flourishing requires more than the affirmation of ordinary life.

What have we gained from looking at one of the signature aspects of Taylor's reading of modern identity? We have seen him manifest his Christian humanist sensibilities as he affirms, simultaneously, the far-reaching ethical contributions of the theme of the affirmation of ordinary life alongside the insistence that its true value can only be realized in an encompassing movement of religious transcendence.

Boyle

Turning to Nicholas Boyle's reading of modern identity, we find a similar attempt to connect the humanist concern for the common good with the religious drive for transcendence, in this instance, through a more economically grounded analysis. A striking example of this attempt is found in his reflections on our differing experience of time as consumer and as producer, which opens up a religiously significant understanding of selfhood. That analysis requires a short introduction.

For Boyle, the roots of our modern identity lie in the bewildering impact of the transition to a global economy, a particularly acute process for postimperial Europe. As global economic activity intensified and the room for imperial expansion ran out in the 1900s, imperial structures crumbled, at first violently in a futile struggle for hegemony; and, from 1945 onwards, by negotiation and political accommodation of the new economic reality, albeit in the context of the cold war. Only recently did the "Seventy-Five Year War" (1914–1989) between the empires finally come to end, when the attempt of the final empire to isolate itself from the world economy (with a wall) ended in bankruptcy. Throughout this process of globalization, the nation state becomes increasingly irrelevant because the flow of capital and labor disregards its boundaries. Its empires, to which poverty and lucrative overproduction were exported, disintegrate. Imperial privilege then vanishes without underprivileged colonies. Former citizens of a nation, who once took pride in their government's administration of an empire, must now endure that government's austerity measures, which discipline the nation's economy to compete in the ruthless, worldwide market.

The intermediate organizations of civil society, such as professional organizations and local authorities, wilt under these market forces, because they are unquantifiable and "unproductive." Their functions are either transferred to state control or exposed to market rigor. The centralizing state accrues more power in order to ensure efficiency, in particular, by making the workforce flexible, that is, unemployable or mobile. Increasingly atomized individuals are subject to ever more intense bureaucratic monitoring, the purpose of which is to maximize competition. As a result, the economy expands, while the public realm, in which competing interests are rationally and morally adjudicated, shrinks. Consequently, the isolated individuals who must live under this regime no longer find shared purpose in belonging to a nation, engaging in work as a lifelong vocation, or even participating in the "little platoons" of civil associations that give depth and substance to life.

All these formerly stable sources of identity, which stand in the way of economic efficiency, are thus whittled away by market forces. But culture abhors a vacuum. And so those fading identities are replaced by the accumulation and spending of money. The corresponding rise of consumerism gives individuals an intoxicating and seemingly limitless freedom to satisfy their material desires at any moment of the day— freedom, of course, constrained by what the market actually offers and limited to those who have money to spend. As the ideological front of the forces of supply, consumerist ideology, with its myth of infinite supply, hides the fact that we live in a finite world. For while the imperial consumer could export the ever-increasing work orders to the ever-expanding empire, the postimperial consumer must trade in the closed, global system and live off his own labor, not the colonies'. Thus, to think oneself *just* a consumer, as the market culture repeatedly invites us to do, obscures one's status as the producer upon whom these consumerist desires eventually retort. For since consumer and producer are now identical, our desires as consumers (for cheaper goods, longer shopping hours, increased travel, more credit, and so on) revisit us, through the system of exchange, as producers (in the form of job insecurity and pay stagnation, longer working hours, more pollution, deeper debt, and so forth). And so "the more choice we give ourselves as consumers the heavier the chains we forge for ourselves as workers."[112] We can all live like kings, as long as we work like dogs.

Crucial for our purposes is what this consumer identity does to our sense of time. It compresses time to the present moment of consumption, in which the past is irrelevant and the consequences are unexamined—since sellers rarely invite us to consider either the conditions under which the product was made, or the ecological damage or unsustainable debt that our purchases entail.

Boyle's strategy to counteract this truncated understanding of our identity is to bring into sight the neglected producer side of our identity. For consumerist ideology obscures our status as producers in a finite world and thus hides the reality of time. But to call to mind production is to reveal a network of relationships that extend over time. For to produce is to take up some past material and work it into a new form for future use. This temporal process involves gratitude for what is taken up and confidence in what will come.[113] It therefore connects the person across time, transcending the instantaneous point of consumption in which the market hopes to corner the buyer. This awareness and appropriation of the fact that we have to work for a living replaces "the infinite depth of bourgeois personality" that lives as a "refined consumer of the pleasures of existence." It thus punctures the consumerist myth that we make "contact with the [economic] system, like butterflies, only in the moment when we sip from it the satisfaction of our desires."[114]

From this greater awareness of the temporal nature of personal identity flows a broader and more religiously significant conception of the self that is able to resist consumer ideology. It recognizes that the blinkered focus on the act of consumption generates a fragmented, punctual self that sets fewer and fewer limits on what it demands and thus lacks a sense of life as an integrated and bounded whole. Baptized by postmodernism, this consumerist self buys into the mantra of "diversity" that, ironically, tends to level all values except those of the market. Consequently, it hides the fact of our growing economic integration and reduces the possibility of understanding our shared history, not least because history, after all, requires a sense of time. From this sense of time comes an awareness of finitude, an awareness that is often lacking in postmodern thought. As Boyle argues,

> Postmodernism betrays its collaboration with global consumerism in its insinuation that all limitations of [moral commitment and death] can be opened up to infinity—an infinity of desires and satisfactions, of life in the shopping mall, of possible rearrangements of the system of language. To assert the relevance of a Christian humanism to the post-modern world is to take on the task of tracing and counteracting this detachment from finitude—in the theory of language which denies the unique importance of literary realism ... and in the obliteration of the thought of death.[115]

The church is well positioned to help downsize consumer ideology by resisting the atomism of the market, its promotion of individual, materialistic desires, and its denial of limits. More positively, the church cultivates a sense of vocation, such as in the vows of lifelong marriage or celibate orders, thereby counteracting the fragmentation and cupidity of the consumer-driven market. Developing Boyle's analysis, Timothy Radcliffe argues that the church thus creates a cultural space in which vows are understood not as a special *moment* that shows the strength and refinement of one's expressive individualism, but rather as communal statements of trust in a providence that guides one through an unknown future.[116] Furthermore, such vows, which are made *usque ad mortem*, summon up the finitude of our one, bounded, mortal life. By doing so, they help us to see our creaturely status and so allow us to appropriate our Christian identity as *viatores*, as pilgrims, as people who transcend the limits of material desires and finite life in a religiously significant manner.[117]

In ways such as this, the church strives to transform culture through its evangelical witness that, as mentioned above, is "inspired by the [Christian humanist] belief that all areas of human life must be reached by the good news and can be bearers of it."[118] Thus, instead of postmodernism as the guide for these confusing times, Boyle advocates the tradition of liberal Catholic humanism: *liberal*, in the political (and especially Hegelian) sense that change is inevitable and needs to be intelligently evaluated so that our freedom be responsibly exercised; *Catholic*, in its appeal to an international religious authority, respected by the secular order, that expresses the unity of the human moral conscience and defends those noneconomic, local identities that the market ignores; and *humanist*, in its conviction that the good news permeates and perfects all areas of the natural order. The answer to the question "Who are we now?" is that we are future citizens of the one, interconnected world, who intend "the only goal compatible with the rational self-respect of human beings who understand their dependence on each other and on the world that has been given to them: a permanently peaceful global order, freely chosen by all its citizens."[119]

Conclusion

Boyle's Christian humanist interpretation of modern identity, like Taylor's, exhibits the twofold concern for the humanizing influence of Christian beliefs and practices alongside some credible movement of religious transcendence. They both therefore stand in the tradition of Maritain's integral humanism, because their religious aspiration to a life of meaningful prayer and credible sanctity is integrally related to—and only truly realized through—some form of commitment to the present good of the world. But because of the different historical conditions in which they write, they give correspondingly different social expression to the basic synthetic aspiration of Christian humanism.

Living through the beginning stages of the Seventy-Five Year War, Maritain wrote at a time when society was so obviously and perilously split between two blocs, capitalist and communist.[120] He therefore shaped the synthetic impulse of Christian humanism into a personalist vision of a social *via media*, which others subsequently tried to realize. By contrast, Boyle, living through the end stages of the Seventy-Five Year War, writes at a time when the individual members of the postimperial global economy, who are increasingly united with each other, fail to see the contradiction—between consumer and producer—at the heart of their self-image. He therefore shapes the synthetic impulse of Christian humanism into a call to recognize and reconcile that internal conflict. Thus, while Maritain proposed a future vision of a social synthesis that remained unrealized in his time, Boyle gives a present account of an economic contradiction that remains unrecognized in ours. Correspondingly, Boyle's appeal to democracy stems not only from the claim that it is a superior *idea*, as Maritain argues on the basis of its recognition of freedom. Rather, democracy's appeal rests also on its fundamental mechanism of voting, by which freedom is given institutional expression.[121] In particular, voting is understood as the point at which one seeks to reconcile (albeit provisionally) the contrary impulses of one's desires as a consumer and one's needs as a producer. For to vote is to choose where to apply the state's monopoly of force: either to increase one's choices as a consumer (for example, by deregulating markets and enforcing labor flexibility, thereby providing more and cheaper goods) or to extend one's protections as a worker (for example, by regulating the conditions of labor and raising taxes for broader health care, thereby providing greater security in and for work). By bringing this contradiction to awareness, Boyle thereby creates the possibility for reconciling it in some Christian, humanistic synthesis that is both informed by the conviction of the transcendent dignity of the human person and engaged with concrete political and economic realities.

One could point to an analogous development of the synthetic principle in Taylor's understanding of the sociology of religion. In his analysis of the contemporary situation of secularization, it is less the case that there are two discrete groups, believers and unbelievers, but rather that members of each group—if indeed they identify clearly with one group, which cannot be assumed—feel the draw of the other. Hence, both are "cross pressured" and need to bring that internal contradiction to awareness if they are to hope for some workable synthesis between concern for the human good and openness to authentic transcendence.

Christian humanism's synthetic impulse, then, has taken on a different style in Taylor's and Boyle's reflections. Shorn of nostalgic appeals to past greatness or triumphant invocations of present strength, their retrieval recognizes that Christians, like everybody else, are subject to the bewildering impact of globalization, and, more than most, to the solvent effects of secularization. To chart a way forward amidst the perplexity left in the wake of these forces, Taylor and Boyle draw more on the thought patterns of Hegelianism than Thomism, in order to identify debilitating contradictions, rather than to offer a reassuring synthesis. For it is only when those painful tensions, personal and social, are faced and understood that they might yield a new, more credible synthesis of being, in our time and conditions, at once fully Christian and fully human.

Chapter Two

THE SOURCES OF CHRISTIAN HUMANISM: THE PROBLEM AND A PROPOSAL

The work of Taylor and Boyle represents a distinct development in, and promising revival of, the Christian humanist tradition. Their reflections on the common good—whether on the affirmation of ordinary, secular life or on the experience of meaningful time in a consumer culture—gesture towards the enveloping movement of religious transcendence in which such ethical concerns must finally be set. But gestures do not tell the whole story. Closer inspection invites further questions and can even reveal assumptions or omissions that require explanation or completion. For while Taylor and Boyle significantly advance the project of Christian humanism, both their accounts, at critical points, require further theological elaboration. In particular, the connection between religious transcendence and the human good remains, at times, unclear or incomplete. To address that problem, I return to the more theologically trained mid-twentieth century authors. Two of the most influential among them, Jacques Maritain and John Courtney Murray, ground Christian humanism explicitly upon faith in the Incarnation, the belief that the Word became human in Jesus Christ out of God's great love for the world. While Taylor and Boyle advert to this doctrinal source of Christian humanism,[122] Maritain and Murray spell out this dependence. Consequently, their thought reinforces the contemporary retrieval of Christian humanism by its sustained attention on the doctrinal paradigm for the relationship between sacred and secular.[123]

Despite the crucial contribution of Maritain and Murray, however, the appeal to faith in the Incarnation does not exhaust the theological sources of Christian humanism. The tradition of Christian humanism, after all, encourages the internalization of religious ideals and the construction of the common good. One must therefore cast a wider net beyond doctrinal assent. I shall propose that Thomas Aquinas's account of the virtue of hope strengthens the theological sources of a Christian humanism that must meet the challenges so acutely diagnosed by Taylor and Boyle. I will then clarify this proposal by way of contrast with another reflection on Christian hope offered by Rowan Greer. Finally, I register some objections to this proposal from influential contemporary theologians who see Aquinas's doctrine of hope as irrelevant, even harmful, to a contemporary Christian humanism. In the chapters that follow, I will develop and defend the hypothesis outlined here.

The Limitations of the Contemporary Renewal of Christian Humanism

The Limitations of Boyle's Christian Humanism

To locate an important area in which Boyle's Christian humanism could benefit from theological elaboration, one must first briefly recall his account of literature that is presented in the final section of *Who Are We Now?* Realistic literature, for Boyle, reveals our sense of self in the local situations that are buffeted by global forces and where personal identity finally resides. It often prepares the way for explicit Christian belief by its common presupposition that each individual has a meaningful personal history. In particular, it describes how purposeful work and personal love can fulfill the time before death, because that death is believed to be transcended. Such literature portrays our secular life—our finite, historical life in the world—as possessing a uniqueness and absolute importance because it is understood in the context of an eternal destiny. It thus bestows upon the secular a relative autonomy or distinctiveness from the sacred that is to be "reclaimed by God."[124] This secular space, the proper sphere of the literary artist, creates room for the fuller expression of the nature which grace is to perfect.

The modern forms of exploring this secularity are the realistic novel and lyric poetry. Both can honestly and accurately depict—and therefore help sustain—that part of our identity that is not overrun by market forces. For example, Gerard Manley Hopkins in particular exhibits that "tragic moral tension" between poetic and priestly vocations, "between sharing in a world that needs redemption and sharing in the [cruciform] agency that is to redeem it."[125] Among the twentieth-century poets, Seamus Heaney gestures towards this sense of secularity. His series of sonnets on his mother's death, "Clearances," explores how being can be revealed through a limit experience of loss and absence.[126] Although not explicitly Christian, it is, like much of his poetry, modulated by the background presence of the sacraments. And while it could not be accused of "tragic tension," his work nonetheless exhibits a Stoic integrity that refuses compromise with the world, perhaps most clearly in his justly famous poem from *The Haw Lantern*, "From the Republic of Conscience":

> When I landed in the republic of conscience ...
> No porters. No interpreter. No taxi.
> You carried your own burden and very soon
> your symptoms of creeping privilege disappeared....
> Their embassies ... were everywhere
> But operated independently
> And no ambassador would ever be relieved.[127]

With admiration for noble sentiments such as these, Boyle concludes his final essay (in a book that would make a stirring manifesto for such a republic) with the following reflection on the prospects of the Christian humanist enterprise and its contribution to our understanding of modern identity:

> The tradition of Christian humanism, even detached from its origins, is old and honorable. The title-poem of [Seamus Heaney's] collection *The Haw Lantern* tells how the hawthorn with its berry "takes the roaming shape of Diogenes / with his lantern, seeking one just man." In the global market Diogenes may have a long search. But Heaney's own example shows us how even in our time it is possible to seek oneself to be just, and that in the end is enough identity for anybody.[128]

But is that "enough"? The closing words of the penultimate essay assert that "only a Christian literature can show us ... who we are," while the subsequent essay, which is to support that claim by articulating "The Idea of Christian Poetry," concludes with the assertion just quoted—that "to seek oneself to be just ... is enough identity for anybody." This yields an odd position for a book advocating Christian humanism: namely, that the distinctive contribution of Christian literature is to reveal the sufficiency of a natural virtue for one's personal identity. At the heart of this tension lies an inadequate differentiation between nature and grace, between secular goodness and religious holiness. In particular, Boyle's emphasis on "secularity" is, as it stands, too accommodating to a Christian humanism that is "detached from its origins."[129]

While the Christian honors the natural virtues,[130] especially justice, she honors more the theological virtues of faith, hope, and charity, which transcend human nature and unite the believer to God. No doubt Boyle occasionally emphasizes the theological underpinnings of a Christian humanism and its literature,[131] and criticizes writers who marginalize them.[132] But any account of the identity of a Christian humanist that fails to integrate the theological virtues is insufficient, for they are the central concepts by which the graced life is described.[133] More pointedly, they allow the meaningful history presupposed by any humanistic literature to be seen and loved in its eternal destiny.

To be fair, Boyle remarked after the publication of the book that it "only intends to knead the issues into such a shape that they are ready for theological consideration."[134] The task for the theologian, then, is to complement Boyle's preparation of the materials by reuniting Christian humanism with its theological origins. Only then might a "republic of conscience" more accurately set its bearings to become a community of saints.

The Limitations of Taylor's Christian Humanism

Before taking up that task, one must first note an analogous shortcoming in Taylor's thought, expressed prior to the publication of *A Secular Age*, and then identify—in order to develop—the trajectory he takes in *A Secular Age* that begins to address that shortcoming. As mentioned, Taylor suggested that credible, authentic "moral sources ... seem to me to involve a God."[135] But that "hunch," although repeated,[136] is never explored at any length.[137] The incompleteness in Taylor's account of the theological context for moral action is most evident in the conclusion of *Sources of the Self*, which explores "the spiritual possibilities in today's culture."[138] There, he judges the "natural humanist" position to be "defective" because it denies the deep moral sources that religious experience offers.[139] More importantly, the modern ideal of universal benevolence may not survive the rejection of the religion that provided the model for that universal benevolence, namely, Christianity.[140] Remove Christian *agape*, Taylor suggests, and one may find one's benevolence "conditional on a vision of human nature in the fullness of its health and strength" that could exclude the "irremediably broken, such as the mentally handicapped" from its care.[141] Thus, "the potential for a certain theistic perspective is incomparably greater" since it has the "moral sources which might sustain our rather massive professed commitments in benevolence and justice."[142]

But this "incomparably greater" theistic perspective receives a mere three pages at the end of the book (which is over five hundred pages long). Even then, it is introduced with a powerful warning of its potential for evil. The perennial corruption of religion would seem to commend "a sober, scientific-minded, secular humanism," in which "prudence constantly advises us to scale down our hopes." But, in the final analysis, Taylor rejects the counsel of secularism on the principle that *abusus non tollit usum*:

> Adopting a stripped-down secular outlook, without any dimension of radical hope in history, is not a way of *avoiding* the dilemma, although it may be a good way to live with it.... It involves stifling the response in us to some of the deepest and most powerful spiritual aspirations that humans have conceived. This ... is a heavy price to pay.[143]

The task, then, for contemporary Christian humanism is to develop Taylor's embryonic recognition of a hope that "affirms"[144] human nature. As Fergus Kerr notes, "Taylor ... works with a surprisingly pared-down theology in his ... profound attempt to rehabilitate an understanding of sources for the self that are irreducibly other."[145] Russell Hittinger, too, finds grounds to "suspect that there is a theology that is crucial to, and yet left inarticulate in, Taylor's treatment of these issues."[146] Thus far, Taylor offers only a generalized religious humanism rather than a theologically informed Christian humanism.[147] But, as he himself admits, the particularities of a religious tradition have more transformative power than the generalities of a Nathan the Wise.[148]

Thus, while the ideal of Christian humanism is clearly a strong influence on Taylor's thought, it is fair to say that its theological grounds are not thoroughly explored. One cannot, of course, blame a philosopher for not being a theologian. And, to be fair, *Sources of the Self* was "philosophical discourse" and therefore addressed to "thinkers of any and all metaphysical and theological commitments."[149] But one can nonetheless detect a hesitation to pursue theological lines of inquiry that his own position entails—so much so that there exists a serious disjunction between, on the one hand, the importance of religious convictions for his reflection on the human good and, on the other hand, the brevity with which he articulates them. This contradiction has not gone unnoticed.

One critic scorns Taylor for presenting the reader with his theistic "hunch, without making any attempt to show us that it amounts to more than whistling in the dark."[150] Bernard Williams suggests that Taylor appears to claim that the skeptic "who is trying to understand [religious] values historically must simply accept the religious belief as their ultimate source, and agree that no further explanation is necessary or possible."[151] Worse, Williams concludes, "though Taylor inhabits, unlike many philosophers, what is clearly and vigorously planet Earth ... his calculations still leave it being pulled out of orbit by an invisible Being."[152] Another critic, responding to Taylor's Marianist Award lecture, asserts that, according to Taylor, "to acknowledge the transcendent, then, is to acknowledge the capricious will of God—something that is more important than either the practical conditions of everyday life or one's own needs and desires. One in effect devalues (or renounces) the ideal of promoting human welfare in favor of upholding God's will."[153]

The fairness or accuracy of these comments is not the issue. They simply indicate that the absence of any systematic theological grounds for Taylor's Christian humanism leaves some wondering why "his theistically inspired moral vision is itself a compelling source for moral motivation."[154] For less charitable critics, the claim that God has anything to do with the human good is met with incredulity. So the failure to spell out the connection between God's grace and human moral action inevitably fuels the suspicion that to rely on God's help is to warp your humanity.

To answer these charges, one must examine what Christian theologians have actually said about that fundamental reliance upon God and why they think such a dependency does not contradict the human good. Only then can one appreciate why personally appropriating these theological claims does not distort one's identity. On the contrary, one can begin to see how such an appropriation fulfills it—or, at least, how it means that one walks through the bitter valley not whistling in the dark, but making it a place of springs (Ps. 84).[155]

At nearly eight hundred pages, *A Secular Age* begins that process as it explores the contemporary "conditions of belief." By "conditions of belief," Taylor means the "whole context of understanding in which our [modern Western] moral, spiritual or religious experience and search takes place,"[156] most fundamentally, a context where "belief in God is no longer axiomatic." This primary meaning of secularity is distinguished from political meanings, whereby religion is largely removed from public, especially state, bodies. This political meaning may or may not involve another, more philosophical sense of secularity, whereby religious belief and practice are explicitly rejected. Thus, a secular age, in Taylor's primary meaning of secularity, is one in which, as a serious and widespread option, human flourishing can be restricted to immanent, human goals. (A religious age, by contrast, is one which recognizes and cultivates the need for some transcendence beyond these goals.) By highlighting secularity in this sense, Taylor exposes the dilemmas and cross-pressures felt by modern believers and unbelievers alike. For believers, one dilemma involves the recognition that belief often becomes less stable when it is no longer a naïve default option, but rather one option among many; and, further, one that does not, seemingly, lead adherents to noticeably better lives than those of nonbelievers. For nonbelievers, one dilemma involves the continuing appeal of transcendence, albeit in muted or fragmented forms, and in the midst of intellectual and moral convictions that deny any transcendent reality.

At the heart of these tensions lies the key distinction between transcendence and immanence.[157] Once this distinction is made, the crucial question of their relation arises: "How [can we] define our highest spiritual or moral aspirations for human beings, while showing a path to the transformation involved which doesn't crush, mutilate or deny what is essential to our humanity?"[158] Throughout the book, Taylor explores this key question from a variety of historical perspectives, arguing that the desire for transcendence can, in principle—and often does, in practice—deepen and transform human flourishing. Expanding his tentative claim at the conclusion of *Sources*, Taylor offers a more sustained argument for grounding modern moral commitments on theological sources of motivation.[159] While there frequently remain difficult tensions between transcendence and immanence, Taylor denies any "constitutive incompatibility."[160] Thus, Christianity is not a closet Platonism that denies the body, but rather, at its best, is the personal and social embodiment of God's compassion shown in Christ.[161] Even the renunciation of human goods for a transcendent goal aims to help others flourish or to lead one to a deeper happiness with God.[162] In a significant shift in vocabulary from *Sources of the Self*, *A Secular Age* thus reformulates the theological project as God's "transformation"—not just "affirmation"—of the human.[163]

The distinction between transcendence and immanence, then, lies near the heart of Taylor's argument.[164] But since his primary goal is to give a phenomenological and cultural description of the emergence of secularization, not a theological critique of its current manifestation, he does not give an extended analysis of this distinction. Nonetheless, Taylor's argument in places reveals a significant debt to theology. In obvious ways, Taylor's discovery of the thought of René Girard (not mentioned in *Sources*) allows him to overcome his previously hesitant appeal to theological ideas: positively, by arguing that "the only way fully to escape the draw towards violence is to enter ... the full-hearted love of some good beyond life";[165] and negatively, to criticize the compromised reality of actual Christian communities on internal, theological grounds.[166] But in less obvious ways, too, one finds important theological developments in his work. For example, in a telling addition to the otherwise verbatim reproduction of most of *Modern Social Imaginaries* in chapters 3, 4, and 5 of *A Secular Age*, he adds a crucial theological dimension to his argument. During a discussion of what the calls the "great disembedding" (from the premodern sense of a social and cosmic participation in a divinely saturated hierarchical order geared towards human flourishing), Taylor adds four and a half paragraphs not found in *Modern Social Imaginaries*.[167] The burden of this surprising addition is to show how the intrusion of the idea of *creatio ex nihilo* disrupts this "felt synthesis" between self, cosmos, and God.[168] Since the Creator God is now sharply differentiated from the cosmos, human flourishing is relativized. But, once again, this does not entail the neglect of the human good. To the contrary, because the cosmos is believed to have been made by a transcendent Creator, evil cannot now be accepted as a part of its inevitable order, but rather must be removed or transformed as its unintended imperfection. Consequently, the very recognition of the transcendent God entails a commitment to the human good.

In a much later discussion towards the end of the book, Taylor tips his theological hand as he gives a concrete example of this dynamic from the other end of the creative process. The Christian narrative of forgiveness offers a "vertical" or eschatological dimension of trust and reconciliation. Inhabiting that narrative can transform the "horizontal" calculations of justice that dominate purely immanent attempts to fix a rational moral code for social relations. It therefore opens up the possibility "to forgo the satisfactions of retribution, or the security which comes from keeping a distrustful distance from the neighbor. It involves people bonding in a new way."[169] In this respect, Taylor furthers Boyle's discussion of the place of justice in contemporary identity, by situating it squarely within the religious experience of eschatological hope in a transcendent God, a hope that does not merely affirm existing social relations, but transforms them.

Between *Sources of the Self* and *A Secular Age*, then, there emerges a theological insight that would shore up Taylor's previously tentative articulation of Christian humanism. How can one consolidate this breakthrough and substantiate his "hunch" about a decisive connection between the desire for the common good and the drive for religious transcendence?

The rest of this chapter takes up that question. It identifies and elaborates specific elements in the theological tradition that are especially well suited to support and sustain the contemporary revival of Christian humanism. Such elements would bring greater theological coherence to the project of Christian humanism and would prevent the adjective from detaching from its noun. For without more explicit anchoring in the tradition, the appropriation of this Christian humanist reflection on contemporary culture may drift from the central texts and claims of Christianity; without a firmer theological foundation, it may sink into the practices and norms of its surrounding culture, to the point where its Christian identity diminishes in the search for contemporary relevance.

A Partial Solution: Jacques Maritain and John Courtney Murray on Faith in the Incarnation

The task of reuniting Christian humanism with its theological origins must surely begin with the doctrine of the Incarnation. Aquinas himself sees in the assent to this doctrine the heart of distinctively Christian faith. His comments on a key text in John's gospel—when Christ says: "Believe in God, believe also in me" (John 14:1)—are revealing:

> Here also the Lord presupposes something of faith, namely, faith in the one God (when he says "you believe in God") and commands something else, namely, *faith in the Incarnation,*

through which one person is God and man. This explanation of faith pertains to the faith of the New Testament. And therefore he adds, "and believe also in me."[170]

Thus, for Aquinas, "our faith principally consists in two things: first, in true knowledge of God, according to Hebrews 11:6 ...; and secondly in the mystery of the Incarnation of Christ, according to John 14:1."[171] This additional component of belief in the Incarnation adds to faith, at one and the same time, its Christianity and its humanism, because the extra dimension believed in is precisely Christ's humanity and its union with God. As heirs to the Thomist tradition, Maritain and Murray give complementary accounts of how faith in this central doctrine constitutes the basic source from which any Christian humanism must flow.

Jacques Maritain

Maritain's *Integral Humanism* conspicuously derives its Christian humanism from the doctrine of the Incarnation and, by doing so, clarifies the connection between moral action and religious belief. It advocates not just "humanism, but theocentric humanism, rooted where man has his roots, integral humanism, humanism of the Incarnation."[172] Why? Because "it is only in the mystery of the redeeming Incarnation that the Christian perceives the dignity of the human person, and what that dignity costs. The idea he has of it ... attains its absolutely full meaning only in Christ."[173] It is on this basis, Maritain argues, that a new Christendom can be built.

Maritain advances his proposal for a new Christendom during a broad historical survey that begins with the dissolution of medieval Christendom. The anthropocentric scission of Renaissance humanism was a reaction to the reformers' pessimistic notion that grace operates, initially, without freedom and, subsequently, without vivifying the believer.[174] "For pessimism detaches the creature from any link with a higher order. And then, *as one must in any event live*, the creature takes his ease and makes himself the center, in his own lower order itself."[175] The human person becomes detached from her "transcendent vivifying principle"[176] and there results a secular civilization which "*separates itself* progressively from the Incarnation ... [and] passes from the cult of the God-man ... to the cult of humanity, of sheer man."[177] The modern humanist, at least initially, considers man naturally good and, reversing the reformers' position, believes in freedom without grace. There results a dualism, "the disassociation of the things of God from the things of the world"[178] and "an age of humanism separated from the Incarnation."[179]

But this dualism cuts both ways. Just as a humanism separated from Christ becomes idolatrous, so a church disengaged from secular life becomes incredible—because it fails to participate in the divine love of the world that the Incarnation manifests:

> The Christian world of modern times has failed in that duty [i.e., of the "socio-temporal realization of the Gospel"]. In general it has shut up the truth and the divine life within a limited part of its existence, within the things of worship and religious practice.... Matters of social and economic and political life it has abandoned to their own carnal law, withdrawn from Christ's light.[180]

As a response to this political irrelevance of Christianity, Maritain advocates a new Christendom characterized by integral humanism. With its greater awareness of "the temporal office of the Christian," it would foster a new style of sanctity directed towards the profane, secular order:[181]

> Doubtless metaphysical anguish, the great anguish of Augustine and Pascal, will always play its part in the human search for God. Yet it seems that in the present situation of mankind it is rather through the actual experience of the basic conditions for personality, justice, freedom, respect and love for our fellow man, that ordinarily we shall be led to the rediscovery of God.[182]

To be sure, the kingdom is an eschatological idea; but "what will come after time is prepared by time."[183] And so "the deepest requirement of a new age of civilization, to the extent to which Christianity inspires it, will be the sanctification of secular life."[184]

By sanctifying secular life, Christians participate in the same love by which "God so loved the world that he gave his only Son" (John 3:16). It is this divine love, embodied in the Incarnate Word, that sustains humanistic care for the world. Moreover, the very union of divine and human in the Incarnation means that secular loves cannot be detached from God. As Maritain argues, to focus on the temporal office of the Christian does not negate the spiritual one. The sociotemporal mission of the Christian is ordered to a transcendent goal. "It prepares for man the terrestrial conditions of a life into which sovereign love can descend and make in man and with him a work divinely human."[185] Such divinely human work makes Maritain's humanism *integral*, because it remains firmly attached to its theological origins when honoring the claims of justice.

> To abstract from Christianity, to put God and Christ aside when I work at the things of the world [is] to cut myself into two halves.... In reality, the justice of the gospel and the life of

> Christ within us want the whole of us, they want to take possession of everything, to impregnate all that which we are and all that which we do, in the secular as well as in the sacred.[186]

So while the common task of the earthly city is to realize a fraternal community, it does so in the context of the more fundamental aspiration to create the conditions for the gospel "to penetrate everything, to take possession of everything, to make its way into the innermost recesses of the world."[187]

By reintegrating humanistic moral demands with the Christian spiritual sources cast aside by modernity, this new Christendom awakens "a cultural and temporal force of Christian inspiration able to act on history and to be a support to men."[188] While conceding the truth in Marx's jibe—"It is easy to be a saint when one has no wish to be human"—Maritain retorts: "But did Marx think therefore that it is easy to be human when one does not wish to be a saint? This would be then the great lie of atheistic humanism: because we are born to tend to the perfection of love ... which is called sanctity."[189] To work for the concrete human good now, then, should not suppress the desire for holiness; to the contrary, that work sets the conditions in which holiness can be realized. Underlying this nuanced relationship between the human good and religious transcendence is a deliberate and careful attempt to preserve the integrity of, and distinction between, the spiritual and the temporal (or secular).[190]

By focusing on the doctrine of the Incarnation, Maritain powerfully restates Christian humanism's classic theological grounds. That intimate and ordered union of humanity with God offers a paradigm from which to articulate a more integrated understanding of the Christian love for the world and the ordering of that secular love to its transcendent goal. As in the classical doctrine of the hypostatic union, the divine and human are united but not confused, and humanity is taken up and perfected by its very union with divinity. On this doctrinal basis, Maritain offers a more precise differentiation between, and hierarchical ordering of, nature and grace. Consequently, one glimpses how Seamus Heaney's "republic of conscience" (which Boyle would baptize a little too quickly) can be transposed into more satisfactory theological terms. For Maritain envisages "a sort of Christian diaspora, a Christendom not grouped and united in a homogeneous body of civilization, but spread over the whole surface of the globe like a network of centers of Christian life disseminated among the nations."[191] This diaspora acts as the leaven by which a "republic of conscience" becomes a community of saints.

But one might still ask whether faith in a doctrine can sufficiently inform a Christian humanism that is shot through with the call to action, to the sociotemporal realization of the gospel. Can another influential mid-twentieth-century Catholic—who was trained in systematic theology, wrote extensively on ethical issues, and confidently promoted the idea of Christian humanism—give fuller theological grounds?

John Courtney Murray

One of Murray's key essays on Christian humanism sports the title: "Is it Basket Weaving? The Question of Christianity and Human Values." Its opening quotation from Pius XII expresses the underlying resonance between human values and Christian faith:

> The profession of Christian truth ... [is] indissolubly bound up with the sincere and constant assertion of human nature's most authentic and exalted values.... True religion and profound humaneness are not rivals.[192]

Murray's comment on this assertion indicates his doctrinal understanding of the foundation of Christian humanism: "This statement touches firmly ... upon the perennial problem of Christian humanism. The problem itself is transtemporal because it is doctrinal."[193] The doctrine in question, which is the source of this mutual implication of humanity and religiosity, is the Incarnation. Murray's succinct, yet imprecise, definition of the Christian humanist draws directly on this doctrine's modeling of the divine-human relationship.

> The Christian humanist [is] the man who, in the image of Christ, respects and develops in himself the two natures, divine and human, and who makes of them a unity.[194]

Because the exemplar, Christ, was fully human, "our affirmation of human nature must be equally total and sincere."[195] Echoing an ancient tradition that stems at least from Irenaeus, Murray asserts that "it is to the Word of God made Flesh that humanity owes its pride in being human, its joy in human life, and its dreams of ever fuller humanity."[196] This doctrinal foundation, then, makes "integral humanism ... our ideal."[197]

What, though, beyond these programmatic statements, is the precise nature and extent of this doctrine's foundational role? At times, it seems the sole foundation. For example, in a discussion of Christian educational theory (whose role is "simply to assist humanity in the realization of itself"), Murray asserts that "the Christology of Chalcedon is its *sole and sufficient* justification."[198] But in another essay, on "The Construction of a Christian Culture," that exclusive foundational role is qualified. There, the Incarnation is offered as the first "creative principle" of a Christian culture.[199] Given Murray's definition of culture as "man's efforts to be fully human,"[200] the doctrine of the Incarnation can be seen as one (but not the only) creative source which empowers the believer to be fully human.

The exclusive foundational role of the Incarnation is similarly qualified in a reflection on Christ's passion entitled "The Humanism of the Cross."[201]

> Christology dictates that the first step in our program of humanism must be the great act of self-abnegation which the naturalist refuses to make: we must lose ourselves to find ourselves; we must go out of humanity in order to possess it; to be human, we must consent to be made divine. Integral humanism is not solely a personal achievement; it is initially a gift from God, the gift of His own Spirit who sets upon us the seal, the character, of Christ. When Christ is formed in us, then we shall be men.[202]

It is the doctrinal convictions of Christology, then, that "dictate the first step" of Christian humanism. Beyond this initial step of self-abnegation, there is required the further step of "self-fulfillment" in being conformed to Christ through the gifts of the Holy Spirit. One senses here the beginning of the answer to the question that arises from Murray's brief definition of Christian humanism: How does one make a unity of the divine and human elements in the believer? It is, Murray acknowledges, "unquestionably ... [the] most difficult task."[203] But tasks pertain to practical inquiry, and difficulty, as we shall see, is central to hope.[204] Thus, one can develop Murray's incipient account by broadening the search for the sources of Christian humanism *beyond* faith's intellectual acceptance of the doctrine of the Incarnation *to* hope's practical embodiment of that belief in the concrete willing of the believer.

Despite his interests in moral questions, however, Murray does not fully develop this practical component of the foundation of Christian humanism. The only virtues he enumerates in this context are "confidence" in "doctrinal affirmations" and "prudence" in practical advice to the world.[205] Doctrinal nerve and worldly savvy are, of course, good things to have. But Christian humanism needs a more distinctively *theological* ethic that combines the Christianity of the first with the practicality of the second. It would account for how a Christian acts *qua* Christian while in the world, rather than as one who acts in the world while happening to be a Christian. This is not to deny that Murray has shown how doctrinal thoughts guide the Christian as she acts. It is simply to point out that he did not describe those doctrinally informed acts in their own right. The faithful thoughts on which the Christian should act are one thing; the quality of those acts *qua* action is another.

This overview of Murray's Christian humanism has drawn on a number of essays written over several years, addressed to different audiences, and engaging different problems. A recurring theme, though, has been the foundational connection between the Incarnation and Christian humanism. Murray also suggested a further link between the Incarnation and Christian hope, for example, in his claim that "It was the historical fact of the Incarnation that certified the eternal hope, something native to the human soul, of becoming like to God."[206] In this nexus between Incarnation, humanism, and hope, Murray explored the interrelation of all these terms, with the exception of the relationship between humanism and hope. But it is precisely here that a connection must be made, if the problem of contemporary Christian humanism—the potential drift between humanistic spirit and Christian conviction—is to be addressed. Murray and Maritain's appeal to faith in the doctrine of the Incarnation, then, provides only partial theological grounds. For it is one thing to assent to a doctrine, another to appropriate it.

A Proposal: Thomistic Hope as Theological Source for Christian Humanism

If Taylor's definition of humanism—"a doctrine, a view, or an attitude, which in any form understands the nature of man on a model and tries to ground a practical philosophy on that model"[207]—is valid, one can see both the strength and limits of the appeal to faith in the doctrine of the Incarnation. For while it undoubtedly shows the model for Christian humanism, it does not provide the means by which one conforms to the model. As Aquinas notes, faith is only "the foundation insofar as it is about knowledge."[208] This theoretical source therefore requires a practical component whereby believers grow into the divine humanity revealed in Christ and so personally appropriate their beliefs. Maritain and Murray, at least in their discussion of the sources of Christian humanism, do not directly address the dynamic element by which the believer conforms to the model. But Christian humanism is just as concerned with the habits and sensibilities by which Christ is imitated, as it is with orthodox belief about the Incarnation. The human person, after all, possesses both intellect and will. Christian humanism, accordingly, seeks not only wisdom but goodness.[209] The doctrine of the Incarnation cannot therefore be its sole, sufficient source.

This need for the practical embodiment of Christian conviction through moral action in the world is the fundamental reason for the *partial* nature of previous theological sources of Christian humanism. For the Christian humanists surveyed thus far are not simply exploring, abstractly, how doctrine clarifies the relationship between the human and the divine. They want faith to issue in acts that address the social conditions of the world. They therefore fall under what Michael Buckley, following Paul VI's *Populorum progressio*, had termed "the search for a new humanism."[210] This "new humanism" is understood as a broadening of Renaissance humanism's "cultivation of human achievements and enrichment as such."[211] Consequently, its sensibility must extend beyond the great human achievements in literature and philosophy, to include a "profound attention to and disciplined appreciation of the world of pain and misery in which so many live,"[212] so much so that

> insensitivity to human pain and sorrow, isolation from the international experiences of exploitation and misery, and indifference to the great questions of economic justice and human rights must mark a human being a savage in the twenty-first century, whatever his or her humanistic conquests in terms of literary skills or refined taste.[213]

Echoing Taylor's article on humanism, which concluded with an appeal to the Epistle to Titus, Buckley asserts that any contemporary understanding of *humanitas* must broaden from παιδεία to include φιλανθρωπία.[214] In light of such ethical imperatives, the theological source of this "new humanism" must go beyond faith's assent. That is, it must not only include the assent to a particular doctrine that makes a humanism distinctively Christian; it must also include the fundamental process whereby this Christian vision of the human person becomes embodied.

Hope, I will argue, constitutes this process whereby one comes to appropriate the belief in humanity's intimate and loving union with God through Christ. As such, it provides crucial grounds for Christian humanism. To understand why, it is helpful to summarize the argument thus far.

Modern Christian humanism makes two fundamental claims about Christianity's beliefs and practices:

(1) they contribute to justice and human flourishing in the present life and so should not be ignored or suppressed in the discussion of the concrete human good; and,
(2) they affirm and promote the human person's religious transcendence towards God, in contrast to any secular humanism.

In Taylor and Boyle's philosophical and cultural *praeparatio evangelica*, these claims understandably had only incipient theological warrant. Indeed, the connection between them remained implicit—even, at times, doubtful. In Taylor's case, the crucially important "hunch"— that the affirmation of ordinary human life must grow into some form of religious transcendence if it is to sustain its highest moral endeavors— remained largely unexplored, thereby inviting criticism that no such connection exists. In Boyle's case, the too-ready affirmation of a Christian humanism detached from its origins seemingly reduced it to a natural moral virtue. Consequently, there arose the danger of some disconnect between working for the human good and moving towards God. In a word, the basic theological justification for Christian humanism remained unclear.

To address this problem, I reviewed the thought of earlier, more theological authors. Maritain and Murray offered a partial solution by advancing faith in the doctrine of the Incarnation as the theological basis for Christian humanism, since that doctrine asserts the intimate union between humanity and God in the person of Jesus Christ. Seeking to complement that position, I propose that the theological virtue of hope should also play an explicit role in the theological sources of Christian humanism. Intuitive and systematic reasons support this proposal.

At an intuitive level, the virtue of hope and the vision of Christian humanism share a distinctive concern for how to live as a Christian in the difficulties of the pilgrim state. Both Taylor and Boyle seek to understand contemporary identity as something that has evolved over time, through arduous historical changes. Focusing on the cultural transition to secularism, Taylor emphasizes the fragility of belief in a context where unbelief is widespread, yet where the possibilities of new forms of belief are emerging in unexpected ways. In particular, Taylor argues that religious transcendence sustains the affirmation of ordinary life precisely when that affirmation is sorely tested by suffering and death.[215] Focusing on the economic transition to globalization, Boyle highlights the reality of human life as extended across time, in contrast to the market culture's emphasis on the instantaneous point of consumption and its concomitant denial of finitude. More generally, Boyle's prophetic temperament poignantly captures the trauma of adjustment and dislocation that accompanies this change, without despairing of its more equitable management. He therefore asserts the importance of hope: "Hope is what we need. Only if we look out on the contemporary landscape in the bleakest winter light will we do justice to the pain and disorientation and collapse that is intrinsic to an age of such rapid change."[216]

Intuitively, then, one senses a basic affiliation between hope and humanism, since the virtue of hope carries the believer through profound change and its consequent difficulties unto a further good. But which account of hope would offer the most suitable theological source? While Hegel provides much of the concrete analysis for Boyle's project, Boyle remains dissatisfied with his indifference to the future: "Hegel marked himself off both from Kantianism and from a Catholic understanding of the modern world by his radical rejection ... of any philosophical concern with the future."[217] Boyle admires Kant's powerful philosophical expression of the hope that is required in the face of inevitable failures, in particular, his postulating of ideals that regulate our action even though they are probably unobtainable. But Boyle does not develop this Catholic "concern with the future."

In the search for the theological sources of Christian humanism, one can fruitfully pursue that Catholic theological concern with the future by investigating the virtue of hope in one of the tradition's most influential figures, Thomas Aquinas. For whereas a Kantian postulate is an extrinsic function that guarantees the coherence of a philosophical system, a Thomistic theological virtue is an intrinsic principle of action infused by God. As such, it promises to be a fitting theological complement to Boyle's and Taylor's *praeparatio evangelica*.[218]

Beyond this intuitive correlation, what precise, systematic reasons specify hope as a source of Christian humanism? What is it about hope specifically that gives Christian humanism both its humanism and its Christianity? In its classic Thomistic rendering, the effect of hope could be summarized most succinctly as follows: it is that virtue whereby the believer becomes a pilgrim. By hoping, one does not just believe things about God; one actually approaches God as *the future, difficult, yet possible good* in the *sure expectation of future beatitude through the assistance of God*.[219] More precisely, hope attains God "as first efficient cause, insofar as it depends on God's help, and as ultimate final cause, insofar as it expects future happiness in God."[220] (The "efficient cause" is the agent responsible for bringing about the effect; the "final cause" is its goal or purpose.) Whereas charity unites the believer to God in terms of God's very goodness,[221] hope anticipates that union as the good for the human person. Hope thus regards God's goodness not so much in itself, but as something participated in by the human, as one's salvation. In a word, hope desires God as the human good. Crucially, this desire for future happiness spills over into the present, such that hope can depend upon God's help now "for anything" in order to attain God.[222]

From this brief overview of Aquinas's understanding of hope, it becomes clear how hope correlates directly with Christian humanism by regarding God under the following two aspects:

(1) as the human good in the present, because hope sustains and animates Christian life in the pilgrim state by allowing the wayfarer to lean on God for any difficult good insofar as it is ordered to God (which manifestly includes the present common goods of social and political life); and,

(2) as the transcendent object of human happiness, because hope moves the believer to God as his or her future good through great difficulties that culminate in death.

Hope's twofold understanding of God—as the source of assistance for the human good in the present and as the good in which humans shall participate in the future—corresponds closely with the two fundamental convictions of Christian humanism—in human flourishing now and in the movement of religious transcendence towards God. On the basis of this correlation, it seems reasonable to suggest that hope can ground a humanism that is genuinely and fully Christian. In fact, hope includes—in a single virtue—the two basic components of Christian humanism that were in danger of drifting apart. It thus promises to give theological support at precisely the area where it is most required.

Clarification by Contrast: Rowan Greer's via media

The following comparison with a recent book on Christian hope, by the Anglican patristics scholar Rowan Greer, suggests how Aquinas's account of hope can give systematic coherence to a suggestive—yet incomplete—set of exegetical reflections.[223] In *Christian Hope and Christian Life: Raids on the Inarticulate*, Greer examines how the desire to be with the transcendent God in a future "there and then" transforms Christian life "here and now." Although not expressed explicitly in the terms of Christian humanism, his sensibilities are closely aligned. He not only argues that hope in God animates the believer's present life, but more radically that "only a hope firmly located outside the world of our experience can give that world meaning and value."[224] Recalling a shared etymology, Greer asserts that the *promissio* of sharing eternal life with God grounds the *missio* of bringing new life to the world.[225] He selects two patristic and two Anglican authors to explore this claim: Gregory of Nyssa, Augustine, John Donne, and Jeremy Taylor.

While this book shares Greer's fundamental intention and complements his textual selection, it does not fully accept his conclusions, which can be summarized as follows. Greer identifies two fundamental theological sensibilities: (1) Augustine and Donne locate the object of hope in a future beyond all futures and consequently understand the Christian life as an *anticipatory* movement toward that goal; (2) Gregory and Taylor understand the object of hope as an eternal reality in which it is possible to *participate* here and now. Theologians who emphasize *anticipation* dwell more on the pitiful conditions of the present life that give rise to hope in the first place; those who emphasize *participation* see hope primarily as the movement into the mystery of God here and now. In a broader theological scheme, these differences mirror the divergence between theologies of redemption, which focus on sin and the cross, and theologies of incarnation, which see Christ as the consummator of creation. True to his denominational roots, Greer advocates a *via media* that does not collapse the tension between these two sensibilities. So while the selection of these four authors across the centuries is somewhat idiosyncratic, their deliberate pairing lends a certain symmetry to the book.

But symmetry does not make a system. The latter requires a principle that intelligibly coordinates its diverse parts, rather than simply offer two contrasting poles between which the truth is said to lie. Greer notes at the beginning that "the various versions of Christian hope we shall encounter are more rhetorical than logical," and his treatment is correspondingly more evocative than explanatory.[226] What the author says of Donne contains more than a trace of self-description: "his writings do not expound doctrines so much as they represent reflections on what those doctrines mean for the religious life."[227] While this approach generates many rich insights—so much so that it seems churlish to criticize his work—it nonetheless results in a book that does not forward an argument so much as offer a set of thematic ruminations by way of textual exegesis. To put the matter more pointedly: if, following the subtitle of Greer's book, one wishes to "raid the inarticulate," then a more orderly plan is required. Is it enough to suggest, for example, a *via media* between opposing poles of anticipation and participation? Greer's omission of medieval scholasticism, in his progression from patristic to Anglican authors, overlooks some of the most coherent attempts to make sense of the relation between anticipation and participation.

The rich yet incomplete nature of Greer's conclusions invites further reflection on the nature of Christian hope and on its potential to give greater theological depth to Christian humanism. It is to the tradition of Catholic theological reflection that this inquiry turns to see if one of its classic treatments of hope can give this support. Aquinas's account, I will argue, can bring systematic clarification to Greer's exegetical insight. For example, Aquinas's notion of hope as a single virtue that includes a twofold relation to God—as final goal and efficient helper—might capture in one concept what Greer parses between different authors, namely, God as anticipated goal (final cause in the future) and as participated helper (efficient cause in the present). Alternatively, Aquinas's account of the intelligible interrelation of all three theological virtues (presented in chapter 4, below), with their culmination in charity, which orders or "informs" the totality of one's moral and religious life, could likewise help. For example, it may be the case that the realities of Christian life that Greer discusses are better explained by a system that charts the transition from hope (anticipation) to charity (participation), rather than setting up a framework of two poles in irreducible tension. In any case, if the point is to understand better the life of Christian pilgrimage, one needs some integrated account of the very change that constitutes pilgrimage.

Objections to the Proposal

This notion of pilgrimage, however, which is often considered the heart of the Christian understanding of hope, presents the following problem for my hypothesis: Why select a virtue that makes one a wayfarer through the world as a source for a humanism that is meant to show one how to live in the world? It is by no means self-evident that the theological virtue of hope is a crucial source for a contemporary Christian humanism. Some suspect that Christian hope, especially when expressed as pilgrimage to another world, cannot enhance the human good in this world; or, if it does, it is not Aquinas's version. I will deal with these general and specific objections in turn by selecting three illustrative, contemporary theologians. Their influential criticisms dismiss Aquinas's notion of hope because they see it as unhelpfully directed towards some future world, at the expense of the concern for this one. If accurate, they would immediately undercut my proposal that Aquinas's idea of hope can help formulate the theological rationale of Christian humanism.

Gordon Kaufman

Gordon Kaufman presents one instance of the general objection that traditional Christian hope detracts from the human good. At the start of his most influential work, *In Face of Mystery*, he argues that human flourishing is the yardstick by which traditional beliefs are measured and, if necessary, rejected.

> Christian theology which does not contribute significantly to the struggles against inhumanity ... has lost sight of its deepest *raison d'être*. But for precisely this reason theologians must always take a thoroughly critical stance toward received traditions, and they must never hesitate to undertake drastic reconstruction when it becomes clear that traditional practices or beliefs can contribute to dehumanization.[228]

Later, Kaufman argues that belief in the promise of future life in heaven more often than not contributes to this dehumanization because it erodes the sense of duty and compassionate service.

> It is not difficult to understand either—human nature being what it is—why in most Christian movements most of the time the triumphalist motif [of Christology, especially the resurrection], with its promise of heavenly (or even earthly) reward, became the dominant one, the motif of service and self-sacrifice sometimes being almost lost to sight.²²⁹

In light of this *de facto* incompatibility between hope for eternal life and authentic Christian compassion, the Christian understanding of hope must submit to "drastic reconstruction," or, to be more precise, drastic reduction.

> [Hope is] an attitude of positive expectation regarding the possibilities for human life that will emerge in the future: the relentless movement of time becomes the gift of openness and the prospect of creativity rather than the threat of dissolution and destruction.²³⁰

Since "traditional" Christian hope—any genuinely eschatological hope transcending time—eviscerates the impulse for human flourishing, one must extirpate it from the tradition.

Prima facie, Kaufman has a point. It is by no means obvious why hope should bear any significant relation to human flourishing in the world. As the graced movement towards an end transcending time and space, hope shapes the believer's basic relation to the temporal-spatial world as one of pilgrimage. But Christian humanism is centrally concerned with the believer's relation to the world. Why, then, should it appeal to a virtue whose central effect is to make one a wayfarer through the world? How can hope bear any intrinsic and substantial relation to human flourishing in the world?

Indeed, Aquinas himself once seemingly held the view that hope bears no relation to the temporal world. In *Quaestiones disputatae De potentia*, written shortly before the prima pars of the *Summa theologiae*, Aquinas discusses the question of whether miracles are imputed to faith or hope. He argues thus:

> Miracles are not properly imputed to hope, since hope is ordered to that which ought to be obtained; whence hope is solely about eternal things. Faith, however, is of eternal and temporal things; whence faith can extend to things that ought to be done.²³¹

Drawing a stark contrast between following something and doing something, Aquinas goes on to claim that "the object of hope is the difficult thing that ought to be pursued, not the difficult thing that ought to be done."²³² At least in his early work, then, Aquinas seems to have believed that hope does not pertain to action, and only pertains to eternal, not temporal, affairs.

Why, then, should Christian humanism—which is centrally concerned with the believer's relation to the world—be grounded on a virtue that, at least according to the early Aquinas, is "solely about eternal things"? Moreover, would not hope for better things in the future detract from the project of human flourishing in the present, and, especially, from the honest recognition of the impediments to human flourishing that are so pervasive in the world? Does not hope dissipate, or at least deflect, commitment to the present human good? Now that Kaufman's general criticisms of traditional Christian hope have been laid out, I can now turn to the more specific criticisms of Aquinas by Moltmann and Wolterstorff.

Jürgen Moltmann

Jürgen Moltmann, one of the most influential contemporary theologians writing on Christian hope, severely criticizes Aquinas's doctrine of hope. He charges that the "*Deus adventurus* of the New Testament" is displaced by the "Aristotelian-Thomist God-idea of the *finis ultimus*."

> As *finis ultimus*, the unmoved mover, in the *appetitus naturalis*, draws all things to himself in virtue of the eros awakened by his perfection. As *Deus adventurus*, however, he comes towards all things with the *novum ultimum* and transforms them. This is the difference between the "theology of hope" of Thomas, which is actually an ontology of desire (including anthropology), and an eschatological theology which wants to appropriate and develop the apocalyptic thought forms of the New Testament.[233]

According to Moltmann, the importance of final causality in Thomas's theology evacuates messianic expectation from his account of hope, and ultimately reduces it to an "ontology of desire."

In a later article, Moltmann expands his criticism. He begins with a series of disjunctive questions:

> Is Christian hope aligned toward its future fulfillment in the historical future or is it, along with faith and love, a "theological," that is, "supernatural" virtue? Is Christian hope a forward-looking, historical force which overcomes the old and creates the new because it is searching for its historical fulfillment in the future, or is it aligned "upward" toward the transcendent God in whom alone it can find blessedness?[234]

Having created this dilemma, Moltmann then impales Aquinas on one of its horns:

> Thomas ... replaces the biblical history of the promise with a finalistic metaphysic. In place of hope, which looks for the fulfillment of the promise, he puts in the natural striving after blessedness which ... can only be realized in God himself. Taking the place of the coming of God (*ho erchomenos, deus adventurus*) is the "unmoved mover" which, through the power of Eros, draws all creation to itself. Taking the place of the eschatological promise of the "new heaven and the new earth"—"Behold, I make all things new" (Rev 21.5)—is the *visio Dei beatifica in patria* ... the bliss of the pure spirits in the hereafter.... Thomas did not translate biblical eschatology into another language or way of thinking—he fundamentally liquidated it. His "theology of hope" is, in fact, not the theology of a biblical "hope," but rather the anthropology of natural desire (*appetitus naturalis*), of humanity's inner self-transcendence which finds its response in the metaphysical theology of the Highest Good (*summum bonum*).[235]

Thomas's metaphysical hope, it is claimed, does not merely eclipse the biblical promise of a renewed creation; it utterly destroys it.

Nicholas Wolterstorff

Nicholas Wolterstorff lodges another biblical criticism of Aquinas's doctrine of hope, but from a prophetic, rather than apocalyptic, angle. In an essay entitled "Seeking Justice in Hope,"[236] Wolterstorff argues that since, for Aquinas, the theological virtues have God for their object, and since hope is the movement of intention to this end, then Thomistic eschatology limits Christian hope to otherworldly consummation. Wolterstorff summarizes and evaluates Aquinas's position as follows:

> [For Aquinas,] Christian hope is hope for consummation—consummation here being understood as a supernatural mode of union with God. Christian hope is not a hope for what might transpire in history but hope for a state of eudaimonia that transcends history. Hence it has nothing in particular to do with the struggle for justice within history. Christian hope is not hope that our struggle for justice will bear fruit; nor is it hope that our longing for justice will be satisfied. I judge that in thus understanding hope, Aquinas is representative of a long and prominent strand of Christian thought.[237]

Although Wolterstorff's primary aim is typological, not exegetical, he does not entirely excuse himself from reading further in Aquinas.[238] He notes a possible rebuttal: Aquinas does in fact say that "hope does not have only God for its object, but also other goods which we hope to acquire from God."[239] But these secondary hopes, Wolterstorff responds, are simply means to what Aquinas clearly states is the "proper and principal object of hope ... [namely,] eternal happiness."[240] From this ordering of hope, along with Aquinas's (apparent) silence on how secondary hopes are actually referred to their primary object, Wolterstorff concludes:

> Aquinas does not explain in what way anything that one hopes for other than eternal blessedness ought to be "referred to" one's eternal blessedness as its proper and principal goal or end.[241] The most natural interpretation is that whatever else one hopes for, one should hope for it as a means to one's eternal blessedness; Christian hope is to be confined to the hope for consummation and to the means for achieving consummation. If, for example, one hopes for justice in history, one does so because such justice, or perhaps the struggle for such justice, is a means to eternal blessedness.[242]

Thus, according to Wolterstorff, Aquinas's version of hope dwells on consummation with God in heaven, but ignores injustice on earth. Aquinas, it is alleged, has reduced the preeminent social virtue to a mere means to an otherworldly and narrowly personal fulfillment.[243]

Conclusion

The renewal of Christian humanism by Taylor and Boyle, while offering a realistic and prophetic diagnosis of Christian identity amidst the twin challenges of globalization and secularization, does not say everything about its own theological sources. In particular, it invites further comment on how, exactly, religious transcendence relates to the common good. Earlier thinkers, such as Maritain and Murray, rightly modeled that fundamental relation on the doctrine of the Incarnation. But in light of the practical exigencies of the Christian humanist enterprise, I propose that it broaden its sources to include the theological virtue of hope, which seeks to forge in life what doctrine proposes for belief. At least in the initial sketch of Aquinas's position, hope would seem to unite in one virtue the desire for transcendence towards God and the concern for the temporal common good. Indeed, Aquinas's systematic approach complements Greer's work on early Church and early Anglican theologies of hope: not by replacing these more literary, patristic-inspired reflections; but rather, by transposing those descriptive accounts, based on images, to explanatory accounts, based on concepts.[244] Aquinas's systematic mode of investigation might therefore extend Greer's achievement by giving a more integrated analysis of this virtue and thus a fuller account of how it bears upon on the good here and now.

But, as with any hypothesis, important objections may be raised. The final section of this chapter registered some of the more influential of these and thus refocused the problem of this inquiry onto how, exactly, Aquinas's understanding of hope might ground this contemporary renewal of Christian humanism. For thinkers no less than Wolterstorff and Moltmann see Thomistic hope as undercutting, respectively, the prophetic call to justice and the apocalyptic expectation of the recreation of the world. To respond to these objections requires a broader look at Aquinas's theological vision.

Chapter Three

PRESUPPOSITIONS OF AQUINAS'S DOCTRINE OF HOPE

If Aquinas's doctrine of hope bears no intrinsic relation to the present human good, then the hypothesis of this inquiry immediately fails. A distinctively Christian humanism cannot be grounded on a general metaphysical yearning; nor could it be truly humanist if it failed to address the fundamental moral demand for justice. How, then, can Aquinas speak to a contemporary Christian humanism that understands religious transcendence to bear directly upon the modern preoccupation with social and political justice? To answer this question requires at least some knowledge and appreciation of the more important presuppositions of Aquinas's doctrine of hope. Without this awareness, the link between Christian humanism and hope will remain weak, especially in light of the preceding objections. But grasp Aquinas's theological vision as a whole, and the force of these objections dissipates. In fact, some of the key claims informing that vision show the deeply humanistic spirit of his theology.

The *secunda secundae*'s account of hope, then, does not exist in isolation; it presupposes several metaphysical, philosophical, and theological claims.[245] Three are crucial for understanding the humanistic significance of hope. (1) *Creator and creation are not competing causes.*[246] On the contrary, creation both participates in God as the source of its being and moves to God as its final good. This noncompeting relationship establishes the metaphysical possibility of the concordance between the present human good and religious transcendence. (2) *The human person naturally desires God*. The philosophical arguments supporting this principle reveal an innate, distinctively human attraction to God. (3) *God's grace perfects human nature*. This classic principle of Catholic theology understands the fulfillment of this natural desire as God's noncoercive, graced elevation of human capabilities.

Together, these three presuppositions undergird the claim that hope can incorporate the present human good and religious transcendence. No doubt, as the history of Thomistic thought shows, these presuppositions and their interpretations are complex and controverted.

Here, I only sketch Aquinas's conclusions as they are relevant to this inquiry.[247]

The Creator-Creation Relationship as Noncompeting

In metaphysical terms, creation can be understood to relate to God in two fundamental ways: through participation in the likeness of God as its source;[248] and through movement toward God as its goal. As Aquinas says in question 1 of the *prima pars*, God is the *principium et finis* of all things.[249] To apply the language of Aristotelian causality, God is creation's efficient cause (that is, the agent responsible for bringing about the effect) and final cause (that is, the goal or end).

Creation's Participation in the Creator as the Origin of Its Being

For Aquinas, to be created is to receive existence from God without any preexisting matter.[250] Creatures therefore exist by participation in the Creator, the source of all existence. Conceiving the relationship between Creator and creation in terms of participation allows one to hold in tension, on the one hand, God's transcendent difference from the world and, on the other, God's intimate presence to the world. This tensive relationship, difficult to grasp, is best approached through a brief introduction to the notion of participation.

The idea of participation arises in response to the metaphysical question of the one and the many, and "lies at the heart of Thomas' doctrine of creation."[251] W. Norris Clarke states this question as follows:

> How [is it that] all beings, compared with each other, are at once many and diverse, yet somehow share in the common attribute of actual existence that joins them in one great all-embracing community of existents that we call "the real order" or simply "reality"[?] ... How must reality be structured in order to remain at once both many and diverse yet sharing in a common unity?[252]

Clarke identifies the essential elements of any participation structure as follows:

> (1) a source which possesses the perfection in question in a total and unrestricted manner;

(2) a participant subject which possesses the same perfection in some partial or restricted way; and
(3) which has received this perfection in some way from, or in dependence on, the higher source....

It [is] St. Thomas's chosen tool for expressing the fundamental relations of dependence of creatures on God both for their origin and their analogical imitation of His divine essence.[253]

As applied to the Creator-creation relationship, the metaphysics of participation indicates that each created, finite being participates in God's uncreated, infinite being, because it receives its very existence from God as the source of being. "All created things, so far as they are beings, are like God as the first and universal principle of being" because, even though God utterly transcends creation, "the effect must in some way resemble the form of the agent."[254] One can therefore speak of an analogical likeness of being between creation and Creator, because "existence is common to all."[255] Thus, if analogy captures a similarity-in-difference relationship, then the similarity of creation with God pertains to *esse*,[256] whereas the difference pertains to their modes of existing: infinite and simple for God, finite and composed for creation. The concepts of the analogy of being and of participation allow one to speak of the relationship of creation to Creator without either identifying or separating them. Just as the notion of analogy, in its linguistic application, lies midpoint between univocal and equivocal predication,[257] so the notion of participation lies midpoint between identifying creation and Creator, and separating them. This crucial idea of participation is best approached by showing, first, why creation and Creator are not identified. Once God's transcendent difference from creation is established, then creation's participation in God becomes more intelligible.

God's transcendent difference from creation can be understood in two ways: first, from a consideration of the nature of God as the source of existence; second, from a consideration of the nature of creation as derived from God. First, a consideration of the nature of God—or, more precisely, how God is not[258]—reveals the radical difference of creation from God. God is not another item in the universe of being, alongside other things, contained in some genus set aside for divinity.[259] Rather, God is "the principle of being."[260] In more technical terms, God is not another particular finite thing or essence that derives its existence from another, possessing an act of existence (*esse*), but not identical with its *esse*. If God were a finite essence whose existence was really distinct from his essence, then a prior agent would have to actualize God's essence with his existence. But that would mean that God is not the first, self-existing being, the source of all that exists. Thus, God's infinite essence must be identical with God's own act of existence; whence God's being is simple, not composed. Consequently, "the fact that the being of God is self-subsisting, not received in any other, and thus is called infinite, shows Him to be distinguished from all other beings, and all others to be apart from Him."[261] As the self-subsistent cause of all things, God cannot be one effect among others. God is distinguished from finite things precisely as the cause of their very existence, and not as another thing alongside them.

God's transcendence from creation can be understood from a second perspective, that of creation. As the emanation of all finite being from God, creation is a production *ex nihilo* that presupposes no prior existing beings.[262] This bestowal of being may be haltingly conceived as the composition of God's processing existence *ad extra* with finite essences.[263] If the existence given by God's creative act were not thus limited by union with finite essences, it would be indistinguishable from its source. But then God would be creating another infinite act of existence, which is impossible.[264] Thus, an infinite difference remains between the modes of existence of the simple, infinite, creative agent (God) and its composed, finite, created effects (everything else that exists). In sum, whether approached from the nature of God or creation, the conclusion remains the same: God radically transcends finite creation as its infinite source.

But this infinite difference between God and creation does not imply separation. For God differs from the world in a radically different way from how things in the world differ from each other.[265] The difference *between* God and the world is unlike any difference *within* the world. If God transcends creation as its source, then God must also transcend the usual distinctions within creation. Thus, God cannot be conceived in terms of any other comparison drawn between finite beings. In fact, the more one tries to bolster God's transcendence by opposing God to the world, the more one will "fail to follow through consistently on divine transcendence by inevitably bringing God down to the level of the non-divine to which it is opposed."[266] Radical transcendence, then, does not automatically exclude immanence. To the contrary, it entails God's intimate presence in all creation.

God's immanence can be seen in two ways: first, through a consideration of the nature of God; and second, through a consideration of the nature of created being. First, a consideration of the nature of God reveals God's presence to creation. God's simplicity (especially the identity of essence and existence), which grounds God's infinite difference from creation, itself indicates creation's participation in God. For since agents produce effects according to their nature, and God's nature is his act of existence, then existence must be God's proper effect. "Now the proper effect of God creating is what is presupposed to all other effects, and that is absolute being."[267] This most fundamental causal relationship, between giver and receiver of existence, means that God is very much present to the finite existents she creates.

> God is in all things; not, indeed, as part of their essence, nor as an accident; but as an agent is present to that upon which it works.... Now since God is very being by His own essence, created being must be His proper effect .... Now God causes this effect in things not only when they first begin to be, but as long as they are preserved in being.[268]

As the finite effect of infinite existence, creation can in no way and at no time be separate from its Creator. If it were, it would cease to exist.

This intimate presence of God in all creation can be seen from a second perspective, that of creation. By existing in their limited, partial way, created finite essences "take part"—i.e., participate—in existence, which existence is found in perfect, unrestricted form in God.[269] As God is the infinite act of existence, there can be nowhere that God is not. And as the infinite source of existence, God is innermost and continually present to each created being, for there is nothing more fundamental to a thing than its existence.

> Therefore, as long as a thing has being, God must be present to it, according to its mode of being. But being is innermost in each thing and most fundamentally inherent in all things since it is formal in respect of everything found in a thing.... Hence it must be that God is in all things, and innermostly.[270]

God's act of creation entails creation's participation in God, since to be created is to receive existence from God as first efficient agent.[271]

Creation's participation in God, then, lies midpoint between separation (which amounts to nonexistence) and identity (which amounts to pantheism). To be brought into existence by God is to participate in the infinite, simple Creator, albeit in a finite, composed mode.[272] This intimate-relation-in-radical-difference between God and creation safeguards, at one and the same time, God's transcendence and immanence. It explains why Creator and creation are not competing causes, for God's mode of existence utterly transcends creation as its absolute origin.[273] God does not need to push created reality out of the way in order to be present to it. As the transcendent cause of its very existence, God is already intimately present in creation. By the same token, finite beings do not need to wean themselves from God to establish their own proper existence. Rather, by fully actualizing their distinctive mode of being, they participate as fully as they can in their divine source.

Even the very finitude of each created thing need not be seen simply negatively, as the dependence of a limited, imperfect being on God. Rather, it should be understood positively as the particular way in which a part of creation manifests an aspect of God's universal perfection.[274] There is thus no intrinsic opposition between creation and God. On the contrary, the good for any particular part of creation entails its movement towards God.

Creation's Return to God as the Ultimate Good

The movement back to God is common to all creation. This return (*reditus*), however, should not be conceived literally as some kind of reversal of creation. *Reditus* is not "rocks clinging to God."[275] Rather, it is creation tending towards the perfect actualization of its proportionate being, which necessarily means more fully participating in the source from which its existence and perfection derive. The reason for this *reditus* more or less follows from what has already been said about God, once the general nature of the good is understood as the movement towards what is perfect.

Something is desired as good inasmuch as it is perfect or complete ("for all desire their own perfection").[276] In fact, desire arises precisely when something is incomplete or imperfect. Something is perfect inasmuch as it is actual ("a thing is perfect so far as it exists; for it is existence that makes all things actual").[277] It follows that goodness belongs to God in the highest degree because, as pure act, all finite existence and perfection comes from God.[278]

Since goodness is a relational term, requiring both a good object that is desirable and a desiring subject, its attribution to God should also be understood, first, in terms of God himself, and second, in terms of creation's relation to God.[279] The general structure of that relationship, understood in terms of cause and effect, warrants the designation of God as good. The premise for this argument was stated above: each thing desires its perfection. But "whatever perfection exists in an effect must be found in the effective cause,"[280] for it cannot come from nowhere. It comes, of course, from the agent, "since every agent makes its like."[281] It follows that the perfection of an effect must consist in sharing "a certain likeness to its agent."[282] In other words, effects, by desiring their own perfection, desire to participate in the source of that perfection, the agent.

The conclusion of this argument—that every effect desires to participate in its agent—can then be transposed to God, the universal efficient agent. All beings desire to participate in God's likeness by actualizing the limited perfections they receive from the unlimited, perfect agent. God can thus be described as perfect because

He originally unites in himself all the perfection of the effects in a higher and more excellent fashion.... God is said to be perfect in the sense that the perfection of creatures, diversified over the many genera of things, are originally and unified [*sic*] present in God, as identical with his simple being.[283]

Once God is recognized as perfect, it follows that God must be understood as the final cause or goal of all things—since God intends "to communicate His perfection, which is His goodness; while every creature intends to acquire its own perfection, which is the likeness to the divine perfection and goodness. Therefore the divine goodness is the end of all things."[284] God as final cause finds special expression in the notion of the divine government of the world, whereby God directs all things to their end of assimilation into divine goodness.

Further, because of God's absolute transcendence, God is not just any good, but is the supreme good.[285] The perfections that flow from God into creation, whereby goodness is attributed to him, do not flow from him as a univocal agent (as one being alongside others) but as the absolutely first agent that transcends its effects both in terms of species and genus. "Therefore as good is in God as in the first, but not the univocal, cause of all things, it must be in Him in a most excellent way; and therefore He is called the supreme good."[286]

This metaphysics of goodness, then, in which all beings tend to God as the supreme good, reveals how final causality permeates Aquinas's worldview. This pervasiveness is hard to overestimate, because the final cause is the *causa causarum*, even prior to being (*ens*) in causality, because an agent does not act except for some end.[287] Thus, the metaphysics of goodness goes beyond the metaphysics of participation. The latter emphasized the reception of being from God as first efficient cause, thereby revealing the nonopposition between creation and Creator. The former shifts the emphasis from this derivation of being to a more active movement of return to God:[288] from participation in God as first efficient cause to movement towards God as the supreme, final goal.[289] Thus, the human person, in common with all created beings, moves to God as the highest good. This is the metaphysical context in which the distinctively human movement towards union with God—a radical modification of this general movement to God—begins to make sense.

But creation's *reditus* or return to God and the nonopposition between God and creation do not show how the specifically *human* good is the movement of religious transcendence towards future happiness with God. No doubt humans, *qua* created, have God as their good; but how, *qua* human, do they deliberately intend some deeper union with God? To answer that question, one must recall what distinguishes humans from the rest of material creation: namely, the possession of an intellect and will. Thus, considered in the most general sense of being created, the human person exhibits only a trace of its divine origins; whereas considered as possessing rational freedom, the human person can be understood as an image of God.

> An image represents something by likeness in species (*similitudinem speciei*) ... while a trace (*vestigium*) represents something by way of an effect, which represents the cause in such a way as not to attain to the likeness of species. For imprints which are left by the movements of animals are called *traces*: so also ashes are a trace of fire, and desolation of the land a trace of a hostile army.[290]

In its choice of similes expressing absence (footprints, ashes, desolation), this passage shows how little a trace reveals of God. Further reasons, based on distinctively human capacities, must be given to show the specifically human movement towards God, beyond the common movement of creation towards God as the universal good. For while all creation tends to God as the last end, only rational creatures aim to use or possess this end, insofar as they can know and love God.[291]

This first presupposition, of the analogical relationship between God and creation, establishes the basic intelligibility of the two following correlative points: the natural desire for God (the second presupposition) and God's grace as perfecting that natural desire (the third presupposition). These final two presuppositions constitute the distinctively human instance of the general claim of an asymmetrical, noncompetitive relationship between creation and Creator.

The Natural Desire for God

Since the human person possesses both intellect and will, the natural desire for God correspondingly involves two aspects. Its first aspect, and the common Thomistic meaning, is the intellect's desire for the vision of God; the second aspect refers to the will's desire for God as the absolute good. But this somewhat clunky distinction between intellect and will, drawn from faculty psychology, should not obscure the fact that, properly speaking, it is the human being that desires. For in the fullness and integrity of both intellectual and volitional aspiration, the human person possesses a single dynamic orientation to God. Furthermore, it is only in relation to this natural human longing that one can meaningfully call God's grace the salvation of the human. So before talking of grace, one must first explore the human capacities that in some way seek it and are able to receive it.

The Intellect's Desire for the Vision of God

Question two of the *prima pars* affirms the existence of God by arguing from observable effects (for example, motion) to a cause that is commonly recognized as divine (for example, the unmoved, first mover). These demonstrations, however, only discover *that* God is, not *what* God is.[292] Unable to grasp God's nature, the human intellect's natural questioning remains unsatisfied. The inference from created effects to their essentially unknown cause does not stop the flow of questions. "When the existence of a thing has been ascertained, there remains the further question of the manner of its existence in order that we may know its essence."[293] As with any cause whose existence it discovers, the inquiring mind seeks the nature of that cause. "For there resides in every man a natural desire to know the cause of any effect which he sees; and thence arises wonder in men."[294] That wonder extends to God's nature.

The beginning of the *secunda pars* states this argument for the natural desire for the vision of God in more detail:

> The perfection of any power is determined by the nature of its object. Now the object of the intellect is what a thing is, i.e., the essence of a thing.... If therefore an intellect knows the essence of some effect, whereby it is not possible to know the essence of the cause ... that intellect cannot be said to reach that cause simply, although it may be able to gather from the effect the knowledge that the cause is [*an sit*]. Consequently, when man knows an effect, and knows that it has a cause, there naturally remains in man the desire to know about the cause, what it is [*quid est*]. And this desire is one of wonder, and causes inquiry.... Nor does this inquiry cease until he arrive at a knowledge of the essence of the cause. If therefore the human intellect, knowing the essence of some created effect, knows no more of God than that He is; the perfection of that intellect does not yet reach simply the First Cause, but there remains in it the natural desire to seek the cause. Wherefore it is not yet perfectly happy. Consequently, for perfect happiness the intellect needs to reach the very Essence of the First Cause. And thus it will have its perfection through union with God as with that object, in which alone man's happiness consists.[295]

Since the object of this desire is God, it must be the supreme desire.[296] The case for its supremacy is made in the opening treatise of the *secunda pars* on the last end of human life. As this case is made, God's desirability is framed in volitional terms.

The Will's Desire for the Absolute Good

The ultimate final cause or perfect beatitude of the person, the "purpose for which" that enjoins him to action, must so fill the appetite that no desire remains. If it did not fill the appetite, there would still be something else to be desired, and so it could not be the last or perfect end.[297] In general terms, then, "to desire happiness is nothing else than to desire that one's will be satisfied";[298] or, in Augustine's terms, that the "restless heart" find lasting peace.

To specify God as the object of this ultimate happiness, Aquinas first deploys Aristotelian arguments to rule out external goods (such as wealth, honor, and power) and bodily goods (such as pleasure) as candidates for the highest good, because they fall below proper human function.[299] Even some good of the soul, such as contemplation (which Aristotle reckons the supreme good) is rejected; for the *object* that makes men happy differs from the soul's *attainment* of it.[300] Neither the soul nor its acts can be the supremely good thing, for the will desires the universal good, not any participated good.[301] Participated goods, such as the soul, point to the source of perfection in which they participate. Consequently, the will cannot rest in them. It follows that no created thing whatsoever constitutes happiness, for every creature has only limited goodness by participation. The will, then, cannot rest until it "reaches out to the universal fount itself of goodness ... the infinite and perfect good," which is God.[302]

Thus, not only the intellect (in its natural desire for God), but also the will (in its desire for the absolute, unparticipated good), intends God as its ultimate object. Made in the image of God, the human person naturally strives to know and love God:

> Since man is said to be the image of God by reason of his intellectual nature, he is most perfectly like God according to that in which he can best imitate God in his intellectual nature. Now the intellectual nature imitates God chiefly in this, that God understands and loves Himself. Wherefore we see that the image of God is in man ... inasmuch as man possesses a natural aptitude for understanding and loving God; and this aptitude consists in the very nature of the mind, which is common to all men.[303]

The theme of the image of God will recur in this overview and is critical for Aquinas's treatment of grace. For now, it is sufficient to note that to be made in the image of God is to be ordered to the knowledge and love of God as the uttermost fulfillment of our innate capacities of intellect and will.

The "Need" for Grace[304]

It is one thing to have a desire, another to fulfill it. Neither the intellect nor the will can attain their divine object through their innate powers. Thus, to fulfill their natural longing, God must elevate human knowing and loving beyond their natural, proportionate range. This "supernatural" assistance overcomes the limitations of human intellect and will, which limitations can be summarized as follows: (1) the object of the intellect's desire transcends its capabilities; and so (2) the will cannot effect any real movement to union with it; and, in addition, (3) the mind as a whole is distorted by sin and thus deflected from God.

God's help is required, first, because the human intellect cannot grasp the divine essence. God's nature transcends human comprehension. For whatever is known, is known according to the mode of the knower.[305] But human knowing is embodied, whereas God's essence cannot be known through matter.

> Our soul, as long as we live in this life, has its being in corporeal matter; hence it knows naturally only what has a form in matter, or what can be known by such a form.[306] Now it is evident that the divine essence cannot be known through the nature of material things. For ... the knowledge of God by means of any created similitude is not the vision of His essence. Hence it is impossible for the soul of man in this life to see the essence of God.[307]

God cannot be known in God's essence through any created similitude for several reasons. One, God's essence is God's existence, whereas no created form's essence is identical with its existence. Therefore, God's essence cannot be grasped through a created form.[308] Two, "the divine essence is uncircumscribed, and contains in itself supereminently whatever can be signified or understood by the created intellect. Now this cannot in any way be represented by any created likeness; for every created form is determined according to some aspect of wisdom, or of power, or of being, or of some like thing."[309] Therefore, God's essence exceeds our mode of knowing.[310] Indeed, because God is infinite, "the vision of the divine essence ... infinitely surpasses all created substance."[311] And so human reason, unaided by grace, encounters the following paradox: an intrinsic orientation towards infinite understanding for which its natural powers are inadequate.[312]

God's supernatural assistance is required for a second reason: the natural desire to see God amounts to intellectual wonder about God's nature, not volitional movement towards beatific vision.[313] As William O'Connor argues in *The Eternal Quest*:

> The natural desire to see God is not a tendency towards beatitude consisting in this vision.... A natural curiosity is aroused which has nothing to do with the actual attainment of this further knowledge, or its lack of attainment. This natural curiosity to see God after we know that He exists is all St. Thomas means by the natural desire for the vision of God.[314]

Thus, although the intellect naturally desires to see God's essence, it does not follow that the will naturally desires perfect union with God as the ultimate good.[315] When one "speaks of happiness according to its specific notion, as to that in which it consists," it is clear that "all do not know happiness; because they know not in what thing the general notion of happiness is found. And consequently, in this respect, not all desire it."[316] Indeed, Aquinas never used the term "natural desire for the beatific vision."[317] Granted, there is a natural desire for happiness in general, for the will to find an object in which it can totally rest.[318] But, as with any other desire, the specific content of this desire must be presented to the will by the intellect, since *nihil amatum nisi praecognitum*—nothing is loved unless it is first known.[319] But the intellect cannot, by its natural power, present the essence of God. Therefore, the will cannot naturally desire to see the essence of God.

No doubt, one can give reasons for why God must be the only satisfactory object of the will's desire and one can describe the natural frustration of the will with anything but God.[320] But abstract arguments and a restless heart cannot present the object (the divine essence) to which the will would move.[321] That presentation must wait on the infusion of grace, which, through the light of faith, strengthens the intellect to believe that the divine essence can be seen. Consequently, the intellect, through faith, can present the will, by way of promise, with a suitable object to desire. The will's desire for the beatific vision is therefore supernatural, not natural. In Stanley Hauerwas's words, "To be Christian is surely to fulfill the most profound human desires, but we do not know what such fulfillment means on the basis of those desires themselves."[322]

Other than wonder about God and frustration with anything but God, the natural desire for God is not yet an actual movement towards eternal union with God. For how could one naturally move towards that which utterly transcends natural capacities? To give reasons why something is desirable does not make that desire actual. Notwithstanding the natural inclination of the will for God because of its frustration with any participated good, the actual movement towards *union* with God can only be caused by God's action, not our wishing it were so. Any coordination of the human good with religious transcendence towards union with God must therefore wait on a consideration of grace.

The arguments for the will's natural inclination for God loosely parallel the proofs for God's existence. Those proofs or five ways (*quinque viae*) affirm God's existence from natural reason but grasp nothing of God's nature, and so are considered *praeambulae fidei*, preambles of faith. Likewise, the arguments or "ways" advanced for the will's natural inclination to God affirm God's desirability, but cannot unite us to God's essence. They could thus be considered *praeambulae caritatis*, preambles of love. Both these preambles, of faith and of love, deploy philosophical arguments to identify God as the ultimate object of the intellect and the will respectively, but both leave those faculties frustrated. Consequently, both require grace to satisfy the longings they arouse.

The third reason why the fulfillment of the natural desire requires God's assistance can be seen in the following response to the question, "Whether anyone without grace can merit eternal life?"[323] This *respondeo* touches on the first two reasons for the insufficiency of the natural desire and then raises the third.

> Everlasting life is a good exceeding the proportion of created nature; since it exceeds its knowledge and desire.... And hence it is that no created nature is a sufficient principle of an act meritorious of eternal life, unless there is added a supernatural gift, which we call grace. But if we speak of man existing in sin ... [another] reason is added to this, viz., the impediment of sin.

Thus, in addition to overcoming the natural limitations of human capabilities, grace is also required to heal their distortion by sin. The theme of sin will be discussed in later chapters that explore how hope specifically heals and elevates human nature. As long as these limitations and distortions remain, the natural desire for God will be frustrated. Since only divine assistance could remove them, one must turn to the notion of grace, God's gratuitous healing and elevation of human nature.

Grace Perfects Nature

Although grace is a complex, analogous term, Aquinas asserts simply that Christ, in his humanity, is its principle, just as God is the principle of existence.[324] In its common usage, grace has three meanings: (1) to be in someone's "good graces" or favor on account of their love; which leads to the giving of (2) a freely bestowed gift; which in turn prompts (3) the response of gratitude.[325] One of the highest points of Christian revelation, 1 John 4:7–5:4, captures something of this ordering in the following announcement and exhortation: "in this is love, not that we loved God, but [1] that he loved us and [2] sent his Son ... [and, therefore, 3] we love, because he first loved us."³²⁶

Turning from this common usage of the term "grace" to a more precise theological analysis, a recurring and important distinction in the treatise on grace reveals two basic components:

> Man is aided by God's gratuitous will in two ways. First, inasmuch as man's soul is moved by God to know or will or do something, and in this way the gratuitous effect in man is not a quality, but a movement of the soul.... Secondly, man is helped by God's gratuitous will, inasmuch as a habitual gift is infused by God into the soul.³²⁷

The distinction appears first in I-II.109.1 and recurs in I-II.111.2 and I-II.112.2. Generalizing and expanding this distinction, one can view grace in two ways: first, as God's moving the human person to their ultimate end; and second, as human participation in God, since the term of this movement—its fundamental effect—is "nothing short of a partaking of the Divine Nature."³²⁸ This twofold description of grace as (1) a directing towards the ultimate end, which end is (2) a sharing in God's nature, can be expanded as follows.

Grace Moves Human Nature to Its End

Grace involves the gratuitous operations whereby God moves the person to his or her good.³²⁹ As such, it is a temporal effect of God's eternal love that takes up and completes the natural human longing for God. Thus, one can say that the human person is in a way capable of grace (*capax Dei*) "since from its having been made to the likeness of God, it is fit to receive God by grace."³³⁰ But to be able to receive something is not the same as being able to attain it. The movement towards the ultimate good lies beyond natural reach. Consequently, grace can be specified as "the outcome of His mercy."³³¹ Why mercy? Because "every conferring of good above due pertains to mercy."³³² As an effect of God's loving mercy that directs the human person to the good, grace can be understood as the principle of a movement that terminates in happiness.³³³

As an operation on a preexisting subject, grace presupposes nature.³³⁴ Early in the *Summa theologiae*, justifying the status of the proofs for God's existence as *praeambula fidei*, Aquinas notes how faith, like grace and perfection, requires a prior subject for its operation:

> The existence of God and other like truths about God, which can be known by natural reason, are not articles of faith, but are preambles to the articles; for faith presupposes natural

knowledge, even as grace presupposes nature, and perfection presupposes something that can be perfected.[335]

These three notions—faith, grace, and perfection—move from the particular to the general. Faith is a particular manifestation of grace, and grace is a particular type of perfection. In each case, God does not create something that previously did not exist, but modifies what already exists. Thus, Aquinas understands the presence of grace in the soul as an accidental quality, not an essential feature, because accidents do not exist in themselves, but only in something else, as a kind of modification.[336] Accordingly, in Jean-Pierre Torrell's formulation, "Grace does not enter into the definition of humanity."[337] If it did, it would not be a free gift and, furthermore, it would mean that one without grace is not human. To call grace an accident, then, is simply to acknowledge that human nature retains its integrity when it encounters God's love. Howsoever deeply it be modified by grace, it is still the human person that receives and lives out this gift.

When talking about grace in particular, during a more comprehensive defense of the role of human reason in *sacra doctrina*, Aquinas specifies that modification as perfection:

> Since therefore grace does not destroy nature, but perfects it, natural reason should minister to faith as the natural bent of the will ministers to charity.[338]

Grace does not just presuppose nature, it perfects it. The difference is significant. Clay, for example, is presupposed by the potter, but has no internal dynamism to become a pot. Human wonder and longing, on the other hand, are not merely the raw material that God knocks into a shape that is foreign to their intrinsic orientation. Rather, they are intrinsically ordered to God. That is why faith is said not only to presuppose natural reason, but to perfect it.

This asymmetrical coordination between nature and grace also allows the intellect's natural movement towards truth to serve faith. For example, reason demonstrates the existence of faith's object and "nourishes and defends" faith by analogies and rebuttals. Likewise, charity not only presupposes the rational appetite, but is served by the will's natural inclination towards the good. Thus, if a young person rejects this inclination in his life-forming decisions, he removes himself from the perfective influence of God's love:

> When he begins to have the use of reason, he is not entirely excused from the guilt of venial or mortal sin. Now the first thing that occurs to a man to think about then, is to deliberate

about himself. And if he then directs himself to the due end, he will, by means of grace, receive the remission of original sin; whereas if he does not then direct himself to the due end, as far as he is capable of discretion at that particular age, he will sin mortally, through not doing that which is in his power to do.[339]

Natural longings, whether to love or to understand, are the place where the human encounters God, and where God perfects the human.

The longest statement of the principle "grace perfects nature" comes in an earlier text, the *Commentary on Boethius's "De Trinitate."* This maxim is again invoked in a discussion on the place of philosophy in theological reflection.

> The gifts of grace are added to nature in such a way that they do not destroy it, but rather perfect it. So too the light of faith, which is imparted to us as a gift, does not do away with the light of natural reason given to us by God. And even though the natural light of the human mind is inadequate to make known what is revealed by faith, nevertheless what is divinely taught to us by faith cannot be contrary to what we are endowed with by nature. One or the other would have to be false, and since we have both of them from God, He would be the cause of our error, which is impossible. Rather, since what is imperfect bears a resemblance to what is perfect, what we know by natural reason has some likeness to what is taught to us by faith.[340]

Assuming that the will ministers to charity (and hope) in the same way that natural reason ministers to faith,[341] what is cast here in terms of the light of faith strengthening the light of natural knowledge can be transposed to a volitional setting in which charity perfects the natural appetite for the good. Thus, one could replace the phrase "natural light of the human mind" with "natural striving of the human appetite," and the phrase "light of faith" with, adapting John Wesley, the "warmth of charity." *Mutatis mutandis*, the passage would read as follows:

> The gifts of grace are added to nature in such a way that they do not destroy it, but rather perfect it. So too the warmth of charity, which is imparted to us as a gift, does not do away with the natural movement towards the good that is given to us by God. While natural goodness cannot attain charity's object, charity cannot contradict the natural desire for the good. And since what is imperfect bears a resemblance to what is perfect, what we naturally desire has some likeness to what is infused though the virtues of charity.[342]

Just as natural reason serves faith and faith perfects reason, so natural love serves charity and charity perfects natural love.

The perfective action of grace can further be seen in the following two considerations: (1) It does not contradict nature because it operates through free choice; and so (2) it can be refused. First, grace does not contradict nature because it moves the person according to their proper operations. Since God moves each according to their own nature, and since free will is proper to man's nature, the infusion of justifying grace moves the free will to accept grace.[343] Thus, secondly, grace does not coerce nature since it can be refused. For "although one may neither merit in advance nor call forth divine grace by a movement of his free choice, man is able to prevent himself from receiving this grace."[344] To illustrate the universality of God's grace and the possibility of its free rejection by some, Aquinas employs the image of a man closing his eyes to the light of the sun.

> Since this ability to impede or not to impede the reception of divine grace is within the scope of free choice, not undeservedly is responsibility for the fault imputed to him who offers an impediment to the reception of grace. In fact, as far as He is concerned, God is ready to give grace to all; "indeed He wills all men to be saved, and to come to the knowledge of the truth," as is said in I Timothy (2:4). But those alone are deprived of grace who offer an obstacle within themselves to grace; just as, while the sun is shining on the world, the man who keeps his eyes closed is held responsible for his fault, if as a result some evil follows, even though he could not see unless he were provided in advance with light from the sun.[345]

Of course, trying to conceive the relationship between human freedom and divine initiative presents difficulties.[346] What is important here is the conviction, however imperfectly conceived, that God's grace brings human freedom to a deeper liberty than it could achieve by itself. Without keeping in mind the crucial distinction between Creator and creation, it would be easy to think that God acts on the same plane as human freedom, and thus displaces it. But recalling that crucial distinction, by which God is acknowledged as *transcendently* immanent, gives some notion of how God can be "totally and actively present *in a divine manner* ... without taking over the role of the agent,"[347] such that the agent becomes a mere puppet in God's hands.

Up to now, grace has been understood as a movement that perfects human nature, and so it has been viewed under the aspect of God's directing the person to their good. But movements have terms and are only finally intelligible in relation to them. Thus, the goal of the movement of grace must now be considered.

Grace as Participation in God's Nature

Participation in God's nature is prepared by God's illumination of the mind, which intends, but cannot comprehend, God. This imagery of light conveys Aquinas's conviction that to see God's essence is in some way to become like God.

> Everything which is raised up to what exceeds its nature must be prepared by some disposition above its nature.... But when any created intellect sees the essence of God, the essence of God itself becomes the intelligible form of the intellect. Hence it is necessary that some supernatural disposition should be added to the intellect in order that it may be raised up to such a great and sublime height. Now since the natural power of the created intellect does not avail to enable it to see the essence of God ... it is necessary that the power of understanding should be added by divine grace. Now this increase of the intellectual power is called the illumination of the intellect.... By this light the blessed are made deiform, that is, like to God.[348]

Deification is a key concept in Aquinas's account of human participation in God. It finds scriptural basis in 2 Peter 1:4's expression of the hope to "become participants of the divine nature." The transforming light by which this happens reveals a radically new level of participation beyond a common participation in God as the source of existence.

> God is said to be in a thing in two ways; in one way, after the manner of an efficient cause; and thus He is in all things created by Him; in another way, He is in things as the object of operation is in the operator; and this is proper to the operations of the soul, according as the thing known is in the one who knows; and the thing desired in the one desiring. In this second way, God is especially in the rational creature, who knows and loves Him actually or habitually.... The rational creature possesses this prerogative by grace.[349]

Whereas in metaphysical terms God is present to all creation as the source of its being, in theological terms God is present to the person through the operation of their distinctive faculties. Grace causes this movement from a metaphysical presence (that is common to all created beings and recognized by human understanding) to a more intimate knowledge and love through the elevation of a person's natural powers.

In creation, God causes to exist what is not God, allowing it to participate in the divine through analogical likeness. In grace, God communicates Godself to humanity, bringing it to share in his essence. These two different levels of participation result in two distinct conceptions of the divine good. In the first, "since God is the first Mover simply, it is by His motion that everything seeks Him under the common notion of the good, whereby everything seeks to be likened to God in its own way."[350] In the second, God "directs righteous men to Himself as to a special end, which they seek, and to which they wish to cling.... And that they are turned to God can only spring from God's having turned them."[351] From this, there follow two distinct types of love for God. In the first, "nature loves God above all things inasmuch as He is the beginning and the end of natural good."[352] From God's perspective, it is a general love, "*whereby God loves all things that are* (Wis. 11:25); and thereby gives things their natural being."[353] Whereas in the second type of love, "charity loves Him, as He is the object of beatitude, and inasmuch as man has a spiritual fellowship with God. Moreover, charity adds to natural love of God a certain quickness and joy."[354] From God's perspective, this is "a special love, whereby He draws the rational creature above the condition of its nature to a participation of the Divine good; and according to this love He is said to love anyone simply, since it is by this love that God simply wishes the eternal good, which is Himself, for the creature."[355] Through grace, natural reverence for the transcendent source and term becomes an unbroken friendship. In Karl Rahner's terms, the silent and "infinitely distant horizon" becomes a forgiving and intimately loving presence.[356] The maxim "grace perfects nature," then, does not imply that grace rounds off what nature would have achieved by itself, were it not for sin. The perfection of human nature involves its elevation to a higher participation in God, as its natural inclination is raised to a finality beyond its ordinary reach.

This higher participation in God, described above in terms of illumination, is also evoked through the imagery of indwelling.[357] A passage that describes this divine indwelling similarly adverts to God's twofold presence:

> For God is in all things ... according to His one common mode, as the cause existing in the effects which participate in His goodness. Above and beyond this common mode, however, there is one special mode belonging to the rational nature wherein God is said to be present as the object known is in the knower, and the beloved in the lover. And since the rational creature by its operation of knowledge and love attains to God Himself, according to this special mode, God is said not only to exist in the rational creature, but also to dwell therein as in His

own temple. So no other effect can be put down as the reason why the divine person is in the rational creature in a new mode, except sanctifying grace.[358]

This description of indwelling occurs in the question on the mission of the divine persons because Aquinas understands the perfection of the human person (the image of God) in terms of its exemplar, the triune God. As mentioned, the human person is an image of the triune God by virtue of possessing an intellect and a will. The relationship between image and exemplar can be understood initially as an analogy of proportion. Thus, the processions of knowing and loving in the human person, as immanent acts of an intellectual nature, reflect the divine processions. More accurately, the formation of the inner word and of love in the human mind correspond proportionally to the eternal processions of Word and Spirit in God. For this reason, in the human person "is found the representation of the Trinity, by way of image."[359]

But the Trinity is not only the exemplary cause of the human mind, just as the mind is not simply a distant reflection of its exemplar. The likeness goes deeper than structural similarity. Grace causes a real conformity of the image to the exemplar. How? It perfects the mind's operations of knowing and loving through the missions of the Word and Spirit respectively. These temporal extensions of the eternal processions gather the human person into the divine life of the Trinity (Rom. 8:14–17). Specifically, human understanding comes to share in the wisdom of the Word. "Putting on the mind of Christ," the person comes to see the world less through the distorted lens of sin, and more as a gift given by God.[360] Similarly, the human heart has God's love poured into it through the Spirit (Rom. 5:5). These two missions, of Word and Spirit, are coordinate, as the Spirit of adoption (Rom. 8:15) is "marking upon us a likeness" to Christ.[361] Flooded with divine love and evermore conformed to Christ, a person's capacity for kindness and forgiveness grows, such that she can now act on what she sees anew. This is what is meant by the indwelling of the Trinity, the divinizing of the human as it shares in God's wisdom and love.

This assimilation implies a more active element in the relationship between image and exemplar, in which the distance—or, more precisely, dissimilarity—between them diminishes.[362] Hence the imagery of indwelling. Beyond proportional similarity of human image to divine exemplar, a certain ontological union occurs:

> According to Thomas, man is the image of the Trinity primarily because he can come to know and love God as God knows and loves Himself.... Through the continuing action of God on the

soul every man reveals that his true personal dignity lies in his capacity to imitate God actively by participating in the personal life of God, the Father, the Son, and the Holy Spirit."[363]

The action of grace on the human person can be summarized in trinitarian terms: "God acts directly on the mind as the object specifying its acts of understanding and love, perfecting the proportionality between the mind and the Trinity by conforming the acts of the mind to the inner activity of the divine Trinity."[364] Thus, the more one is directed to God and therefore participates in God's self-knowledge and self-love, the more one can become fully human, that is, the more one can truly *image* God in the world.

Conclusion

The previous chapter concluded with several influential objections to the notion that traditional, especially Thomistic, hope bears any relation to a contemporary Christian humanism. This chapter therefore presented some of Aquinas's key theological presuppositions of his doctrine of hope. These presuppositions have profound consequences for any religious humanism.[365] Creation, as originating from God, the source of all perfection, is good. It is therefore to be approached positively, as the place in which to discover God. Conversely, to disparage creation is to detract from God.[366] Moreover, as distinct from God, creation possesses a relative autonomy. Its own order of causation is not vitiated by God's action. Divine causation does not operate on the same ontological plane, as it were, but rather as the transcendent, sustaining cause behind and within any being at all. Providence therefore "does not do away with secondary causes."[367] To the contrary, "there are certain intermediaries of God's providence; for He governs things inferior by superior, not on account of any defect in His power, but by reason of the abundance of His goodness; so that the dignity of causality is imparted even to creatures."[368] Thus, created being is founded and respected as a relative good, and it retains its own proper value and dignity as it participates in God's action. That divine action does not remove human action, but, to the contrary, is its precondition. In the words of Philippians, "it is God who is at work in you, enabling you both to will and to work" (2:13). It follows that hope in such a God, *pace* Kaufman, should not detract from the human good but, to the contrary, should enhance it.

Clarifying the distinction and relation between God and creation also has important consequences for a distinctively Christian humanism that rests on the doctrine of the Incarnation. For if God and humanity were not radically distinct and were instead on the same plane of being, then their union would *either* displace one of the "parts" thus united *or* spawn a hybrid that is neither God nor man. That purported union between God-as-part-of-the-world and humanity could then only be a myth, perhaps expressing another truth, but not the one it claims to express about the real union of God and humanity in Christ.[369] This crucial metaphysical account of creation's relationship to the Creator, then, underlies the Christian humanist conviction that humanity and divinity stand in direct, not inverse, proportion.

Moving from the Incarnation to the human sharing in Christ through the Spirit, one sees how the noncoerciveness of grace gives a specific, historical instance of the general, metaphysical principle of the noncompetitive relationship between Creator and creation. And just as that principle shows God to be not one object alongside others, but the source of all existence, so the movement towards God cannot be one act alongside other acts, but must pervade all human action. It involves, after all, the perfection of the intellect and will—all that makes the human person distinctively human. Grace therefore possesses a comprehensiveness that embraces all human flourishing. The movement it initiates toward the vision of God need not contradict other acts, but rather will encompass and perfect them. One becomes a more perfect human agent by being more perfectly directed to God. To Wolterstorff's complaint that Aquinas fails to give a particular instance of what might be referred to our beatitude in God, Aquinas's response would be "everything."

In the action of grace, then, God begins and fulfills the process whereby human nature is perfected. The natural wonder of the intellect that desires to see the essence of God is aided by the infusion of the light of grace, and, consequently, the natural longing of the will for ultimate happiness moves from frustration to the beginning of fulfillment. This elevation of the innate human desire for truth and goodness hopes for union with, and delight in, God. As Aquinas makes abundantly clear, such a hope surpasses any "natural striving" or "anthropology of natural desire," to recall Moltmann's objection—an objection which even the very generous commentator Jean-Pierre Torrell states rests on "a deep misunderstanding based on a very narrow consultation of the works."[370] Rather, since the hoped for goal can only be eschatological, the good for the human person in this life cannot be attainment of, but only movement towards, this term. This, in very general terms, is how grace provides the theological condition for the possibility of uniting the human good *in via* with transcendence towards God.

So we see, in fact, that Kaufman, Moltmann, and Wolterstorff fail to appreciate the humanistic nature of Aquinas's theological system as a whole, and, as a result, too quickly dismiss his notion of hope as irrelevant to the present human good. If one instead grasps Aquinas's broader theological vision, then one must grant the antecedent probability that Aquinas's doctrine of hope could have much to say to a contemporary Christian humanism. So we must now sharpen our exegetical focus from Aquinas's general presuppositions to his specific teaching on hope.

Chapter Four

AQUINAS ON HOPE

The presuppositions explored in the previous chapter illustrate the deeply humanistic spirit of Aquinas's theological system. But one cannot remain at their level of generality. Even the natural desire for God is a pre-Christian potency whose completed act (the beatific vision) is a post-temporal state. But Christian humanism principally concerns the distinctively *Christian* contribution to *this* life. One must therefore narrow the focus from the comprehensive treatment of the human person (from natural desire to the beatific vision) to the specific examination of the theological virtues *in via*. For as Aquinas wrote at the beginning of his most succinct and accessible summary of Christian thought and life, the *Compendium theologiae*: "The Apostle, in 1 Corinthians 13:13, taught that the whole perfection *of this present life* consists in faith, hope, and charity, as in certain brief headings outlining our salvation: 'Now there remain faith, hope, and charity.' " Why these three? Aquinas's answer to that question gives a prospect for this chapter's study of hope: because "human salvation consists in knowing the truth [faith] …, in the intention for a fitting end [hope] …, [and] in observing justice [charity]."[371] But before examining these virtues, one must first distinguish them from grace, the last presupposition examined in the previous chapter, to see their distinctive contribution to Christian humanism.

From Grace to Virtue

Even to focus on grace—the source of the human movement towards God—is still too broad a compass for a study of the theological sources of Christain humanism. One must pay closer attention to the dispositions and operations that flow from grace, if one wishes to understand better how the human person approaches God as her ultimate good. For acts pertain to the operation of the soul, whereas grace, strictly speaking, transforms the soul's essence. But Christian humanism looks beyond the healing and elevation of the soul, to the concrete actions that flow from this renewal of heart and mind. And to talk of the soul's operations, one must use a new category, that of virtues, whose acts manifest grace.[372]

Aquinas addresses the relationship between virtue and grace in I-II.110.3, "Whether grace is the same as virtue?" There, he rejects Lombard's identification of virtue and grace.

> It is clear that the virtue of a thing has reference to some pre-existing nature, from the fact that everything is disposed with reference to what befits its nature. But it is manifest that the virtues acquired by human acts ... are dispositions, whereby a man is fittingly disposed with reference to the nature whereby he is a man; whereas infused virtues dispose man in a higher manner and towards a higher end, and consequently in relation to some higher nature, i.e., in relation to a participation of the Divine Nature, according to 2 Peter 1:4.... And thus, even as the natural light of reason is something besides the acquired virtues, which are ordained to this natural light, so also the light of grace, which is a participation of the Divine Nature, is something besides the infused virtues which are derived from and are ordained to this light.[373]

Thus, in order to grasp more fully how the graced human person acts, one must consider the effect of grace in its intellectual (faith) and affective (hope and charity) moments.[374] These virtues reveal the active transformation arising from grace, as the human person knows and loves in a way that attests to a new life that can only come from God.

To consider grace alone, abstracted from its (theologically) virtuous acts, is thus to stay in the realm of generality. Aquinas makes this clear in the following justification for the distinction between the *prima secundae* and the *secunda secundae*.

> Since therefore happiness is to be gained by means of certain acts, we must in due sequence consider human acts, in order to know by what acts we may obtain happiness, and by what acts we are prevented from obtaining it. But because operations and acts are concerned with things singular, consequently all practical knowledge is incomplete unless it take account of things in detail.[375]

Since grace remains at the level of general principles, it is treated in the *prima secundae* and does not explain how the human person attains his or her good through particular acts. For that, one must turn to the *secunda secundae*, which begins with a detailed consideration of the theological virtues, those dispositions and acts that flow from the transformation of the soul's essence that is wrought by grace. These virtues more richly describe the graced life as it is appropriated through a renewed understanding and loving.[376]

To see the role of hope in this process, one must grasp the following four things:

(1) how the theological virtue of hope derives its name and definitional characteristics—but nothing else—from the passion of hope;
(2) how the infused theological virtues differ from the acquired natural virtues;[377]
(3) how the three theological virtues are distinguished; and,
(4) how they are ordered and related.

From these four exegetical tasks emerge the distinctive properties of the theological virtue of hope, which properties can then be applied, in subsequent chapters, to the problematic situation of contemporary Christian humanism.

The Passion of Hope

Although the two differ vastly in context and application, the theological virtue of hope nonetheless derives its name and definition from the passion of hope. It is helpful, therefore, to understand the properties of that passion. To do so, one must first review the structure of the passions, that is, of the sensitive appetite that humans share with other animals.

At its most basic level, the sensitive appetite comprises two different kinds of passions: concupiscible passions, which seek pleasure and flee pain; and irascible passions, which resist obstacles to seeking pleasure and fleeing pain. Inasmuch as the irascible part of the sensitive appetite overcomes obstacles, its object is arduous, and it wins the title "protector and defender of the concupiscible."[378] But its arduous tasks always arise from the more fundamental concupiscible passions and terminate in them. In the animal kingdom, for example, fights arise over concupiscible things, namely, food and sex, and end with the victor claiming the concupiscible object. Such, then, are the two basic components in human sensuality, from which the following passions, including hope, are derived.

From the concupiscible part, there arise six passions.[379] Love (*amor*) is the fundamental inclination or aptitude for the sensible good; desire (*desiderium* or *concupiscentia*), the movement towards it when absent; joy (*gaudium*), rest in it when present. Contrary to these three passions are, respectively: hatred (*odium*), the fundamental dislike of the sensible evil; aversion (*fuga*), the movement from it; and sorrow (*dolor* or *tristitia*), the result of its presence. The irascible passions are five in number, all of which pertain to difficulty. Insofar as the arduous good is good, one tends to it in hope (*spes*); but if it is so arduous as to be impossible, one turns from it in despair (*desparatio*). Insofar as the arduous evil can be overcome, one boldly approaches it with daring (*audacia*); but as difficult to avoid, one shuns it in fear (*timor*). Insofar as the arduous evil is present, it causes anger (*ira*).[380]

From this schematic overview of the passions emerge the distinctive properties of hope. It is worth quoting the relevant passage at length:

> The species of a passion is taken from its object. Concerning the object of hope, there are four conditions. First, that it be good; for, strictly speaking, hope is not for anything except a good. And in this, hope differs from fear, which concerns an evil. Second, that it be future; for hope is not for a present thing already obtained. And in this, hope differs from joy, which concerns a present good. Third, it is required that it be something arduous, obtainable with difficulty; for someone is said to hope minimally for something that is immediately in his power to obtain. And in this, hope differs from desire or cupidity, which is of a future good absolutely, whence it pertains to the concupiscible appetite, whereas hope pertains to the irascible. Fourth, that that arduous thing be possible to obtain, for no one hopes for that which he cannot in any way obtain. And in this, hope differs from despair.[381]

From these four distinctive conditions of hope's object, one may extract a precise, formal definition of hope: the movement towards a future good that is difficult, yet possible, to obtain. As an irascible passion, it originates from more fundamental concupiscible passions: specifically, from desire, which is the movement towards good. Hope is thus the opposite of fear, which flees evil. Since hope includes *movement* to a good, its object must be future, unlike joy, whose object is present. And while desire moves towards any future good, hope intends an *arduous* good. It therefore adds to desire "a certain endeavor, a kind of elevation of the soul to attain the difficult good,"[382] as it rises to the challenge.[383] Finally, since it moves towards something as *possible*, it is contrary to despair, which shuns a good that is impossible to attain. Despair does not regard evil *per se*, since it can arise from the mere excess of good—for example, the despair of attaining union with God. Both despair and hope presuppose desire for the good, because you can only hope for, or despair of, what you want. But whereas hope moves towards that future good, despair withdraws.

Passions, however, differ from operations of the mind. Unlike the intellect and will, they are not *capax Dei*. Sensitive appetite does not consider the common notion of the good, because sense cannot apprehend the universal; whereas the rational appetite (the will) regards the common notion of the good. Insofar as they are movements of the irrational appetite, passions are neither good nor bad considered in themselves. It is only as ordered by reason that they become morally significant.[384] The passions also differ from the rational appetite in that they are commotions of the soul (as well as of the body); whereas acts of will, as simple affections, are without passion or commotion of the soul. Therefore, the theological virtue of hope, which lies in the will, has only formal similarities with the irascible passion of hope. It approaches a difficult good, but from a judgment informed by grace, not from an instantaneous passion.[385] The significance of this distinction between sensual and rational acts can be measured by the difference between the passion of daring (*audacia*) and the virtue of courage (*fortes*). Daring responds in the moment to particular sense data and dissipates as quickly as it arose; courage, by contrast, endures with firmer purpose because it proceeds from a judgment of reason.[386]

Thus, the claim "grace perfects nature" means that human nature is perfected *qua* human, that is, in its rationality, and not simply *qua* animal, that is, in its sensuality. This does not mean, however, that grace circumvents man's sensuality in its perfection of the human person. Rather, as it heals and elevates the mind, the mind in turn can order the lower appetites. In this way, the effects of grace "overflow" into the body.[387]

The passion of hope, then, gives only its name and general definition to the theological virtue. Beyond that, it contributes nothing to the theologian's understanding of hope: its object is sensible, it is held in common with dumb animals, and, worse, it abounds in youth and drunks, for "all fools and persons not using deliberation try everything and have great hope."[388] These attributes are not the most promising material for a theological virtue. But before explaining how hope becomes virtuous when it pertains to God, one must first grasp the similarity and differences between the acquired, moral virtues and the infused, theological virtues.

Hope as an Infused, Theological Virtue

The similarity between the natural and theological virtues rests in the shared designation "virtue." A virtue, whether acquired by human acts or infused by God's grace, is a good habit, a positive quality of the mind by which one lives righteously.[389] According to Aristotle, "the virtue of man will be the state of character [i.e., the disposition] which makes a man good and which makes him do his own work well."[390] It disposes the powers of the human person to their perfection. In the words of Josef

Pieper, virtue is "the enhancement of the human person in a way befitting his nature ..., the perfecting of man for an activity by which he achieves his beatitude."[391]

A virtue, then, is a settled disposition that is the source of those good acts which lead to happiness.[392] The infused theological virtues and the acquired natural virtues, despite their different goals, operate through the same innate human capacities of intellect and will. Just as the person naturally inclines to temporal happiness through knowledge and love, so she is supernaturally inclined to eternal happiness through the perfection and elevation of the same two powers.[393] In both cases, the happiness they bring is humanly possessed.

But the differences between the theological and the natural virtues vastly exceed their similarity. These differences stem from their differing finality: an imperfect happiness proportionate to human nature, and a perfect happiness consisting in "a certain participation in divinity."[394] The moral and intellectual virtues intend the imperfect happiness proportional to human nature and attainable in this life, while the theological virtues intend the perfect happiness of the vision of God in the next. This fundamental difference in their objects, derived from the twofold nature of happiness, determines the differences in their origin and acquisition, as well as whether or not they follow the mean.

The moral and intellectual virtues originate in us by nature—at least by aptitude and inchoation—and can be acquired through acts that follow the rule of human reason. The theological virtues, by contrast, come totally from without and must be infused solely by divine operation, because perfect happiness exceeds natural capacity.[395] Consequently, just as the goal of the theological virtues exceeds nature, so do their habits: "Because a habit must be in proportion to that which it disposes a person, ... it is necessary that a habit disposing to such an end exceed the power of human nature."[396] The difference between the natural virtues and the theological virtues is reflected in the different place of reason in their respective operations. The theological virtues intend God insofar as God exceeds human cognition, while the moral and intellectual virtues intend anything which human reason can comprehend.[397] Thus, while both sets of virtues perfect the human person, the moral and intellectual virtues do so "proportionate to human nature, but the theological virtues do so supernaturally."[398] One can now see whence the "theological" virtues derive their name: God is their object (and not the imperfect, proportionate happiness in this life); God infuses them by grace (as opposed to our acquiring them through following the rule of reason); and thus they are known only through scripture.[399]

From what has been said already, it should be clear why the theological virtues are "in us, without us" (*in nobis sine nobis*): they belong to us, because it is the human intellect that believes and the human will that hopes and loves; but they originate from outside us, because God infuses them.[400] Thus, one cannot charge them with any extrinsicism that renders them irrelevant to concrete human experience. As an example of their intrinsic nature, consider the claim that "by divine influence some principles are superadded [*superaddantur*] to the human person, through which one is ordered to supernatural happiness."[401] These "superadded" principles develop existing human capacities and operations. They are not some free-floating, extrinsic feature. They are "in-fused," not imputed; divinely given yet humanly possessed.

Because of their divine object, the theological virtues do not exhibit one of the fundamental characteristics of the acquired virtues, namely, observing the mean. To understand the importance of this difference, one must recall the nature of the mean. In the context of the virtues, the mean signifies the point at which something ruled attains its rule, rather than exceeds or falls short. When an act reaches its proper rule or measure, it is called good (just as a coat is called good when it reaches its proper measure, and is no good when it is too long or too short). The goodness of the moral virtues consists in the fact that, through them, the passions are ruled by reason.[402]

To give a general example: in the moral virtue that pertains to the irascible passion (which overcomes obstacles to avoiding pain and seeking pleasure), the mean is that point at which this passion attains the measure of reason (in courage), rather than falls short (in cowardice) or exceeds (in rashness). To specify this example: A soldier may face a painful obstacle to a desired good, such as attacking an enemy to win a just war. Reason dictates, say, a flanking assault at dawn. If the soldier's irascible passion is ruled by reason, he will courageously attack as mentioned; if it falls short of the rule set by reason, he will cowardly decline to attack; and if it exceeds reason's measure, he will rashly launches a frontal assault in broad daylight (i.e., his irascibility will overshoot any reasonable measure.)

Returning from this example to a general understanding of the mean, one sees that whenever something is ruled by something else, the mean of what is ruled consists in attaining the rule, as opposed to exceeding or falling short of it. The rule itself, however, does not have a mean and extremes. In the case of the moral virtues, it is not reason that lies in the mean, but the appetitive power as controlled by reason. Therefore, it belongs intrinsically to moral virtue to exist in the mean with regard to its proper object, that is, with respect to appetite ruled by reason.[403]

The theological virtues, by contrast, do not properly share this crucial feature of the mean, since their rule and object is God, "the first rule itself, not ruled by any other rule."[404] Whereas the moral virtues have as their object the ruling-of-appetite-by-reason, the theological virtues simply have God for their object. Consequently, whereas a passion may fall short or exceed rational measure, a theological virtue cannot, in itself and with respect to its object, attain the mean between two extremes, for God does not lie midway between two extremes. Hope, for example, cannot overestimate its object, namely, God's infinite goodness. (The theological virtues may, however, *per accidens* and from the side of the subject, admit a mean and extremes. Thus, hope can veer to extremes with respect to the hoping subject who either presumes to obtain what is above her capacity, or despairs of what is within her capacity.)[405]

Insofar as the measure of a theological virtue is taken from its object, God, it follows that it

> surpasses every human power, whence the human person can never love God as much as God should be loved, nor believe and hope in God as much as God should [be believed and hoped in]. Much less, therefore, can there be excess in these matters.[406]

Consequently, the theological virtues are said to exist not in the mean, but in an extreme.[407] By contrast, the object of the moral virtues, the passions, can be controlled as much as they should be rationally controlled; and, furthermore, they can exceed the measure set by reason. Thus, whereas a person may exceed in the attempt to find some balance in her irascible passions through rashness, and thereby overshoot the mean of courage, there is no such vicious excess in any theological virtue's approach to its object. Aquinas therefore changes the metaphor that describes these two different types of virtue: "the good of such a [theological] virtue does not consist in a mean, but grows as it approaches the summit."[408] Whereas one can attain the measure and object of moral virtue (appetite ruled by reason) and, likewise, of intellectual virtue (accurate correspondence to the reality being judged), one cannot attain the measure and object of the theological virtues, because it infinitely exceeds human capability.

A brief consideration of this change in imagery—from measuring the mean to approaching a summit—conveys something of the distinct nature of the theological virtues. The mean, as something measured, seems within one's control. To take the image of measuring literally, one stands above and apart from the object measured. The imagery of approaching a summit, however, is quite different, for it inverts the subject-object relationship. The subject no longer stands above and apart from the object that he measures by reason. Rather, he approaches an immeasurable object that cannot be grasped by the human mind. This shift in imagery shows how the different objects of the natural and the theological virtues alter the very character of virtue. Instead of rational balance between extremes, the basic tenor of the theological virtues is transcendence. Their object cannot be attained by reason but always remains something greater.

Hope Distinguished from Faith and Charity

In order to grasp the distinctive role of hope in scaling this summit, one must set it in the context of the other two theological virtues by which it is flanked. Understanding the specificity of hope and its ordered relation to faith and charity allows one to more precisely articulate its distinct contribution to Christian humanism.

Specification

What makes each theological virtue distinct? Aquinas succinctly distinguishes them in his commentary on 1 Timothy: "Faith shows the end, hope causes one to move towards it, charity unites [one to the end]."[409] The basic argument that specifies them is laid out in the third article of the sixty-second question of the *prima secundae*. Its *sed contra* appeals to the authority of the Apostle (1 Cor. 13:13) to affirm that faith, hope, and charity are fittingly reckoned as theological virtues.

The two powers of intellect and will, which differentiate the natural virtues at their most general level, partially account for the distinction between the theological virtues as well. Thus, one must recall how these faculties naturally order the human person to their proportionate end, since the theological virtues operate through these same faculties. The intellect "contains the first universal principles known to us through the natural light of the intellect, from which reason proceeds, both in speculative and in practical matters"; while the will "naturally moves to the good as given by reason."[410]

These natural powers only achieve their divine object if something be "supernaturally added."[411] "With respect to the intellect, certain supernatural principles are added to the human person, and are grasped through divine light. These principles are the things worthy of belief (*credibilia*), with which faith is concerned."[412] Thus, one can initially understand faith as an infused perfection of the intellect by which one assents to those truths necessary for supernatural happiness.[413]

The remaining two theological virtues elevate the will's potency for the good, for whereas "faith is in the intellect, hope and charity are in the appetitive power."[414] These "appetitive" theological virtues direct the person to supernatural happiness in two stages: first, the "motion of intention, tending towards the end itself as that which is possible to attain (which pertains to hope)"; and, second, "with respect to a certain spiritual union, through which the will is, in a certain measure, transformed to that end (which is through charity)."[415] This twofold operation of the will—moving to the end and conforming to it through love—distinguishes hope from charity.

Such are the basic arguments that specify the three theological virtues. Since the question under consideration falls under the general treatment of the habits in the *prima secundae*[416] and, moreover, since that general treatment follows the extended analysis of the subject's voluntary and passionate nature (qq. 6–21 and 22–48 respectively), question 62's discussion of the theological virtues is correspondingly general and, for the most part, focuses on the subject. It does, however, give some indication of the distinctive objects of each theological virtue, that is, of the particular divine attributes by which each virtue is measured. Specifically, it claims that "our faith is ruled according to divine truth; charity according to [divine] goodness; and hope according to the greatness (*magnitudinem*) of [divine] omnipotence and compassion."[417] Thus, each virtue approaches God under different aspects: *veritas* (faith), *bonitas* (charity), and *omnipotentia et pietas* (hope).

Immediately, one notices something curious about hope in this brief characterization. Not only is this intermediate virtue treated last, but it comes with a designation of size (*magnitudinem*) that seems redundant. Are not God's goodness and truth also great?[418] And if hope pertains to God's power and compassion, and charity to God's goodness, why does the response to the third objection of the very same question discuss hope in terms of God's goodness, and not in terms of God's power and compassion?[419] In fact, in his earlier writings, Aquinas struggled to express consistently the proper aspect under which hope attains God. While it is always clear that faith regards divine truth and charity divine goodness, hope is variously described as it relates to divine "abundance and majesty,"[420] or to God as "the highest difficult object,"[421] or to divine "kindness,"[422] or with special reference to the Father because it regards divine power "according to the sublimity of his majesty."[423] This is not to question the accuracy of the above correlation between the theological virtues and certain divine attributes; it simply shows why one must look beyond the *prima secundae* for a fuller treatment of the nature of the specific theological virtues. For this characterization of the theological virtues falls within a question asking whether the theological virtues observe the mean—which is an inquiry into the general properties of the theological virtues—and so should not be read as a definitive statement on the specific nature of any theological virtue. For that, one must turn to the *secunda secundae*.

Faith

Since dispositions are only revealed through actions, and actions are only intelligible in the context of their purpose or objective, the habit of faith can only be defined after identifying its object and examining its act.[424]

As mentioned, the theological virtues all have God for their object, but in different respects.[425] The aspect under which faith approaches God is First Truth (*prima veritas*), who reveals that to which our mind, commanded by the will, assents. Since faith is a cognitive habit, it has two objects: what is known (the material object) and that through which it is known (the formal object).[426] Faith's formal object can only be God as *prima veritas* because it assents only to those things divinely revealed as true. Faith is not virtuous unless it is faith in something revealed by God:

> The faith of which the Philosopher speaks depends on human reasoning that infers from something that is not necessary—from which it can be subject to error. And therefore such faith is not a virtue. But the faith of which we now speak depends on divine truth, which is infallible, and so it cannot be subject to error. And therefore such faith can be a virtue.[427]

Faith cannot include any intermediate or secondary object as its formal object, even the church. Accordingly, Aquinas suggests that the fourth article of the creed be understood as "I believe in the Holy Spirit sanctifying the church."[428]

Faith's material object, by contrast, is not only God, but many other things, such as "those things which pertain to the humanity of Christ and the sacraments of the church and the condition of the creatures."[429] These other things, however, can only be faith's material object inasmuch as through them we are ordered to God, that is, "insofar as through some effects of the deity, we are helped to tend towards divine enjoyment."[430] Nothing, then, falls under faith except as referred to *prima veritas*.

The manifold diversity of the material objects to which faith assents can be reduced to the relatively few propositions in the creed. "Because faith is principally of those things we hope to see in heaven ... therefore those things that directly order us to eternal life pertain in themselves to faith, such as the three persons, the omnipotence of God, the mystery of Christ's Incarnation, and other like things."[431] These principal objects comprise the distinct articles of faith.[432] Crucially, faith does not terminate in these articles, but rather in the reality to which they refer, namely, God. For, as in science, we form propositions in order to know reality through them, not for the sake of assenting to propositions.[433] Faith, then, is more than propositional assent.[434] Affirming the articles of the creed is an intermediate, albeit necessary, stage of the act of faith, for that act ultimately intends "the union of the human mind to divine truth."[435]

These distinct articles of faith may themselves be distilled to two fundamental, encompassing categories. "All the articles of faith are implicitly contained in some primary *credibilia*, namely, so that it is believed that [1] God exists and that [2] God has providence over the salvation of man."[436] This twofold core of the *prima credibilia* finds biblical warrant in Hebrews 11:6, as the quotation continues: "according to Hebrews 11: 'He that cometh to God, must believe that he is, and is a rewarder to them that seek him.' " In other words, what faith "shows"[437] is that God exists and God cares. These two most fundamental objective components of faith—in God's existence and providence—are, from the subject's perspective, (1) the goal of happiness; and (2) the way to the goal: "In God's existence are included all the things which we believe to exist eternally in God, in which our happiness consists; but in faith in providence are included everything God arranges, in time, for human salvation, which things are the way to happiness."[438] The same point is expressed more succinctly as follows: "Those things in themselves [which] belong to faith [are] [1] the vision that we will enjoy in eternal life and [2] that through which we are led to eternal life."[439]

Having considered the object of faith, one can explore its act, defined briefly in the *prima secundae* as "to believe in God."[440] To believe, generally speaking, is "to think with assent"; it is a particular kind of thinking "before the intellect arrives at its perfection through the certitude of vision."[441] Despite its conviction, faith falls short of science. In fact, it lies midpoint between opinion and science: "Faith occupies a middle position, for it is superior to opinion in that it has firm adhesion, but it falls short of science in that it does not have vision."[442] Thus, while faith is essentially an act of the intellect (because it yields knowledge), its insufficient evidence means that the will must determine the intellect to its object. "The intellect of the believer is determined to one thing not by reason, but by the will. And thus 'assent' is meant here as the act of the intellect insofar as it is determined by the will to one thing."[443]

Although a single reality, the act of faith comprises three elements. On the part of the intellect essentially, faith (1) believes God (*credere Deum*) as the material object, since nothing is proposed for belief unless it pertains to God; and (2) believes God as revealing (*credere Deo*), that is, as the formal object, the medium on account of which one assents to the articles of faith. On the part of the intellect as moved by the will, faith (3) believes or trusts in God (*credere in Deum*), since God as *prima veritas* has the additional aspect of an end.[444] Thus, expanding on the terse definition in the *prima secundae*, one could define faith's act as "the act of the intellect assenting to divine truth from the command of the will moved by God through grace."[445]

Having treated faith's object (q. 1) and its act (qq. 2 and 3), one can now define the virtue of faith. Hebrews 11:1 provides a quasi-definition: "Faith is the substance of things hoped for, the evidence of things that appear not." There are two clauses in this definition because the act of faith involves two faculties: the assenting intellect and the commanding will. "Thus the act of faith is ordered both to the object of the will (i.e., the good and end) and the object of the intellect (i.e., the true)."[446] Since faith is properly an intellectual act, that aspect will be treated first.

Faith is primarily an intellectual act because "the object of this act is the true, which properly pertains to the intellect. And therefore it is necessary that faith, which is the proper principle of this act, is in the intellect."[447] Since faith is infused by God so as to elevate the mind beyond its natural capacity, it may be termed the "perfection of the intellection."[448] As an intellectual act, faith is called "evidence" in the sense that it yields the result of evidence—or, better, the conviction—of nonapparent things. Why? Because God convinces the believer of the truth of these things, even though they remain unseen (i.e., unproven).[449] Thus, it is the intellect that firmly adheres to the *credibilia* precisely because they are held as true. A definition of the intellectual aspect of faith that is more exact than the one presented in Hebrews runs as follows: "a habit of the mind ... making the *intellect* assent to what is not seen."[450]

In addition to this primary intellectual aspect, the act of faith includes a volitional component because it is also ordered to the object of the will (i.e., to the good).[451] Hebrews expresses this volitional aspect as "the substance of things hoped for." Aquinas interprets "substance" loosely as "the initial germ of whatever thing, especially when the whole following thing is virtually contained in the first beginning."[452] Thus, hope is included in the definition of faith because faith's goal (*prima veritas* and other things believed in reference to God) is unseen, and hope involves the striving of the will to see what is unseen.[453] "In this way, therefore, faith is said to be the 'substance of things hoped for' because it is evident that in us the first beginning of hoped-for things is through the assent of faith, which contains virtually all hoped-for things. For we hope to be made happy when we shall see with clear vision the truth to which we [now] adhere through faith."[454] Thus, a more exact definition of faith's volitional aspect is "a habit of the mind whereby eternal life is begun in us" because faith initiates the hope for eternal life. To recap both the intellectual and volitional components in faith, one can see how the analysis of Hebrews 11:1 yields a precise definition of faith as "a habit of the mind whereby eternal life is begun in us, making the intellect assent to what is not seen."[455]

As this definition suggests, faith is only a beginning. It reveals the object, but does not move towards it. "Faith does not regulate the appetitive motion tending to God, which pertains to the theological virtues; but it only shows the object."[456] It will require a new, distinct virtue to move towards the object.

Hope

As an act of the will, hope is the "motion of intention tending towards the end itself as that which is possible to attain" as a future, difficult good.[457] The treatise on hope in the *secunda secundae* (qq. 17–22) expands on this general account.

Just as faith has God for its object in two ways—as material object (what is known) and as formal object (that through which something is known)—so hope's relation to God is similarly twofold. But since hope is an appetitive, not cognitive, virtue, it is more accurate to distinguish this twofold relation in terms of the final and efficient causes that move the will, rather than in terms of the material and formal object by which the intellect knows.[458]

> Hope ... considers two things, namely, the good that it intends to obtain and the help through which that good is obtained. The good that one hopes to obtain, however, has the intelligibility of final cause; the help through which one hopes to obtain that good, on the other hand, has the intelligibility of efficient cause.[459]

Hope, then, relates to God as final cause (the hoped-for object) and as efficient cause (the helper through which that object is obtained). Specifically, hope regards God as ultimate final cause by expecting God as eternal happiness; and as first efficient cause by depending on God's help to obtain the hoped-for object.[460] Thus, hope's final cause may be termed "God as my eternal happiness" and its efficient cause may be termed "God as helping."[461] In hope, then, a Christian regards God in two ways: as future goal and present helper.

As helper, God is the efficient cause of the virtue of hope. Hope becomes virtuous—that is, it makes someone good—when it relies on God's help to attain some good.[462] Why does this reliance make someone good? Because human acts are virtuous when they attain their proper measure or rule.[463] But God is the ultimate measure of human acts.[464] Therefore, when "we hope for anything as being possible to us by means of divine assistance, our hope attains God himself, on whose help it depends. And therefore it is clear that hope is a virtue, since it makes a human act to be good and to attain its fitting rule."⁴⁶⁵ Depending on God's help to attain a future, difficult good is therefore termed the efficient cause of the virtue of hope because it causes the effect of the hoped-for thing and makes hope virtuous.⁴⁶⁶ It does not matter whether one hopes to win eternal happiness or lose some weight; if one depends on God to hope "for anything"⁴⁶⁷ it is reckoned virtuous.

This point may be expressed negatively and by comparison with the theological virtue of faith. Just as faith without the formal object of "God as revealing" would not be a virtue, so hope without the efficient cause of "God as helping" would not be virtuous. Faith is only a virtue when what is believed is made known by God; likewise, hope is only a virtue when what is hoped for is expected through God's power.⁴⁶⁸ It is not a sign of human excellence, for example, to believe in the creed from one's own reason (since faith's conviction outstrips the evidence). It is, rather, a sign of poor judgment—or worse, pride, because one believes on the basis of one's own judgment, not God's revelation. Similarly, it is not a sign of human excellence to hope for something through one's own power, either for eternal happiness or temporal goods. If one hopes for eternal happiness from one's own power, it is a sign of wishful thinking (since the object exceeds human nature).⁴⁶⁹ And if one hopes for temporal goods from one's own power, it is not necessarily vicious, but neither is it virtuous. For while more mundane hopes may be normal and attainable, they are not yet virtuous. Anyone can hope, for example, to pass a difficult exam. But only a dedicated student possessing the requisite intellectual and moral virtues can actually pass. And if a student hopes to pass, it is his intellect and dedication one admires, not his hope.⁴⁷⁰ For if a lazy, unintelligent student hoped to pass from his own power, one would hardly think him virtuous. One does not, therefore, attain the proper rule of action (either reason or God) by hoping in one's own powers. Hope's virtuousness—the fact that it attains God as a rule of human acts—consists in hoping for anything as being possible to us by means of divine help. It is only the act of relying on God in the present, not simply wanting something from God in the future, that brings the person into actual contact with God.⁴⁷¹

But to be a *theological* virtue, hope must not only depend on God's help, it must also intend *beatitudo aeterna* with God as its proper object.⁴⁷² Depending on God's help to lose some weight or pass an exam would not qualify as a theological virtue, even though it be virtuous, because theological virtues have God for their object. To be a theological virtue, hope must not only depend on God's help as efficient cause (article 1), but it must also intend eternal happiness with God as final cause (article 2). If God were just the helper, then hope would attain God only as measure, but not as object. If God were just the goal, then hope would indeed have God as object, but without proper measure (i.e., presumptively). Only when these two claims (articles 1 and 2) are combined can one conclude that hope is a theological virtue (article 5). The two intervening articles (articles 3 and 4) address subsidiary issues that must be considered before one can conclude from hope's twofold cause to its status as a theological virtue.

Article 3 asks to what extent the object of hope refers beyond its subject; that is, it asks who one may hope *for*. The goal of someone's hope (eternal happiness with God) is indirectly reflexive because the subject who hopes primarily hopes for his own eternal happiness, not the happiness of others.[473] For whereas charity, as a form of union, necessarily regards another subject, hope, as motion, must regard its own term of movement. Hence it principally concerns the good "for me." Only secondarily, when united to someone else through the union of love, does hope regard another's eternal happiness. It is in this way that one hopes for a friend, "considering him as one's own self."[474]

Article 4 broadens the inquiry by asking whether hope considers intermediary objects. To the question, "May one hope only in God or also in creatures?" Aquinas responds that one must hope principally in God, but one may also hope secondarily in creatures. As principle efficient cause, God is the first agent that brings hope into existence, since hope depends principally on God's help to attain happiness. As secondary efficient cause, a creature (for example, a saint) may be an instrument of God's action moving us to happiness.[475] Similarly, as primary final cause, God is the ultimate end of hope. As secondary final cause, some other good may be an intermediate end that is ordered to the ultimate end.[476] Thus, although one may hope for something besides God, "whatever else hope expects to obtain, it hopes as ordered to God as the ultimate end and first efficient cause."[477]

Having clarified the ordering of primary and secondary causes for hope by the end of article 4, one can then combine the two claims of articles 1 and 2—on the twofold object of hope as efficient and final cause—in article 5, "Whether hope is a theological virtue?" In particular, article 4 prepares the ground for article 5 by providing the response to the first objection of article 5. That objection argues that hope cannot be a theological virtue because it "does not have God alone for its object, but also other goods we hope to obtain from God."[478] The response, drawn from article 4, counters that hope expects these other goods as ordered or referred to God, whether as instrumental efficient causes of God's action or intermediate ends ordered to God.[479] Having dealt with that objection, the *respondeo* can combine the claims of articles 1 and 2 in order to assert that hope is indeed a theological virtue.[480]

Moving from this twofold object, which makes hope a theological virtue, one can identify hope's twofold act: depending on God's help (and, secondarily, on the help of others, such as the saints, who are God's instruments) in the expectation of attaining the difficult, possible, future good of my own eternal happiness with God (and, secondarily, attaining other goods that are referred to that eternal goal).[481] Hope then evolves into charity when that goal is held through some kind of present union, rather than desired as a distant, future object.

Charity

Charity is first and foremost a friendship (*amicitia*) in which we dwell with (*convivere*) God in fellowship (*conversatio*).[482] Friendship is a particular kind of love that requires two additional components beyond ordinary *amor*: benevolence and mutuality. Benevolence entails loving some*one* so as to desire *his or her* own good (as opposed to concupiscence, which loves some*thing* for *my* own good).[483] Charity therefore considers God as a good in itself, rather than as a good for me (as in hope).[484] It loves God not for what God has done for me, but simply on account of God's goodness itself.[485]

The second component beyond ordinary *amor* is mutuality (*mutua amatio*), which follows from the fact that friendship is between friends.[486] For this mutuality to exist, friends must be in some kind of communication (*communicatio*, a "making in common" or participation). In the case of the theological virtue of charity, God communicates or shares his happiness with us. This sharing of happiness grounds charity, which is the friendship of the human person with God.[487] One can therefore love God as the object of eternal happiness because God loved us first by sharing his eternal happiness with us (cf. 1 John 4:10).

Because charity is a friendship based on the participation of a shared object (eternal happiness) through which one lives with God in fellowship, it unites the believer with God. For not only does "friendship imply union, since Dionysius says 'love is a unitive power,'"[488] but charity itself "is that which, by loving, unites the soul immediately to God with a bond of spiritual union."[489] And since one attains what one is united to, charity attains God, and therefore is a theological virtue.[490]

As a kind of union with God, charity clearly surpasses any natural love for God. Like the other theological virtues, it is infused by God's grace, not acquired by human effort.[491] As Romans 5:5 has it, "God's love has been poured into our hearts through the Holy Spirit that has been given to us."[492] Charity therefore elevates our participation into the trinitarian life of God: "Charity cannot exist in us naturally nor be acquired through natural powers, but through the infusion of the Holy Spirit, who is the love of Father and Son, whose participation in us is created charity itself."⁴⁹³ Thus, through charity, one enters the infinite, perfect relationship of divine love. In the words of Jean-Pierre Torrell:

> God not only wants us to be happy, he wants us to be happy with the happiness with which he himself is happy, his beatitude. Charity associates us then with the good already possessed in common by the three persons of the Trinity, in their very life, their happiness, and makes us participate in their eternal exchange.⁴⁹⁴

This intimate union with God differentiates charity from faith and hope.⁴⁹⁵ The latter two virtues cling to God "as a certain principle from which something comes to us": specifically, "knowledge of truth [and] attainment of perfect goodness."⁴⁹⁶ Charity, on the other hand, clings to God "on account of Godself, uniting the mind of the human person to God through the longing of love."⁴⁹⁷ So while all three virtues attain God in some way, charity excels because, through its union, it attains God in Godself, and not through something else.

> Faith and hope indeed attain God insofar as from him comes to us either knowing the true or obtaining the good; but charity attains God himself in order to rest in him, not to gain something ... from him.⁴⁹⁸

Put simply, charity attains God not as a means to the end, but as the end in itself.

The significance of this difference should not be underestimated. Loving someone because she gives me something is not the same as loving someone simply because she is good in herself, independent of what she does for me. These very different kinds of love underlie a crucial difference between hope and charity: hope seeks eternal happiness for oneself, whereas charity wishes eternal happiness for all.⁴⁹⁹ Consequently, while hope is more like concupiscence, charity is true friendship. "Hope presupposes the love of that which one hopes to attain for oneself, which is the love of concupiscence, by which love the one desiring the good more loves himself than anything else. Charity, however, means the love of friendship."⁵⁰⁰ By promoting our relationship with God from one based on reward to one based on friendship, charity has the following effect that radically alters the motive and goal of human life: "Charity, properly speaking, makes us tend to God by uniting the longing of the human person to God, so that we live, not for ourselves, but for God."⁵⁰¹ Similarly, charity extends the reach of hope, which, when formed by charity, desires another's eternal happiness, insofar as that other person is united with oneself through love.⁵⁰²

These differences between hope and charity account for the different aspects under which they approach God: God's power and mercy for hope, and God's goodness for charity. For while they both desire the same good[503] (i.e., God's eternal happiness), they nonetheless relate to it under different aspects: hope conveys a certain distance, whereas charity implies nearness because it unites the mind to God.[504] And if an object is distant and difficult to obtain, one needs a powerful and merciful helper to overcome that difficulty and distance. And so hope is measured by the divine attributes of omnipotence and mercy,[505] through which God is recognized as able and willing to fulfill hope's expectation. Charity, on the other hand, pertains to union with God through friendship. It does not regard this goal as difficult because it already unites the believer, in some fashion, to it.[506] Since it enjoys God in Godself, as something intrinsically good, and not as something useful for me, charity is measured by God's goodness (*bonitas*) rather than God's mercy and power.[507] Thus, one may functionally define charity as follows: Charity "consists in this, that God is loved above all things and that the human person totally submits himself to God, by referring everything he has to God."[508]

Thus, while charity, as with faith and hope, regards not only God but also extends to created goods (in particular, one's neighbor), nevertheless one's neighbor is loved insofar as she is referred to God. "The reason for loving the neighbor is God, for what we ought to love in the neighbor is this: that he be in God."[509] Consequently, one loves one's neighbor not as a final end, but *propter Deum*.[510] This is not to say that love of neighbor and love of God are two different loves. To the contrary, it is "with the same love of charity that we love all neighbors, insofar as they are referred to the one common good, which is God."[511] But it is to say that God must be loved more than our neighbor. For friendship mainly pertains to that which causes the good that grounds the fellowship. The friendship of charity, therefore, principally pertains to God, who is the cause of happiness, but extends to the neighbor who participates in the same happiness. Thus, when one loves a neighbor, one participates in God's love: "The charity by which formally we love our neighbor is a certain participation in divine charity."[512] And while neighbor love ranks after love of God, a neighbor, because more visible, is the first thing to demand love—which is why someone who claims to love God, but fails to love his neighbor, is lying.[513]

Returning to the principle meaning of charity as friendship with God, one must address the following problem before moving from the specification of the virtues to their ordering. The difficulty is as follows: If charity unites the believer to the object, would it not vitiate, rather than perfect, faith and hope? For how can hope and charity coexist at the same time and in the same person, since the advent of union (charity) nullifies distance (hope)? The solution to this problem lies in the fact that charity's union admits degrees. For example, on the part of the subject, charity can be considered perfect in three ways: when the whole heart is carried to God (which happens only *in patria*); when there is an earnest endeavor to scorn the world (*qua* sinful) and give one's whole time to God (possible but not common *in via*); or when one habitually loves God and does not desire anything contrary to God (common to charity *in via*).[514]

It follows, then, that as long as charity's union is incomplete, one can still hope for its completion. Thus, charity does not vitiate hope because charity's consummation only happens *in patria* through the beatific vision. It is only then that faith and hope come to an end. But *in via*, that vision remains unseen, and so one still needs faith to apprehend God and hope to continue moving towards that distant, future goal. Consequently, some form of imperfect union with God as object of eternal happiness (charity) can coexist alongside the desire for yet fuller union (hope). Furthermore, not only does charity's imperfect union *not* vitiate hope, but, to the contrary, it perfects it, because formed hope, possessing at least some union with its object, rejoices as it moves towards full union with an object it already partially possesses.

Hope Related to Faith and Charity

Having specified the three theological virtues, one can now see how they interrelate. Article 4 of the sixty-second question of the *prima secundae*, which asks "whether faith precedes hope, and hope, charity," gives the basic strategy for their ordering and relation. Making a determination on this issue is more difficult than simply establishing whether "faith, hope, and charity are fittingly accepted as theological virtues" (the task of the previous article). The same scriptural text appears in this *sed contra* as in article 3 (1 Cor. 13.13). But whereas this verse from 1 Corinthians clearly supplies the answer to the correct enumeration and identification of the three virtues, it does not immediately suggest their order, unless the mere sequence of their presentation suffices. Clearly, settling the order of the theological virtues requires further theological argumentation.

The key distinction that underlies Aquinas's ordering of faith, hope, and love invokes two meanings of order: generation and perfection.[515] In the order of generation, the imperfect precedes the perfect, just as matter precedes form. For example, a lump of wet clay comes before a pot. In the realm of rational operations, apprehension precedes appetitive movement, which in turn precedes union. One cannot move towards, or be united with, an object that one does not first apprehend, for "those things which are in the intellect are principles of those things which are in the appetite, inasmuch as the apprehended good moves the appetite."[516] You cannot want something unless you first have some notion of what you want. Thus, "the principle of all appetitive motions is the apprehended good or the apprehended evil. Whence it is necessary that some apprehension be the principle of ... all appetitive motions."[517]

Likewise, in the theological life, intellectual assent (faith) comes before the movement towards the end (hope), which in turn precedes union with the end (charity).[518] It is impossible for fear and hope to precede faith "because if we were totally ignorant with respect to the rewards and punishments (about which we are instructed by faith), we would in no way [hope for or] fear them."[519] Furthermore, since hope is only for the possible, one must first believe in the possibility of divine help and eternal happiness before one can hope for it.[520] Therefore, faith (apprehension) precedes hope (motion) and charity (union).

Next, hope precedes charity. The reasoning for this claim—that charity emerges out of hope—involves three steps. First, we only love a thing once we regard it as our good (*bonum suum*).[521] Second, we will, by extension, regard the person through whom we hope to attain this good as himself *quoddam bonum suum*.[522] Third, a love for this person emerges from our hope in him, precisely because we regard him as our good.[523] Charity, then, can in no way exist without the preceding virtues of faith and hope:

> Just as someone cannot have friendship with anyone if he disbelieved or despaired of being able to have some fellowship or intimate conversation with him, so someone cannot have friendship with God (i.e., charity) unless he has faith, through which he believes in this fellowship and conversation of the human person with God, and hopes to attains this fellowship. Thus charity cannot in any way exist without faith and hope.[524]

Thus, in the order of generation, faith precedes hope, and hope precedes charity.

In the order of perfection, however, charity precedes the other virtues. As shown above, it unites the believer to God as an inherently good friend in whom we can rest, as distinct from faith, which opaquely apprehends God, or hope, which self-interestedly approaches God. Charity is therefore the "greatest of the theological virtues" because it

> comes nearer to the object than the others. And in this way charity is greater than the others. For the others, in their proper intelligibility, signify a certain distance from the object: since faith is of what is not seen and hope is of what is not held. But the love of charity is of that which is now possessed, for the beloved is, in a certain way, in the lover; indeed, the lover is drawn through longing to union with the beloved.[525]

Because charity unites the believer to the goal shown by faith and approached by hope, it is the form of the virtues. Why "form"? The notion of form is applied from physics to human acts.[526] "In morals, the form of an act is taken principally from the end" because whatever gives an act its order to its end, gives it its intelligibility (that is, its form).[527] Why? Because acts only make sense in the context of the final goal they intend. But charity has the ultimate end for its proper object, namely, the enjoyment of God.[528] Therefore, charity in-forms faith and hope because it in some way attains the goal they both intend. In fact, charity is the form of *all* the virtues, because it directs them all to the ultimate and universal good.[529] It therefore puts order into every aspect of one's moral life, forging its intelligible, unified purpose, such that it can be given over in its totality to God. As such, "charity gathers the effective power for the good present already in the moral virtues to guide them to the ultimate end that transcends the natural tendency of the will."[530] Since charity causes this ordering, it is said to operate as formal cause *effective*, that is, after the manner of an efficient cause that brings about a certain effect.[531] The next chapter will elaborate on the significance of charity as the form of the virtues in the context of Christian humanism. For now, it is sufficient to show how Aquinas, in his reply to the objections in I-II.62.4, uses the distinctions between the orders of perfection and generation, and between formed and unformed virtue, to resolve some apparently contrary statements in scripture, Augustine, and Aquinas's own account of the passions regarding the ordering of the theological virtues.

First, when scripture likens charity to the root of the other virtues, this must be read as referring to the order of perfection, not generation. For in the order of perfection, charity is the "root" because it perfects faith and hope; whereas in the order of generation, charity presupposes faith and hope, and cannot exist without them.[532]

Second, when Augustine argues that hope is the result of belief and loving, this hope must be understood as already formed by charity, and therefore arising from it, unlike unformed hope, which precedes charity in time.[533] For "faith and hope, like the moral virtues too, can be considered in two ways: in one way, with respect to a certain inchoateness; in another, as being complete virtues."[534] The distinction derives from the second book of Aristotle's *Ethics*, in which an imperfect virtue is described as the source of a good action but one that is not done easily or happily; whereas a perfect virtue makes one perform a good work well, that is, as the good person would do it—promptly, with pleasure, and according to prudence. That distinction applies to the first two theological virtues. Faith and hope are imperfect when they laboriously and lovelessly intend their object: for example, when one assents with difficulty to a doctrine that is obscure and bears no fruit in one's life; or when one tentatively hopes for salvation in the absence of any merit. These same virtues, however, are perfect when their acts are informed by charity and therefore are done well: for example, when one believes in the same doctrine with ease and when that belief issues in good works, or when one hopes for salvation based on merits already acquired.

When formed, faith is no longer dead, but living ("faith without works is dead," James 2:20; and "faith works through charity," Gal. 5:6[535]); and hope, although still intending a difficult object, is itself no longer arduous, but is instead joyful ("rejoicing in hope," Rom. 12:12).[536]

The third and final apparent contradiction arises during Aquinas's discussion of the passions, in which love (*amor*) was the principle of hope. The response to this objection begins with a distinction between the object of hope and the person in whom one hopes. The priority of love only holds when hope considers the *object*, namely, the good hoped for. In this case, love does indeed precede hope, for we only seek to attain something we desire or love.[537] But when we consider the *person* from whom we hope to obtain some good, then hope precedes love, for our love for that person develops from a prior hope for a possible good we may receive therefrom. Thus, hoping for a good object differs from hoping in a person who can give us that object. In the former, our love for the good object prompts our hope to attain it; in the latter, our hope in the power and mercy of the person who grants the good object blossoms into love for that person as they share the good thing with us.[538] And since God is a person, not an object of concupiscence, then theological hope falls under the latter category; wherefore it precedes charity. The respective priorities of hope and charity (in the order of generation and perfection) are captured elegantly by William Hill: "Charity, wherein the will does not seek God for its own personal happiness but rests tranquilly in the divine goodness for its own sake, is the consummation of this love begun in hope."[539]

The same distinction between love as causing hope and love as emerging from hope occurs in article 8 of question 17. This article makes essentially the same point concerning the different kinds of hope (either for an object or for a person) but in broader terminology that distinguishes between perfect and imperfect. As with every appetitive motion, hope is indeed derived from *amor*. But there are two kinds of *amor*: imperfect and perfect. Imperfect *amor* does not love something in itself, but only insofar as it gives something to the one loving. This love of concupiscence pertains to hope because he who hopes intends to obtain something for himself. Perfect *amor*, on the other hand, loves someone (not something[540]) in him- or herself, as, for instance, when someone wishes the good for someone, as a person loves a friend. This perfect *amor* belongs to charity, which clings to God in himself. Therefore, while hope is prior to charity in the order of generation—because someone who hopes to receive a reward from God is thereby roused to love God and keep God's commands[541]—charity is prior to hope in the order of perfection, because hope becomes perfect when it is placed in friends, and someone can only be a true friend when they are truly (and not just concupiscently) loved.

Conclusion

The three theological virtues are the central Christian dispositions and acts that flow from the gift of grace. Faith is the "foundational" act of Christian life because of its critical assent to God's existence and providence, especially as shown in the Incarnation.[542] Next, hope is the providential movement toward the future, difficult, yet possible goal of eternal life with God, a journey already "pioneered" by Christ.[543] Finally, charity unites the person to God, a union modeled on Christ, through which the pilgrim can experience, even now, the peace and joy that will come with the journey's end. Taken together, Aquinas's account of the theological virtues shows how the infusion of grace transforms human knowing and loving.

This examination of hope and of its position within the theological virtues completes the exegetical chapters of this book. What they have achieved and what remains to be done? The previous chapter's exegesis showed the general humanistic spirit pervading Aquinas's theological system. It therefore demonstrated why, in general terms, Aquinas's doctrine of hope cannot be dismissed as irrelevant for a contemporary Christian humanism. This chapter's exegesis showed Aquinas's specific understanding of the nature of Christian hope. But it does not yet demonstrate how Aquinas's notion of hope informs a contemporary Christian humanism. As it stands, it cannot be straightforwardly applied to a contemporary Christian humanism without some creative appropriation. Recall that one of the distinctive features of contemporary Christian humanism is the shift from a synthetic to a dialectical style: that is, *from* winsome appeals to axioms such as "grace perfects nature" that are based explicitly on the doctrine of the Incarnation (and implicitly on assumptions about the Church's purported social harmony, past or present), *to* more realistic diagnoses of cultural tensions and contradictions, caused by the twin dislocations of globalization and secularization, that unsettle any harmonious vision of Christian identity. In light of this dialectical awareness, the preceding exegesis seems too neat. And while Aquinas rightly and carefully distinguished the theological virtues, they still need to be seen as a whole (beyond the limited discussion of their unity in terms of their relative priorities in the orders of generation and perfection). In the light of this inquiry into the theological sources of a contemporary Christian humanism, the theological virtues need to be seen as the differing modalities of the single graced way of living in the face of change, perplexity, and sin. The next two chapters will therefore seek to appropriate Aquinas's notion of hope for a contemporary Christian humanism that can, without losing its dialectical sensibilities, nonetheless more clearly articulate the integral relation between religious transcendence and the present human good.

Chapter Five

HOPE AND RELIGIOUS TRANSCENDENCE

The preceding exegesis of Aquinas's account of the theological virtues forms the basis of the following constructive reflections on the significance of hope for a contemporary Christian humanism. In this chapter, I explore how Christian hope specifies and deepens the idea of religious transcendence; in the next, how it underlies the task of constructing the present human good. These two chapters put to the test the guiding hypothesis of this study: namely, that since contemporary Christian humanism insufficiently integrates its two principal features of religious transcendence and the human good, the virtue of hope provides a critical theological source because it both moves toward God as future happiness (final cause) and relies on God's help now for any good (efficient cause). Hope thus promises to integrate in a single virtue what is potentially disparate in contemporary Christian humanist reflection. Can that promise be fulfilled? Does Aquinas's doctrine of hope articulate a credible movement of religious transcendence toward God alongside convincing grounds for moral action in the world? Can it inform and deepen what is meant by religious transcendence?

The task of this chapter—to explore how Aquinas understands hope as the movement of religious transcendence toward God and to unpack the significance of that understanding for Christian humanism—is approached in three stages. The first develops the exegetical findings of the previous chapter to show that hope, unlike faith or charity, essentially pertains to motion and thus can be thought of distinctively as religious transcendence. The second offers what I consider to be a legitimate development of Aquinas's account of the theological virtues. I argue that if hope be the motion that constitutes the transcendence advocated by Christian humanism, then faith and charity may be considered, respectively, the potency and the act of Christian humanism. This interpretation of faith, hope, and charity as the potency, motion, and act of Christian humanism helps to articulate how the theological virtues, in distinct yet related ways, mutually inform Christian humanism. In the third and final stage, I argue that a consideration of hope's distinctive kind of motion—as pertaining to difficulty—underscores the specifically

Christian character of Christian humanism, not least by giving a cruciform shape to its otherwise generic appeal to religious transcendence. For if the emphasis on faith in the Incarnation allowed a previous generation of Christian humanists to articulate the transcendent dignity of the human person, then the emphasis on hope allows contemporary Christian humanism to insist that such faith only becomes credible when it faces the difficulties which distort that vision and impede its realization.

From Religious Transcendence to Theological Hope

By drawing the person beyond his or her natural capabilities towards God, all three theological virtues unquestionably involve religious transcendence. Aquinas recognizes this shared movement of faith, hope, and charity in his early *Quaestiones disputatae De veritate*, in which he reckons them as "one complete motion, insofar as one is included in another."[544] Hope, though, differs from faith and charity because it distinctively and in its essence moves to union with God. While such transcendence is clearly not exclusive to hope—since faith and charity also approach the divine—neither faith nor charity are essentially constituted by motion towards union with God. To justify this claim, one must show how faith and charity pertain only indirectly to motion towards God, whereas hope comprises the heart of this movement.[545]

Unquestionably, faith involves religious transcendence because it glimpses realities that exceed the natural capacity of the intellect. But an important qualification, based on the difference between the intellect and the will, must be made:

> The motion towards things concerns the appetite. But the action of the cognitive power is completed not by the movement of the knower toward the things, but rather insofar as the things known are in the knower.[546]

In other words, the intellect "takes in" what it apprehends, whereas the will "moves out" to what it desires. The transcendence of the intellect, then, is not towards real union with the reality considered. Rather, it is an intentional movement that brings the reality considered into the mind. The will, on the other hand, moves towards real union with the reality desired. Again:

> The act of the cognitive power is perfected by the known being in the knower. The act of the appetitive power, however, is perfected through the appetite being inclined to the thing itself.[547]

Thus, since faith is in the intellect, it cannot, properly speaking, be called a *movement* of transcendence towards God, even though the intellect undergoes some undeniable religious transcendence in grasping the *credibilia*. It is more accurate to say that, through the graced illumination of the *lumen fidei*, the intellect glimpses something that it would otherwise not see. As the image of light suggests, one is seeing better, not moving closer. Faith "shows" the object, but does not "move" towards it.[548] And while this "showing" clearly transcends what the intellect naturally attains, it does not yet move the person towards real union with God, only intentional union. Faith is only a restricted form of religious transcendence, more intentional than real, more assent than ascent.

That hope centrally involves motion was seen in the previous chapter, which detailed the numerous places in which Aquinas specified hope as movement, in contrast to faith as "showing" and charity as "uniting."[549] In addition to those instances, the following examples confirm this characteristic: "The act of hope is a certain motion of the appetitive part, since it has the good for its object."[550] "Hope conveys a certain motion towards that which is not possessed."[551] "Love and hope differ as follows: love conveys a certain union of the lover and beloved; hope, however, conveys a certain motion or stretching forth of the appetite to any difficult good."[552] Furthermore, since desire is the movement towards a *future* good, hope is again seen as pertaining to motion: "For motion regards the future, while rest is in something present."[553] In this way, hope contrasts with charity, which finds fulfillment by resting in the desired object that is present. Hope, then, centrally pertains to motion. The precise meaning and significance of the term "motion" will be addressed in the next section after considering how motion is not of the essence of charity.

Charity, in contrast to hope, rests in an object that is already, to some extent, possessed.[554] Whereas hope moves to a distant end that is difficult to obtain, charity unites with the end in joy.[555] Since hope pertains to the end as distant, it essentially entails motion to overcome that distance. Since charity, by contrast, pertains to the end as already possessed, it does not essentially involve motion. Rather, its distinctive trait is transformation to that end.[556] Its operation, therefore, is not a restless movement, contending with difficulty, towards that which is not yet possessed. Instead, in its perfect state, it rests in a goal that is possessed. Unlike faith and hope, charity can possess its object, and the measure by which it is united to the object will be the measure it can rest therein.

Since that union, however, is never complete *in via*,[557] it follows that motion is not completely absent from the charity of the wayfarer. Charity moves, for example, between its different stages of beginning, progress, and perfection.[558] This development is even compared to motion: "Just as we also see in physical movement: first, withdrawal from one term; next, approach to another term; and thirdly, rest in this term."[559] Charity's motion, in the sense of its increase, can be understood "according to the intensity of act, namely, whether something is loved more or less."[560] Motion towards God, then, does not suddenly halt with the advent of charity. But that enduring motion within charity is not its essence. Rather, what is essential to charity is the union with and enjoyment of God, howsoever intense those activities be. It is only because that union and enjoyment admit degrees that movement arises within charity. But when that union and enjoyment are complete, motion will end, but charity will remain.

No doubt Aquinas occasionally suggests that motion is predicated of charity's essential operation, not just its accidental increase.[561] But that seeming difficulty can be met by distinguishing two senses of motion. Strictly speaking, motion is the reduction from potency to act. It is in this proper sense that hope is said to be a motion. But motion can also have a broader meaning, more properly called "activity" (*energeia*), which refers to many operations beyond the specific process of the reduction from potency to act. Aquinas follows Aristotle in distinguishing these two types of motion:

> As said in book 3 of *De anima*, "motion" is said in two ways. In one way, in the proper use of the term, according as it means the going forth [or egress] of potency to act, as an act of something incomplete.... In another way, "motion" is said of an act of something completed, that is, of something existing in act, as understanding or feeling are said to be a certain motion.[562]

Thus, in *actus*, becoming gives way to being, and there is no more essential imperfection that characterizes *motus*. Motion proper (the reduction from potency to act) differs from motion broadly understood (as activity).[563] When Aquinas describes charity as motion, the broader meaning of motion[564] is understood.

Thus, while both hope and charity tend to God, hope tends to God as a good to be obtained, whereas charity tends to God through ever-deepening union.[565] Hope's motion (which is the proper meaning of motion as reduction of potency to act) has the imperfection of striving towards a goal that is not yet present, whereas charity's motion (which is the broader meaning of motion as activity) has the character of perfection in that it unites one to God.

The same point applies when discussing charity's act. *Dilectio* differs from benevolence because it presupposes the union of affection between lover and beloved "insofar as the lover values the beloved as in some way one with him, or belonging to him, and thus is moved to him."[566] This movement of love is based on union, in contrast to the movement of hope, which is based on distance and absence. Charity's movement, then, is a movement from fullness, not emptiness.[567] It is therefore the broader sense of motion, a kind of perfect operation. Its motion may also be considered an increase or augmentation, by which the Holy Spirit more deeply takes root in its subject through the intensification of charity's act.[568] Even when Aquinas uses the terms of reduction from potency to act in the context of charity, thereby suggesting the first, proper, kind of motion, he explains that usage as the reduction to the last, perfect act, based on all the previous acts, which brings a motion to completion.[569] Whatever motion is ascribed to charity, then, is best understood as motion in the broader sense, as perfect act or operation, because the essence of charity is union with God. Thus, any motion it exhibits is its very operation or the intensification of its act.

The burden of this section has been to show, positively, how hope in its very essence moves the human person towards God and, negatively, how that movement is not an essential property of either faith or charity. Insofar as hope constitutes the heart of this graced motion towards God, it can be understood as the "religious transcendence" that Christian humanism advocates. Consequently, as a theological virtue integrally connected to faith and charity, hope promises to give greater theological specificity to Christian humanism's appeal to transcendence. In order to develop this promise, the next section argues for a new understanding of the interrelationship among the theological virtues precisely insofar as they inform the Christian humanist enterprise. This creative appropriation of Aquinas's thought allows one to identify more precisely the significance of hope for a contemporary Christian humanism. For it is not enough to appeal to the various images, scriptural or otherwise, that Aquinas uses to describe hope—for example, the walls built upon the foundation of faith;[570] or a column of smoke rising to heavens;[571] or an anchor, for just as an anchor secures a ship, so hope secures the soul in God while it exists in this sea of troubles,[572] thus making it the "strongest of the virtues,"[573] and so on. While such images may evoke the existential reality of hope, they do not meet the exigency of articulating a precise, conceptual account of how faith, hope, and charity variously relate to a Christian humanism they wish to inform. Setting out from the reliable starting point that hope is motion, I propose that one can not only *describe* hope through various images, but also *conceive* of hope as the process by which the humanistic potential of Christian faith moves towards its full actualization in charity.

Faith, Hope, and Charity as the Potency, Motion, and Act of Christian Humanism

The claim that faith, hope, and charity constitute, respectively, the potency, motion, and act of Christian humanism finds significant, if not complete, grounding in Aquinas. To establish the validity of this correlation, I first consider the nature of hope as motion. During the course of these initial comments, the technical meanings of the terms potency, motion, and act are given. Next, I draw on Aquinas's text to propose faith as the potency for Christian humanism, a potency that hope moves into the act or fullness that is charity.[574]

The Meaning of Hope as *motus*

The appropriateness of naming hope a motion becomes apparent when one grasps motion's proper definition. As mentioned in the previous section, motion, strictly speaking, is the passage or reduction from potency to act. For Aquinas, "motion ... properly speaking ... means the going forth [or egress] of potency to act, as an act of something incomplete."[575] As defined by Aristotle in the *Physics*, motion is "the fulfillment of what exists potentially, in so far as it exists potentially."[576] Motion, then, is neither potency, nor completed actuality, but the process of going from potency to act. It is therefore "thought to be a sort of *actuality*, but incomplete [because] the potential whose actuality it is, is incomplete. [Hence it is] ... hard to grasp, but not incapable of existing."[577] For example: a pile of bricks and some mortar are in potency; the process of building is motion; and the completed building is the act.[578] Before the building began, there was no actualizing of the potential; and once finished, there remains no more potential to be actualized. Only in the process of building is there said to be motion, that is, the process of the actualization of what exists potentially. "Thus, it is part of the nature of movement that the potential has not yet completely lost its potentiality and become actual."[579] To take another example: an acorn is in potency to become an oak tree; the process of growth from seed to fully developed tree is the motion; the oak tree existing as a fully developed oak tree is the act. From both these examples, it is clear that motion is a kind of act, but imperfectly so. Aquinas accordingly describes motion as follows:

> Motion is the actualization of something existing in potency. This is clear because, receding from one contrary, it does not, while it is moved, reach the other contrary that is the term of motion. Instead, it is in potency to it. And because everything

that is in potency is, as such, incomplete, motion is therefore the act of something incomplete.[580]

Clearly, hope exhibits the qualities of motion. It is the movement towards a term that is not yet possessed, and so, in that respect, it is imperfect (i.e., incomplete). "Hope conveys a certain defect, namely the futurity of happiness, which defect is removed when [that happiness] is present."[581] It is not simply a potency for that actual state of happiness; nor is it the completed and perfect act of happiness that has attained the goal. Rather, it is the passage from the potential for that act to the act itself; it is the process of actualizing the potency to be united with God, without having yet reached that goal.

Hope's Motion as the Process of Actualizing the Humanistic Potency of Faith

If hope, then, is a motion towards union with God, the following question arises: what, precisely, is the potency that it actualizes? Motion does not arise *ex nihilo*; it is the actualizing of something that already exists in potency. The motion that is the growth of an oak tree can only arise from an acorn (not a stone or a coconut), just as the motion of building can only arise from the materials of brick and mortar (not sand and water). Likewise, a person who can potentially build must be a builder (not a plumber or a theologian). In other words, for something to be in potency, it must have the capacity to be moved to an actual completed state because motion does not arise from nothing. What, then, is the potency that hope's motion actualizes? Three reasons support the claim that the content of faith may be understood as the potency of Christian humanism that hope moves into act. The first two reasons derive from specific properties of faith, as understood by Aquinas, that can be correlated with specific properties of potency; the third derives from a close examination of Aquinas's interpretation of a key scriptural passage. Together, these three reasons justify my "creative appropriation," in the context of Christian humanism, of Aquinas's understanding of the three theological virtues as a kind of potency, motion, and act.

First, the infusion of faith enables the very motion of religious transcendence towards union with God because it shows the end. In this way, faith differs from the intellect's natural desire for God because it actually gives the will some apprehension of the end of eternal happiness (at least by way of promise), which apprehension the natural desire cannot give.[582] (In this respect, one could consider the natural desire for God as the remote potency of hope's movement towards God, in contrast to the proximate potency of faith, which brings one into a qualitatively closer relationship with God.) Faith is therefore a crucial precondition for hope because the will cannot move to the end unless that end is first shown.

But faith is not itself that motion. Therefore, one might understand faith as supplying the *potency* for that motion of hope, since it presents the content (or "substance," as Hebrews puts it) of what is hoped for. For example, someone who knows how to build, but is not actually building, has the potency to build;[583] similarly, an acorn has the potency to become an oak tree, but is not in the process of becoming an oak tree. Likewise, someone possessing the virtue of faith is in potency for union with God, but, unless this potency be informed by charity, one is not actually united to God, nor, strictly speaking, in the process of moving towards that union. For that union to occur, one must undergo some motion or development from the potency of faith. Hope, it is proposed, is that motion.

A second reason supports the argument that faith is a kind of potency: it possesses another crucial characteristic of potency, namely, some intrinsic lack. For example, the potency that is an acorn is certainly not an oak tree, nor can it, of itself, move to become one. It requires a change in soil and climate conditions to move towards actuality. Likewise, a builder is only in potency to build. Without a reliable promise of financial reward (a contract), he will not begin the motion of building. Potency, then, entails some fundamental lack. What is simply in potency cannot, of itself, initiate motion towards act.

If the content of faith, then, is a kind of potency, it, too, will possess a certain incompleteness. Faith's lack with respect to action, as seen above, stems from the fact that it only shows the end, but does not move towards it. But faith's imperfection does not end there. The severity of faith's limitation derives, further, from its very relation to its proper object. For faith is less a "showing" of the end than it is an assent to an object that remains unseen because it exceeds the capacity of the human intellect *in via*. Faith remains a *cognitio aenigmatica*,[584] whose obscurity "does not pertain to the impurity of guilt, but rather to the natural defect of the human intellect according to the state of the present life."[585] So not only does faith, insofar as it is an intellectual virtue, not immediately move the person to God, but its central act is itself opaque. "The knowledge of faith does not calm desire, but arouses it."[586] Faith therefore makes the believer restless. It reveals an object that the intellect barely grasps, let alone approaches. But the believer wants to know more about the object to which she has given assent. Thus, "theological faith remains radically incomplete with respect to ... final fulfillment."[587]

A distinct virtue is therefore required that brings the believer closer to the divine object that exceeds faith's opaque vision. That new virtue, which issues from faith's inquietude, must be volitional rather than intellectual, since the will is the appropriate power for an object that is higher than the human person:

> In those things that are above the human person, love is nobler than knowledge. For knowledge is perfected insofar as the known is in the knower; but love [is perfected] insofar as the lover is drawn to the reality beloved. But that which is above the human person is nobler in itself than it is in man, because each thing is in another according to the mode in which this other thing exists. The opposite is true for those things which are below the human person.[588]

As primarily a cognitive relation to God (and therefore inferior *in via* to volitional relations to God), faith must be supplemented by a virtue of the will that remedies that deficiency. One cannot fully attain the object of faith by the act of faith. Believing that God is one's eternal happiness does not unite (or even move) one to eternal happiness. In this respect, faith is in potency to a new, distinct virtue that can begin the process of actualizing the virtualities that faith shows, namely, the *credibilia*. Faith therefore generates what might be called a supernatural desire for the beatific vision, analogous to the way in which intellectual wonder generates a natural desire for God.

A third reason supports the argument that faith is in potency to hope's motion: the presence of significant textual support, specifically, Aquinas's discussion of Hebrews' definition of faith as "the substance of things hoped for." Here Aquinas interprets "substance" loosely as the

> initial germ [*prima inchoatio*] of whatever thing, especially when the whole following thing is potentially [*virtute*] contained in this first beginning [*in primo principio*]. For example, we could say that the first indemonstrable principles are the substance of science because the beginnings of a science that are in us are principles of this kind, and in them are contained in potency [*virtute*] the whole science. In this way, therefore, faith is said to be "the substance of things hoped for," because it is evident that the initial germ of the hoped-for thing in us is through faith's assent, which contains in potency [*virtute*] all the hoped-for things.[589]

Similarly, in *De veritate*, Aquinas argues that faith "in potentiality [*virtute*] contains in itself those motions [of hope and charity] and is included in them."[590]

The words *inchoatio* and *virtute* require comment. Both suggest that faith involves potency. *Inchoatio*, as a "beginning" or, especially, "germ,"[591] suggests the idea of potency. The verbal root of the word—*inchoo*—means "to lay the foundation of a thing, to begin," and its past participle, *inchoatus*, conveys the contemporary meaning of "inchoate," in the sense of the imperfect beginning stages of something. Thus, although faith's content is not named as potency, the use of the word *inchoatio* suggests that such a designation is not inappropriate.

This suggestion is strengthened by the immediately subsequent use of the word *virtute*, an adverb derived from the noun *virtus*, to describe the manner in which faith contains the hoped-for things. According to Deferarri's *Latin-English Dictionary of Aquinas*, *virtus* has for its first meaning "*power, faculty, aptitude* ... [and it is a] synonym of *potentia*, *potestas*." The dictionary lists the third meaning of *virtus* as "*power, might, potentiality* in a being, [and it is a] synonym of *potentia* and *potestas*, the opposite of *actus*." Thus, *virtute* should not be confused with its English cognate "virtually," meaning "nearly" or "almost," which fails to capture the sense of potency that *virtus* conveys.[592]

Indeed, Aquinas himself interchanges the phrases *in virtute* and *in potentia* on occasion. Earlier, in I.4.2, Aquinas writes, "Manifestum est enim quod effectus praeexistit virtute in causa agente," translated correctly as "This is because effects obviously pre-exist potentially in their causes."[593] In the very next sentence, Aquinas discusses the same issue but substitutes *in virtute* for *in potentia* mid-sentence: "Praeexistere autem *in virtute* causae agentis non est praeexistere imperfectiori modo sed perfectiori, licet praeexistere *in potentia* causae materialis sit praeexistere imperfectiori modo" (emphasis added). An accurate translation need not differentiate the terms: "to preexist *potentially* in the efficient cause is not to preexist in a more imperfect way but in a more perfect way, although to preexist *potentially* in the material cause is to preexist in a more imperfect way."

Again, Aquinas's usage in the *Commentary on Posterior Analytics* confirms that *virtute* refers to potency and is justly translated "potentially." During the course of a comparison between efficient causes and self-evident principles, both of which contain within themselves a certain kind of potency, namely, effects and demonstrations respectively, Aquinas twice uses *virtute* to refer to potency.[594] In fact, in the same text, when discussing the nature of principles as potentially containing their conclusions, Aquinas treats *virtute* and *potentia* as synonyms:

> [The conclusion (or, what someone learns)] was known *potentially or virtually* [*potentia sive virtute*] in the pre-known universal principles, but unknown in actuality as particular knowledge. And this is what it means to learn, namely, to be led back from *potential or virtual* [*potentiali seu virtuali*] or universal knowledge to particular and actual knowledge.[595]

Thus, ample evidence indicates that *virtute* and *potentia* are synonymous terms in Aquinas's lexicon, and that *virtute* may be translated as "potentially" or "in potency."

To return to the argument: If faith is in potency, then the motion by which it becomes actualized must engage the very things that faith, in its incipient and inchoate way, shows. The virtue of hope fulfills this expectation because its twofold object directly correlates with faith's twofold *prima credibilia*. As shown above, faith's fundamental *credibilia* are

(1) God's eternal existence, which includes "all the things we believe to exist eternally in God, in which our happiness consists"; and,
(2) God's providence, that is, "everything God arranges, in time, for human salvation, which things are the way to happiness."[596]

Correlatively, hope's twofold causal relation to God intends

(1) God as the final cause of eternal happiness in the beatific vision in the next life; and,
(2) God as the efficient cause whose providential help *in via* moves the person to eternal happiness.

This duplex correlation between faith and hope derives from their shared appeal to the same biblical passage, Hebrews 11:6: "The one approaching God must believe that he is and that he is a rewarder of those seeking him." Just as this text provided scriptural warrant for asserting the two most fundamental items of the *prima credibilia* (God's existence and divine providence), so the same text justifies the two basic modes of hope's object (God as eternal happiness and God as helper). As Thomas says:

> The object of hope is, in one way, eternal happiness, and, in another way, divine help.... And both of them are proposed to us through faith, by which is made known to us that we can reach eternal life and that, for this, divine help is prepared for us, according to Hebrews 11.[597]

This use of the same text to establish the object of faith and hope shows, specifically, how faith is "the substance of things hoped for"—that is, how faith's content is in potency for hope's motion—since hope's twofold act directly engages the very two things that constitute the heart of faith's assent. Faith shows the existence of the eternal God in whom our happiness lies and the way thereto, while hope moves the believer towards that end through God's providential help. Indeed, "among the doctrines of the faith we say ... God has providence over human things; from this, the motion of hope arises in the heart of the believer."[598] Hope thus puts the potency of faith's content "into motion" (if not yet "into action"). This correlation confirms, then, that faith is in potency for the motion of hope and that hope is the process of actualizing the potency of belief.

If faith and hope constitute Christian humanism's basic potency and motive force, can charity be seen as its perfect act or complete operation?

Charity as the Act, or Culmination, of Christian Humanism

As a kind of completed operation or perfect motion, charity may be considered the culmination of Christian humanism (although the final consummation of Christian life remains unfulfilled until the beatific vision). The manner in which charity perfects Christian life *in via* is obvious from what has been said about charity up to this point. And since this inquiry focuses on the source, not the culmination, of Christian humanism, it is sufficient to recall briefly the main reasons for this claim.

As the form of the virtues, charity puts order into all the virtues, theological and moral, and thereby informs the totality of a person's life through this ordering of every action.[599] As the fulfillment of the law (Rom. 13:8–10, Gal. 5:14, James 2:8, and so forth), charity not only contains all other precepts,[600] but "extends to all human acts."[601] Thus, whereas faith and hope are preambles to, or foundational for, the law, charity is the goal of the law.[602]

While the other two theological virtues can exist without charity,[603] in this unformed state they are inchoate and therefore lack the perfection that is, properly speaking, required of a virtue. Why? Because a true virtue "not only does what is good, but also does it in a good way."[604] Charity enables faith and hope to act fully and completely, that is, perfectly.[605] With the onset of charity, the two preceding theological virtues are perfected or "quickened" or come alive; if charity is absent, then they are not yet virtues, but only formless beginnings of virtue.[606] In this way, charity is said to "quicken" faith because it causes it to come into full, mature, and pleasant possession of a formerly laborious, opaque, and incipient virtue. Thus, faith "works through charity" and, without works, "is dead."[607] Likewise, charity informs hope because one now hopes on the basis of merits already possessed, not on the basis of merits one hopes to acquire in the future.

The theological virtues thus possess a certain feedback quality. For just as faith and hope dispose the person to charity,[608] so charity turns back on hope and faith, and perfects their acts. Thus, from charity arises formed hope, in which someone hopes for a good from God as from a friend:[609]

> [The theological virtues] overflow back onto themselves in a certain holy circuit, because when anyone is already led to charity from hope, then indeed one hopes more completely and

> fears more purely and believes more firmly. Therefore, to say that hope is from charity is not said with respect to the first generation of charity, but with respect to a second pouring back of charity, insofar as already implanted in us, it makes us hope and believe more completely.[610]

The perfective function of charity can be seen, further, from its intrinsically social character (as one would expect from a virtue that is essentially a form of friendship). Unlike hope, which primarily regards one's own salvation, charity essentially involves union with the other,[611] and therefore more readily lends itself to the concern for one's neighbor. The fullness of Christian moral action in the world flows from charity, as is clear from the account of its principal act (*dilectio*) and its effects or fruits (joy, peace, mercy, beneficence, almsdeeds, and fraternal correction).[612] Indeed, with the advent of charity comes the infusion of all the moral virtues:

> With charity are infused at the same time all the moral virtues.... Charity, insofar as it orders the human person to the ultimate end, is the principle of all good works which can be ordered to the ultimate end.[613]

By uniting the believer to God, charity constitutes the heart of the Christian enterprise and vivifies the entire moral life of the person. It therefore culminates the Christian humanist aspiration to transform secular life through a deepening participation in God's love for creation.

Benefits of Understanding Faith, Hope, and Charity as the Potency, Motion, and Act of Christian Humanism

If hope can be characterized as the motion that sublates the humanistic content of faith to its own dynamics, then one can offer a more precise indication of how these virtues, together, ground Christian humanism; more precise, that is, than any of Aquinas's other images. For one may now conceive the relationship between Christian humanism and its theological foundation in faith and hope as follows. The content of faith establishes the *potential* for Christian humanism by revealing the transcendent dignity of the human person, specifically, her eternal destiny that is to be achieved through participation in Christ's paradigmatic union of humanity and divinity. Hope begins to actuate that potential through its *motion* towards union with God, or, in more familiar and generic words, as religious transcendence. (As Aquinas notes in a discussion of the creed, "acts of faith are shown through acts of hope.")[614] Finally, charity is the culminating *act* of Christian humanism because it unites the believer-pilgrim to God, and, in doing so, patterns the whole of the moral life *in via* on Christ, the divinely-human embodiment of God's love.

From this correlation between, on the one hand, the theological virtues of faith, hope, and love, and on the other the metaphysical terms potency, motion, and act, one can present the close relationship between faith and hope without collapsing them into each other. The temptation to collapse them can be seen in an otherwise laudable attempt to integrate the reality of historical change into an understanding of faith. Explaining how historical consciousness alters our understanding of faith, Roger Haight asserts that

> as the theology of faith is adjusted to the framework of historical consciousness, it becomes more and more difficult really to distinguish faith and hope. Indeed, hope can be considered as faith within an historical context. What I am suggesting here is not a substitution of hope for faith, but a view of faith that fuses it with hope on the deeper level at which they cannot be distinguished.... [O]n a deep level, faith and hope are indistinguishably one.[615]

While Haight correctly argues that greater recognition of historical consciousness entails a closer relationship between faith and hope, his appeal to an unspecified "deep level" in which faith and hope are identical obscures their meaningful distinction. Perhaps that "deep level" could be understood in Thomistic terms as the transformation of the soul's essence by grace, from which flow the distinct acts of the theological virtues. In any case, distinguishing faith and hope as potency and motion captures their tight unity-in-distinction without collapsing them into each other. The distinct but mutually reinforcing aspects of the three virtues are captured poetically in one of Ratzinger's reflections for a retreat, published as *The Yes of Jesus Christ: Spiritual Exercises in Faith, Hope, and Love*:

> Hope is the fruit of faith ...; in it our life stretches itself out towards the totality of all that is real, toward a boundless future that becomes accessible to us in faith. This fulfilled totality of being to which faith provides the key is a love without reserve.... Christian hope approaches [this divine love] in the light of faith.[616]

From this integrated account of the theological virtues, there results a firm insistence on their unity: "Hope and love therefore belong immediately to each other, just as faith and hope are not to be separated from each other."[617] This image of light, way, and goal conveys the interdependence of the theological virtues as they form an *ensemble vivant*.[618]

Another advantage of this correlation between faith, hope, and charity and potency, motion, and act is that it captures the dynamic interrelation of all three theological virtues. This may be seen through a contrast with another, less satisfactory correlation to which one might have appealed. That inferior correlation would begin on strong grounds by conceiving charity as the form of Christian humanism, because charity is the form of all the virtues, and thus is the intelligible structure of a life that seeks human excellence in all its dimensions. On more tenuous grounds, this correlation would then conceive the foundational role of faith and hope as the material cause of Christian humanism, based on Aquinas's claim that "the foundation and root have the *ratio* of a material cause."[619] While this correlation conveys how faith and hope are like formless matter insofar as they lack charity (cf. 1 Cor. 13:2, "if I ... do not have love, I am nothing"), it nonetheless fails to capture the dynamic relationship between all three theological virtues, and crucially, the motion that constitutes hope (not to mention any distinction between faith and hope).

To understand why the analogy *matter : form :: hope/faith : charity* fails to capture the growth inherent in a life infused with the theological virtues requires a brief explanation of the four causes. For Aquinas, following Aristotle, matter and form are intrinsic causes that explain that out of which a thing is made (material cause) and the intelligible structure that makes a thing to be the kind of thing it is (formal cause). These causes are therefore intrinsic because matter and form comprise what a thing is. On the other hand, the agent that brings about the change or the effect (efficient cause) and the goal towards which some thing moves (final cause) are extrinsic, in the sense that they do not comprise the very thing that is being explained, but must be some other, external reality responsible for change. Thus, restricting the explanation of the theological virtues to material and formal causality alone overlooks the reality of the extrinsic source and goal that, respectively, efficient and final cause explain.

Perhaps this inadequacy of material and formal cause to account for change explains a curious development in Aquinas's account of hope. Between *De spe* and the *Summa theologiae*, Aquinas alters the terminology he uses to conceive hope's twofold relation to God, as helper and goal. In the earlier work, *De spe*, Aquinas explained hope's twofold relation to God with the same terms he used to explain faith's twofold relation to God, as formal object (the revealer) and material object (the revealed). Thus, God as the helper who brings hope into existence was termed formal object; God as the goal towards which hope moves was termed material object.[620] But in the *Summa theologiae* a significant shift occurs. There, God as helper is termed efficient cause (not formal object); and God as goal is termed final cause (not material object). This development in the conceptualization of hope's twofold relation to God suggests that, in the later *Summa theologiae*, Aquinas was striving to express more clearly hope's nature as motion, for efficient and final cause account for change in a way that material and formal object do not.[621] This development more forthrightly conveys the reality of hope as motion, because God is no longer related to statically, as material and formal object, but dynamically, as efficient and final cause.

But if this speculation is true, why not then use all four causes to explain the interrelation of the theological virtues? Why not regard faith as material cause, hope as efficient and final cause, and charity as formal cause? Why map the theological virtues onto a different set of explanatory terms, namely, potency, motion, and act? To justify this move, a brief explanation of the difference between the four causes and the terms potency, motion, and act is required.

In brief, the four causes give a kind of snapshot account of a process at any given moment in time, whereas the terms potency, motion, and act capture the intrinsic dynamism of a process *qua* process.[622] Thus, the four-cause analysis will explain a thing in terms of what it is made from (material), what it is (formal), what brought it into existence (efficient), and what its purpose is (final). By contrast, the potency/act analysis attempts to capture a process, extended across time, in which a thing evolves from one state to another. Thus, it describes an initial, inchoate state that has the potential to become something else (potency), the very development or process of change (motion), and, finally, the completed state in which a thing actually exists in its fullness (act). If the four causes are like a snapshot, the potency/act terms may be compared to a video clip. Their greater attention to process and temporality can be seen by the fact that the very concept of time derives its intelligibility from motion, since time is simply the measure of motion. Consequently, even though efficient and final cause presuppose change, they do so only by naming its extrinsic source and goal. They do not, however, account for the inner dynamism through which the thing itself changes. In our instance, they account for the reality of God impinging upon the subject as a mighty and merciful helper, as well as the reality of God enticing the subject as final goal. But they do not convey the subjective changes wrought by hope, precisely as a process that transforms the person as she comes, over time, to appropriate faith and grow into charity.

For these reasons, the correlation I propose between faith, hope, and charity and potency, motion, and act simply develops a trajectory begun in Aquinas. That trajectory—which heightened the emphasis on hope's motionality by reformulating its twofold relation to God as efficient and final cause—is extended here in order (1) to emphasize hope's intrinsic nature as motion; and (2) to integrate that motion into the overall dynamism of all three theological virtues. This proposal therefore gives a more coherent account of how hope's "religious transcendence" is precisely the movement from the divinely-humanistic potential given in faith to its actual flourishing in *caritas*.

Understanding faith, hope, and charity as the potency, motion, and act of Christian humanism not only emphasizes the role of hope as the graced motion of religious transcendence, but also clarifies the conceptual relations between the theological virtues and Christian humanism. That conceptual clarification bears existential significance.

The Existential Significance of Specifying Transcendence as Hope

Once Christian humanism's religious transcendence is understood in terms of hope, one can more precisely and meaningfully specify the *Christian* nature of the transcendence that Christian humanism wishes to promote. Why? Because motion brings into act what exists in potency. Thus hope, as the motion that brings faith into act, can be understood as the process whereby faith's content becomes realized. Consequently, this hope-formed transcendence entails much more than the generic transcendence of the natural desire for God. The transcendence of hope moves the believer to realize the very claims that are believed: principally, the existence of God and God's providence that guides us to himself— paradigmatically through Jesus Christ, the pioneer who, in his divine humanity, has gone before us to that end. Hope, therefore, is the process whereby the intellectual assent of faith begins to be appropriated in the concrete willing of the believer. In Benedict XVI's words in *Spe salvi*, what is "informative" now becomes "performative."[623] The incalculable attitudinal shift that faith brings—because God is believed to be intimately involved in our personal and social history—now enters the very fabric of the believer's desire, as union with God becomes the ultimate goal of human longing. Whereas faith brings the mind to assent to truths otherwise beyond grasp, hope moves the will to ascend to goals otherwise beyond desire.

As the motive force that begins the long journey of realizing faith's conviction, hope is the point at which the believer becomes a pilgrim. That believer-pilgrim is not transcending in a generic way through her own efforts, but rather moving towards an eschatological goal along a Christ-like path through grace. Conceiving transcendence in terms of hope's motion, then, intimately links it with the Christian content of faith. It thus brings Christian specificity to the Christian humanist insistence on religious transcendence. That specificity is most evident in its cruciform way and its eschatological goal.

The Way of Transcendence as Cruciform

Hope is motion specified as difficult. It therefore suggests the cruciform nature of Christian humanism's religious transcendence. The significance of this claim can be seen by distinguishing the generic and specific potency of faith, and then working towards a similar identification of hope's generic and specific qualities.

Faith constitutes the originating potency for Christian humanism in a general and a specific way: generally, because it reveals the unsurpassable dignity of humanity's goal of union with God; and specifically, because it reveals Christ's divinely united humanity as the paradigmatic manifestation of God's providentially arranged way to that goal.[624] To appropriate faith's conviction in the transcendent dignity of the human person, however, is to encounter great and numerous difficulties, most fundamentally, finitude and sin. For it is one thing to believe in God and the possibility of union with God;[625] another to act on that conviction in a finite, fallen world that is manifestly separated from God. But it is precisely the reality of difficulty that hope engages as it moves from potency to act, from faith to charity, from conviction about God to union with God. Therefore, hope constitutes the foundational movement of Christian humanism: generally, because it moves believers toward the goal that faith shows; and specifically, because it supports them along the cruciform way toward that goal as it is sought in a finite, fallen world.

If faith shows the way by presenting the transcendent dignity of humanity, then hope moves along the way by confronting and overcoming the difficulties that undermine that dignity. If faith reveals the Incarnation and thus the greatness of God's love, then hope recognizes the cross and thus the unconditional nature of God's love as it enters a world that often crucifies whoever embodies that love. If faith opens up the transcendent horizon that gives human life its meaning and dignity, then hope realistically focuses on the suffering through which finite, fallen being must pass on its way to union with God. Hope thus allows the believer to go on when the splendor of faith meets the squalor of sin or the sadness of taking leave. It is therefore the point at which the conviction of faith begins to convince the world. For it is one thing to claim belief in providence; another to accept that providence is at work in life's difficulties. It is one thing to believe in the coming of God's kingdom; another to want it when it comes at a price.

> The sign of the strength of the hope we have on account of Christ is that not only do we rejoice in the hope of future glory, but also in the evil that we endure for it.[626]

Hope thus manifests what one really believes, as distinct from what one says one believes. Without it, suffering and difficulty undermine faith's conviction in the transcendent dignity of humanity. With it, suffering and difficulty, although realistically acknowledged as such, no longer constitute the final, tragic word, but rather something that can be endured, even transformed, through sharing in Christ's cross.

Insofar as hope encounters difficulty, it deepens the engagement with the Christian narrative, from assent to the doctrine of the Incarnation to appropriation of the reality of the cross. Precisely as emerging from faith, hope's transcendence contrasts sharply with the transcendence associated with the natural desire for God. That desire arose from intellectual curiosity about God's nature and relies on human effort. Consequently, as Aquinas notes in *De spe*, desire does not cling to God in the present and so lacks "spiritual contact" with God.[627] Hope, by contrast, arises from existential difficulty about enacting faith and relies upon God's grace. Consequently, hope's transcendence is, in the words of Karl Rahner, less like the eros of the mind that "opens upwards" to God and more a "falling into the abyss" that one encounters in the limits imposed by death and sin.[628] These limit situations, whether they be the severance of personal love or the corruption of moral failure, radically expose the inadequacy of any natural solution to the problem of human meaning. Hope arises precisely in the unflinching recognition and patient endurance of these limits. And by so acknowledging and approaching those limits, and correspondingly relying upon God's help to overcome them, it makes "spiritual contact" with what lies beyond them.

Consequently, any Christian humanism explicitly grounded upon hope is well positioned to follow Boyle's prescription that "to assert the relevance of a Christian humanism to the post-modern world is to take on the task of tracing and counteracting ... [the] detachment from finitude" that an increasingly consumer culture promotes.[629] By reckoning with the inescapable reality of the cross, a Christian humanism grounded on the virtue of hope can internalize de Lubac's sobering caution in the final chapter of his *Catholicism: Christ and the Common Destiny of Man*, entitled "Mysterium Crucis": "Humanism is not itself Christian. Christian humanism must be a *converted humanism*. There is no smooth transition from a natural to a supernatural love. To find himself man must lose himself."[630] Something of this sensibility was evoked, too, in John Courtney Murray's 1940 lecture at Loyola College in Baltimore, significantly entitled "The Humanism of the Cross,"[631] and in Walter

Kasper's 1972 address on "Christian Humanism," which concluded that "the death of Jesus on the cross stands at the center of Christian faith."[632] To ground Christian humanism on hope is to give the subjective, existential correlate to this objective, doctrinal emphasis on the cross.

Perhaps this explains why a faith that has yet to be tested by difficulty may, at times, seem to the observer to be more a possession than a gift. After all, insofar as faith relates to God as material object (what is revealed) and formal object (the revealer)—and thus in terms analogous to the "intrinsic" material and formal causes—faith could mistakenly convey a relationship with God that emphasizes God's presence as something intrinsically possessed by the believing subject (at least in the intentionality of knowledge). Prior to the emergence of a hope that sustains faith through difficult times, there always remains the danger of claiming faith as a possession. The advent of hope, however, makes Christian belief more believable, since it not only proclaims God's truth, but manifests God's mercy and power through a nonpossessive attitude of humble reliance and patient expectation. In Cardinal Newman's words, it teaches that Christian life is less about "giving glowing accounts" of the cross and more about patiently bearing it.[633] Whereas faith causes a radical shift in one's view of the world, hope appropriates that intellectual conversion by causing a correspondingly radical shift in one's way of life, especially in the attitude to suffering and death, which, as Taylor suggested, are no longer seen simply as evils to be combated but are instead set within a broader horizon of significance and meaning that lies beyond the limits of our finite, fallen vision.[634]

The Goal of Transcendence as Eschatological

Insofar as hope specifies transcendence as cruciform, it reveals its radical nature. For to encounter the limits of death and sin symbolized by the cross is to come before the abyss that lies beyond them. To freely and faithfully pass through those limits is to hope that one is entering not into nothingness, but into the depths of God's love. It is a twofold act that at once cedes control over the future and totally relies upon God's transcendent help. This ability to transcend in hope is most clearly shown in Jesus' death on the cross, as Rahner writes:

> For precisely this radical quality inherent in the "outwards of self" movement into the absolute incalculability and uncontrollability of God as our absolute future, is based upon that grace of God which finds its unique historical manifestation in Christ precisely as crucified, and thereby surrendering himself in the most radical sense to the disposing hand of God.[635]

In that reliance upon what lies beyond finite reality, the radically eschatological goal of hope becomes clear: namely, union with the transcendent, infinite God. The ultimate fulfillment of hope lies beyond finite creation and secular time.

Aquinas's designation of God's twofold relation to hope—as efficient and final cause—emphatically conveys the transcendence of God in the experience of hope. As extrinsic, these causes relate the person to God not as something possessed in faith's knowledge (however opaquely) or united with in charity's love (however imperfectly), but as something relied upon beyond one's power and moved toward while yet still out of reach—and therefore as something radically transcendent. Of course, any experience of grace, any theological virtue, lies beyond the limits of natural human abilities. Conversely, any experience of hope is precisely that, an immanent experience of God as merciful helper and possible goal. But what differentiates hope from faith and charity is a greater accent on God as something extrinsic, as the terms "efficient cause" and "final cause" convey. Hope thus brings into awareness the sheer transcendence of God, whether as the ultimate source of help in a world where no finite thing can offer salvation, or as the final goal of happiness in a world where no finite thing can satisfy human longing. Faith and charity, although also exceeding ordinary human reach, nonetheless give something that is intrinsically possessed, such as knowledge of God's truth or union with God in love. Hope, by contrast, does not give any sense of intrinsically possessing God. It gives instead a real experience of God as beyond, as radically transcending the world, and so, for that very reason, as the appropriate source of help and the fitting goal for desire.

As Benedict XVI asserted repeatedly and forcefully in *Spe salvi*, Christian hope is more than hope for a better world. Eschatological hope cannot be reduced to secular hope. In fact, there remains a crucial contrast between these two hopes. Christian hope begins when secular sources of help fail. Since the need for God's help arises precisely when secular longings reveal their intrinsic limitation, any description of Christian hope must emerge from the contrastive realization that one cannot finally rely on anything finite (*qua* finite) but must rely instead on that which is not limited by finitude or compromised by sin, i.e., God.

The following contrast with charity illustrates this point. Any discussion of charity can more readily begin with natural love (as Benedict's first encyclical, *Deus caritas est*, in fact begins) in order to explore how it is connected with and perfected by divine love, since the neighbor, not God, is the first thing to evoke love, and it is through our love of neighbor that we reveal whether or not we love God.[636] By contrast, hope only becomes virtuous when it relies upon God, not upon a neighbor or myself.[637] Consequently, the account of theological love can build on the experience of neighborly love, whereas the account of theological hope will, at least initially, contrast with ineffective hopes in anything finite. For hope without God is more like the optimism that withers in the face of difficulty. That is why, for Aquinas, spontaneous hope without reference to God is not virtuous and is only found in the young or the drunk: that is, in those who have little experience or those who evade the difficulties experience brings.[638]

The difficulty and unhappiness that prompt the need for hope explain why this virtue approaches God under the aspect of mercy and power. For when a goal is distant and difficult to obtain, only a powerful and merciful helper can overcome that difficulty and distance. The one who hopes, therefore, acts on the belief that God possesses the means (power) and the motive (mercy) to overcome the impotence and difficulties of creaturely existence as it seeks happiness with God.

In the experience of hope, then, the believer encounters that very transcendence of God that is discontinuous with our experience of limitation and brokenness. In fact, dissimilarity is written into the essence of hope because one seeks a goal that is not yet, by relying on a power that is not ours. That is why hope in particular appeals to the idea of motion and to the metaphors of journey and wayfarer (*viator*), all of which convey the subject's correlative transcending through the world.[639]

Conclusion

Hope gives theological depth to the Christian humanist appeal to religious transcendence. Intimately bound to faith, it specifies religious transcendence as cruciform and eschatological. It thus contrasts sharply with any generic, natural desire for God. This heightened emphasis on transcendence also prevents the reduction of Christian hope to a mere buttress for social progress.

But precisely because of that emphasis, hope would seem to obscure the second dimension of Christian humanism, the emphasis on the temporal human good. For if it moves the person to eternal life in the future, how is it really contributing to the human good now? Chapter 3's examination of the presuppositions of Aquinas's understanding of hope defused, in very general terms, the criticisms of contemporary theologians, such as Wolterstorff and Moltmann, who rejected Aquinas's notion of hope as having nothing to do with the present good. Can one now sharpen that rebuttal and develop specific aspects of Aquinas's understanding of hope that show why it contributes to the present human good? If not, one would be forced to choose between (to use Murray's terms) "incarnational humanisms," which emphasize the Christian contribution to the world, and "eschatological humanisms," which emphasize the apocalyptic judgment on the world.[640] But this is simply a theological transposition of the modern atheistic humanism dilemma that opposes the secular and the religious. How, then, can one give more precision to general appeals to balance hope in creation with hope for redemption,[641] and develop what Zachary Hayes calls a "dialectic understanding"?[642] To do so, one has to spell out how secular hopes relate to eschatological hope, and argue that Christian hope encompasses both. For although hope unmistakably conveys the transcendence of God and the cruciform path to him, it nonetheless remains a virtue in which God is felt as immanently present and in which we can rejoice, here and now. How, then, might Thomistic hope, *pace* Wolterstorff, order and perfect secular hopes, especially those concerning justice; and how, *pace* Moltmann, might it indicate what it means to hope for the recreation of the world?

Chapter Six

HOPE AND THE PRESENT HUMAN GOOD

Christian hope binds together the secular and the eschatological. Exploring the nature of this connection will reveal, in two parts, how Christian hope builds up the temporal human good. First, eschatological hope, precisely because it radically differs from and transcends secular hopes, protects and sustains them, especially as they encounter difficulty. It therefore grounds human moral action *in via* as its underlying modality, not least by counteracting despair. Second, secular hopes can themselves anticipate and participate in eschatological hope by preparing the person for God. In fact, Christian hope gathers those secular hopes into eschatological hope as the very means of realizing that transcendent goal. Thus, contrary to Wolterstorff's objection, Thomistic hope is not a narrowly "other-worldly" hope detached from earthly justice. Rather, the intimate participation of secular hopes in eschatological hope demonstrates the appropriateness of this virtue as a key source for a contemporary Christian humanism. To illustrate that participation, two examples, drawn from Aquinas's discussion of the law and of the beatitudes, develop the contention that Christian hope supports and empowers the construction of the temporal human good—not despite, but because of, its promotion of religious transcendence.

Throughout this chapter, Benedict XVI will be an important conversation partner. His opening brace of encyclicals, on love and hope, powerfully restate his influential reflections on eschatology and manifest his intention as pope to focus on the core aspects of Christian identity. In his 1988 set of retreat lectures, he described the theological virtues—the theme of the retreat—as "those fundamental attitudes in which human existence opens itself up to God and thus becomes truly human."[643] His views on these virtues are therefore important to this study on Christian humanism. But while his recent document, *Spe salvi*, shows how eschatological hope differs from and sustains secular hopes, it does not sufficiently account for how secular hopes participate in eschatological hope. Perhaps this reticence stems from his Augustinian theological sensibilities—heightened by his firsthand witness of a totalitarian regime—which emphatically caution against the perennial tendency to place ultimate hope in finite goods. Operating within a Thomistic framework, this book acknowledges that contrast between these two hopes while still advancing their intimate connection.[644] But it does not do so through winsome appeals to Thomistic principles (such as "grace perfects nature") that can gloss over the reality of suffering or diminish the transcendent difference and unpredictable newness of God's action. The examples from the law and the beatitudes are selected precisely because they reveal the cruciform way in which Aquinas understands grace to perfect nature.

These discussions aim to give a robust account of how secular hopes participate in the comprehensive movement towards union with God. For the weaker that account, the more one detaches the secular human good from, in Taylor's terms, the deepest theological source of moral motivation. That detachment, in turn, can lead to a theological misconstrual of, and pessimistic acquiescence in, the suffering to which hope responds. Articulating and developing Aquinas's position avoids that detachment. It also responds to Moltmann's charge that Aquinas lacks any sense of the renewal of creation. To the contrary, it shows that Christian hope entails not resignation from the world, but its re-creation.

Before beginning this argument, some basic terms require clarification. By "secular hopes" are meant those temporal aspirations that properly belong to the world (for example, hopes for social justice and moral virtue) as distinct from the radically theological hope for an ultimate, eternal fulfillment with God that transcends time. Thus, the distinction is not between supernatural and natural hope, that is, between hopes that are explicitly graced and hopes that are proportionate to, and attainable by, ordinary human capabilities. Rather, the distinction is between the hope that intends a divine goal utterly transcending time (which must be graced) and the hopes that intend temporal realities in the world (which may or may not be graced).

Eschatological Hope Protects and Sustains Secular Hopes

At a very basic level, eschatological hope contributes to the temporal human good because the very intention for a future goal has consequences in the present. As Benedict XVI states at the beginning of *Spe salvi*, hope is the disposition "by which we can face our present, [since] the present, even if it is arduous, can be lived and accepted if it leads towards a goal."[645] If eschatological hope intends what is good for the human *in patria*, then proportionally similar effects could be expected *in via*. By analogy, the intention to dine with good friends, for example, can make one happy throughout the afternoon. It could focus work by setting a clear deadline for its completion, reduce spending on snacks in the afternoon, and kindle a happy anticipation of a pleasant and meaningful conversation. Increasing productivity, reducing expenditure, and raising spirits are all present goods that derive from the intention for a future good. In principle, then, there are no necessary grounds for thinking that hope in the future diminishes concern for the present. Even if the hoped-for good is future happiness with God, one could only think that theological hope diminishes concern for the present if one erroneously thought that God and creation were competing causes. More positively, one could argue that to intend God as my future good—that is, as something that will accrue to me and be enjoyed as my human happiness—will bring present effects that correspond to that future happiness. For even though this good might be future in reality, it can still be present in some form in the imagination and anticipation.[646] In fact, one could argue that hope makes action more intense because the difficulty of its object excites our attention while its possibility prevents us from giving up.[647] There is an antecedent probability, then, that to hope for God as the human good *in patria* will contribute to the human good *in via*. To move towards future union with God in heaven, then, is not necessarily to recede from present obligations on earth.

But neither is it necessarily to engage them. For to claim that hope does not necessarily detract from the temporal human good is only a first step. It does not, of itself, explain why hope might in fact positively contribute to the human good of the *viator* state. To return to the example of hoping to meet friends for dinner: that anticipation for a future good might encourage one to overlook looming deadlines or it may serve as an excuse for laziness, and so on. It is possible (although not necessary) that an expectation for the future can dissolve one's sense of duty to the present. Likewise, the hope for eternal happiness could entail a Stoic resignation to human suffering. If you believe everything is going to turn out all right in the end, then why worry too much about problems now? It is not enough, then, to make the negative claim that hope does not, in principle, erode concern for present goods. Even the fact that hope squarely faces difficulty—and therefore cannot be dismissed as facile optimism—is insufficient. For it is one thing to possess an unflinching realism about the human condition; another to contribute to its healing. Stronger reasons are required to demonstrate why hope's motion to God as a future good builds up the human good here and now.

To see Christian hope in its cruciform and eschatological dimensions is to grasp the radically transcendent nature of God. More acutely, to recall the origins of hope in the contrast between God's omnipotent mercy and human impotent misery deepens that recognition of transcendence. But the deeper the sense of transcendence, the greater the hope for humanity, for two reasons. One, a fully transcendent hope relativizes all human projects and ambitions, and thus *protects* secular hopes from becoming absolute and, in political form, totalitarian. Two, a fully transcendent hope connects the person to a power that is capable of a deeper liberation, and thus *sustains* secular hopes when secular sources of help fail.

Eschatological Hope Protects Secular Hopes

By directing human longing to God, eschatological hope acts as a powerful solvent on any absolute claims of secular politics. In Aquinas's words, "Man is not ordered to the politic community according to all that he is and possesses.... All that a human person is, all that he can do, and all that he possesses, must be ordered to God."[648] Caesar is not God, and the state is not to be worshiped. This insistence carries particular urgency in the context of modern, especially twentieth-century, European history. The primary factor in modernity that warrants sharply distinguishing eschatological from secular hope is the need to counteract what Eric Voegelin has called the "immanentization of the eschaton,"[649] especially Enlightenment faith in material and moral progress, and the more radical Marxist hope for the kingdom of man. The vicious failure of the latter, and the inability of moral progress to keep pace with material progress in the former, exhibit the folly of restricting hope to solely human efforts to create a perfect society in this world. Christopher Dawson's reflections on totalitarianism capture the principle at stake very clearly:

> If we believe that the Kingdom of Heaven can be established by political or economic measures—that it can be an earthly state—then we can hardly object to the claims of such a State to embrace the whole of life and to demand the total submission of the individual will and conscience.[650]

In light of the European traumas that followed upon the collapse of the distinction between eschatological and political hopes, Benedict XVI has repeatedly urged their radical discontinuity. For "when this kind of duality does not exist, the totalitarian system is unavoidable."[651] From this conviction issues the striking and forceful claim of his 1977 book *Eschatologie—Tod und ewiges Leben*: "the setting asunder of eschatology and politics is one of the fundamental tasks of Christian theology."[652] The desire for a goal that transcends creation and exceeds natural human capabilities cannot be shrunk to a temporal political settlement achieved by human hands alone. The political relevance of eschatology derives from the fact that it empties politics of absolute claims.

> The Kingdom of God is not a *political* norm of political activity, but it is a *moral* norm of that activity.... The message of the Kingdom of God is significant for political life not by way of eschatology but by way of political ethics. The issue of a politics that will be genuinely responsible in Christian terms belongs to moral theology, not eschatology. In this very distinction, the message of the Kingdom of God has something very important to say to politics ... [namely, that] its own content is not eschatological.[653]

In a word, politicians are not messiahs. And in the post-1989 global market, it should be said that neither are economists, as has become clear since the financial crisis beginning in late 2008. By relativizing allegiance to political and economic projects, eschatological hope prevents the distortion that results from misdirecting the desire for the infinite towards finite goods.

Eschatological Hope Sustains Secular Hopes

Hope arises from impotent misery and so seeks liberation in God's omnipotent mercy. Precisely because its goal is radically transcendent, eschatological hope promises a liberation that the world cannot offer. For only a God who fully transcends finitude and sin could effectively liberate from finitude and sin. That is why eschatological hope not only protects secular hopes, but also sustains them. The very difference between these two hopes is the condition of the possibility for their relation.

This argument simply transposes into eschatological terms the classic Thomistic account of the relationship between Creator and creation. Aquinas argues that it is precisely the transcendent difference of the creator God *from* the world that establishes God's full presence *in* the world, or, otherwise put, creation's participation in God. In eschatological terms, this noncompetitive relationship between Creator and creation means that hoping for future union with the transcendent God does not enfeeble present commitment to hopes for the world. To the contrary, the very difference between God and the world is the reason why eschatological hope supports and sustains secular hopes. For the God who is the object of eschatological hope is not distant from the world, but, in the words of *Spe salvi*, "encompasses the whole of reality and ... can bestow upon us what we, by ourselves, cannot attain."[654] Correspondingly, the consummation of that hope—the Kingdom of God—"is not an imaginary hereafter, situated in a future that will never arrive; his Kingdom is present wherever he is loved and wherever his love reaches us."[655] That is why, in his earlier work *Eschatology*,

Ratzinger forcefully argued that the Kingdom is "not ... a heavenly reality but ... something God is doing and will do in the future *here on earth.*"[656] Eschatological hope, therefore, does not remove one from the world, but should, to the contrary, draw one into the agency of the God who redeems it.

Despair Reveals Hope as the Underlying Modality of Secular Action

The importance of eschatological hope for secular hopes can be seen by what, according to Aquinas, results from its opposing vice of despair, the absence of any transcendent hope in God's mercy and power. Despair is the contrary movement to hope, arising from an opposing judgment in the intellect.[657] Thus, while hope is the appetitive motion conformed to a true affirmation (i.e., "that from God comes salvation to humanity and God gives forgiveness to sinners"), despair is the opposite appetitive motion conformed to a false affirmation (i.e., "that God denies forgiveness to the repentant sinner, or that God does not turn sinners to Godself by justifying grace").[658] In essence, to despair is "to prefer one's own guilt to the divine mercy and goodness, [and therefore] to deny the infinity of God's goodness and mercy."[659]

Despair has comprehensive and catastrophic effects upon the human good, as Aquinas clearly recognizes:

> That through which people are led to sins seems to be not only a sin, but the foundation [or beginning, *principium*] of sins. But despair is of this kind, for the apostle says in Ephesians 4:19 of certain people: "They, despairing, have handed themselves over to lewdness in every work of impurity and avarice." Therefore despair is not only a sin but also the source [*principium*] of other sins.[660]

Aquinas develops this assertion concerning the perils of despair as follows:

> Through hope, we are drawn away from evil things and led to seek good things; and therefore when hope is removed people fall into sin without restraint and are drawn away from good works.[661]

An intimate bond thus exists between eschatological and temporal hopes.[662] Since despair totally removes any hope of reaching eschatological happiness, it scatters the unity of the moral self that would integrate its secular projects within some overarching theological goal. Remove that final goal, and the secondary goods ordered to that end lose their coherence and purpose. Consequently, since despair pulls one away from good works *in toto*, it is not merely one sin alongside others, "but the source of other sins."⁶⁶³

By moving the person in the opposite direction to despair, eschatological hope is presumably not merely one virtue alongside others, but, in some fashion, the origin of all other virtues as it orients all acts towards the final good. Since the term of its motion is God—who is not one thing alongside others, but the source and goal of all that exists—hope may be considered in some way the comprehensive and underlying modality of all moral intention.⁶⁶⁴

A further reason for despair's deleterious effect upon the human good derives from a distinctive feature of hope. Among the theological virtues, hope especially (although not exclusively) regards human participation in divine goodness. For whereas faith pertains to divine truth, and charity regards the union with God's goodness in itself,⁶⁶⁵ hope anticipates that union as the good for the human person.⁶⁶⁶ Consequently, hope has the character of concupiscence, while charity is true friendship.⁶⁶⁷ Hope thus approaches God not disinterestedly as goodness itself, but self-interestedly as something that the person can benefit from and participate in—that is, as the human good. As Ratzinger himself claims, "By its very essence, hope refers to the person." ⁶⁶⁸ It therefore awakens the sense that the *humanum* is capable of participating in God's goodness.

It is precisely for this reason that sin arises when hope fails, because in despair "man does not hope that he participate in the goodness of God."⁶⁶⁹ Remove eschatological hope, and secular hopes are severed from their ultimate goal with vicious results. It follows that "from our point of view, despair is more dangerous [than infidelity and hatred of God] because through hope we are drawn away from evil things and led to seek good things."⁶⁷⁰ Eschatological hope, then, reverses sin and grounds the present good precisely because it recognizes God as the ultimate human good.

Hope therefore informs the human good fundamentally and comprehensively. That influence can be seen in its relationship to the law. In the first article of the final question in the treatise on hope, question 22, "Of the precepts concerning hope and fear," Aquinas asks: "Whether there ought to be given any precept concerning hope?" He replies that hope and faith are not only explicit, particular precepts in the law—that is, something directly commanded—but also crucial preambles without which law is impossible.⁶⁷¹ Why?

> Because through the act of faith the mind of the human person is inclined such that it might recognize the author of the law as such to whom he ought to subject himself; while through the hope of reward, he is incited to the practice [*observantiam*] of the law.⁶⁷²

There is no point giving laws about how to live rightly unless the one receiving the law is "already subject and prepared to obey," that is, "unless someone already believed and hoped."[673] Thus, just as faith (as a preamble) had to be given in the form of announcement or reminder, so hope (as a preamble) had to be given in the form of promise:

> The precept of hope in the first promulgation of the law had to be proposed through the mode of promise; for the one who promises rewards to those who obey, incites them by this [promise] itself to hope. Whence all the promises contained in the law arouse hope.[674]

Hope, then, along with faith, plays a foundational role in any understanding of the law. Faith is the precondition for accepting or receiving the law;[675] hope is the precondition for acting on it. It is not difficult to apply these foundational properties to Christian humanism, if one understands the law as the obligatory core of the moral life in the present with which Christian humanism is concerned. So, just as faith is a necessary, but not sufficient, source of Christian humanism, so hope expands this source by moving faith's acceptance of the law into observance or practice. Hope, then, contributes decisively to the Christian humanist concern for the good of the present life. When one considers how the vices opposed to hope undercut the incentive for all good works, it is a short step to claim that hope is therefore a basic mode in which all action is done. That action, as always, is woven together with faith, which provides the prior intellectual awareness and assent; and with charity, which, as the end of the law, fulfills the movement towards the good in the present life.[676]

The comprehensive contribution of hope has been seen from a negative perspective (in the consequences of its absence) and from a minimalist perspective (in its relationship to the law). There remains the task of developing a fuller and more positive account of the connection between its secular and eschatological dimensions.

Secular Hopes Participate in Eschatological Hope as the Means of Its Realization

In light of the arguments presented above, the unity between eschatological and temporal hopes may be understood in terms of participation. Consequently, instead of two hopes, it would be more accurate to think in terms of a single, all-encompassing hope whose primary, eschatological goal includes and perfects secondary, temporal goals by gathering them into the one, comprehensive movement towards

God. In this respect, Aquinas's position resonates with that of Christian thinkers from as early as the second century, whose eschatology, according to Brian Daley, "insisted on the continuity of its hope with *this* world and its history."[677] The following reflections, derived from Aquinas, elaborate this continuity within the twofold finality of a single hope.[678] Before exploring those reflections, however, the following contrast with *Spe salvi* shows how Thomistic hope broadens and deepens Benedict's Augustinian position.

Clarification by Contrast: *Spe salvi* on the Relationship between Eschatological and Secular Hopes

Spe salvi's emphasis on the difference between secular and theological hope can be seen, interestingly enough, in the very places where it clearly affirms their connection. Consider Benedict's assertion that eschatological hope, although "directed beyond the present world, as such ... also has to do with the building up of this world."[679] As evidence for this claim, he cites the agricultural labor of medieval monks. While not wishing to slight their work, it seems strange that other fruits of medieval religious life that directly engaged human suffering were not mentioned, such as the foundation of hospitals or the formation of mendicant orders, both of which responded to the poverty attendant upon urbanization. It seems strange, too, that the one example offered here for the transformational nature of Christian hope now is agricultural development eight hundred years ago. One might, therefore, surmise that the invocation of medieval rustic purity serves more as a contrast to modern scientific hubris—the theme of the immediately following section of *Spe salvi*, "The transformation of Christian faith-hope in the modern age"—than as a viable model for contemporary Christians.[680] In any event, this passage certainly leaves plenty of room to develop the claim that eschatological hope builds up the world.[681]

Further instances show how the very assertion of the connection between secular and eschatological hope reveals a deeper emphasis on their difference. Consider, for example, the very clear and seemingly promising claim that would signal a fuller exploration of how secular hopes connect with Christian hope: "All serious and upright human conduct is hope in action," which is the opening sentence of the section entitled "Action and suffering as settings for learning hope."[682] But once again, this claim is left undeveloped and hedged round with warnings of the emptiness of hope without God (e.g., it ends in fanaticism or burnout). In fact, of the six paragraphs in this section, only one deals with action, the rest with suffering. The promised discussion of "hope in action" is largely missing.

Consider, finally, how even the affirmation that "we must always be committed to the improvement of the world" is (1) set in a concessive clause that (2) follows upon another warning of the illusory nature of purely secular hopes and (3) is followed by the unambiguous caution that "tomorrow's better world cannot be the proper and sufficient content of our hope."[683] That caution is, of course, valid, but its negative phrasing does not express the positive content and role of secular hope. Granted, secular hope is not the proper and sufficient content of Christian hope, but how might it participate in, and even contribute to, its realization?

Spe salvi thus remains incomplete, because however clearly and forcefully the *connection* between theological and secular hopes is made, it remains overshadowed by the even clearer and more forceful insistence on their radical *discontinuity*. The structure of the document itself supports this reading. Whereas *Deus caritas est* began with the unity between natural and graced love, *Spe salvi*'s first major section[684] focuses on the difference between Christian hope and contemporary secular hopes ("The transformation of Christian faith-hope in the modern age"). The next major section—which is meant to articulate "the true shape of Christian hope"—does so by way of contrast with false worldly hope that suffers from overconfidence in structural reform or in science. Only after the fourth mention of Ephesians 2:12—"having no hope and without God in the world"—is the "true shape of Christian hope" presented. Indeed, Ephesians 2:12 is mentioned five times and is by far the most cited scriptural text. By contrast, Romans 8:24, from which the encyclical derives its name, is cited just once near the beginning.[685] So important is this Ephesians text that Benedict glosses it as follows to leave no doubt as to his interpretation: "The Ephesians ... previously ... were without hope and without God in the world—without hope *because* without God."[686] Later, in one of the tersest statements in the document, Benedict says: "Let us put it very simply: man needs God, otherwise he remains without hope."[687] Given the centrality of this message for Benedict, it is not surprising that the emphasis of the encyclical falls on the vast difference between hope in God and hope in secular projects.

A final comparison between the two encyclicals encapsulates this difference. In *Deus caritas est*, the full verse of the scriptural text that gives the encyclical its name signals the notion of participation ("abides") that runs through the document, specifically in the account of how human love anticipates divine love, and how divine love heals and perfects human love. The consequent claim of the unity between love of God and love of neighbor is thus presented as the crucial hinge section (paragraphs 16–18, entitled "Love of God and love of neighbor") on which the bipartite document turns. In *Spe salvi*, however, the scriptural text that gives the encyclical its name signals the broken situation and frustrated worldly hopes from which only God-given hope saves. The consequent claim of the difference between secular and eschatological hope is thus communicated through the repeated citation of Ephesians 2:12.

As argued above, there are sound theological reasons for emphasizing this contrast. But the question remains: How can the relationship between secular and eschatological hope, which is overshadowed by *Spe salvi*'s insistence on their difference, be brought into the light? For while one fundamental task of theology is undoubtedly to "set asunder eschatology from politics," there remains the equally fundamental task of relating them.[688] As N. T. Wright points out in *Jesus and the Victory of God*, "the scandal inherent in this announcement [of the Kingdom] lay not in its *religious* but in its *eschatological* and therefore *political* meaning."[689] It is not enough to claim that politicians are not messiahs. For if eschatological insight is to make a difference to political ethics—no matter how circuitous the route or how dangerous the pitfalls—some kind of relationship must be elaborated. And so, in the final analysis, one cannot hide their connection because one fears their conflation. Yes, Benedict's well-placed concern over the disorder arising from any messianic conflation is indisputable. But the very judgment of their disorder presupposes some understanding of their proper order. By failing to make explicit that understanding, their connection unravels. And with that unraveling comes the following question: Why expend energy on a detached and distant "great hope," when the "greater or lesser hopes" so urgently demand attention? As noted earlier, a similar question lies behind Wolterstorff's criticism of Aquinas's notion of hope as unhelpfully and narrowly focused on a "supernatural consummation" that has "nothing in particular to do with the struggle for justice within history."[690] Aquinas's position, as we shall now see, is quite different.

Eschatological Hope Orders Secular Hopes to Their Transcendent Goal

Aquinas lays out the basic structure of the unity between eschatological and secular hopes in his response to the question "Whether someone can legitimately hope in a human person?"[691] That response begins by arguing that one must hope principally in God, but one may also hope secondarily in creatures. As principle efficient cause, God is the first agent that brings hope into existence, since hope depends principally on God's help to attain a happiness that exceeds human power. But as secondary efficient cause, a creature may be an instrument of God's action moving us to happiness.[692] Similarly, as primary final cause, God is the ultimate end of hope. But as secondary final cause, some other good may be an intermediate end that is ordered to the ultimate end.[693] Accordingly, finite goods proportionate to temporal human life can be caught up in hope's fundamental orientation to eternal beatitude. Hope for a more just earthly city, for example, can be a legitimate auxiliary object of the theological virtue of hope.[694]

In fact, the range of secondary objects that may participate in eschatological hope is, in principle, unlimited, for it is when "we hope *for anything* as possible to us through divine help, [that] our hope attains God himself, on whose help it depends."[695] Aquinas's comments on prayer suggest some examples:

> Prayer is the interpreting of hope…. But man prays to God lawfully not only for eternal happiness, but also for goods of the present life, both spiritual and temporal, and indeed for liberation from evil, which will not be in eternal happiness, as shown in the Lord's Prayer.[696]

The provision of the necessities of life ("our daily bread") would be another example.[697]

Precisely how secondary hopes participate in eschatological hope can be seen by exploring what it means to say that they are ordered or referred to the primary hope of eternal happiness. The term *in ordine* refers to a commonplace Aristotelian understanding of the hierarchy of goods. In book 1 of the *Nicomachean Ethics*, for example, the good of bridle making is said to be referred to horsemanship, which in turn is referred to military science, which in turn is referred to politics. Bridle making is a subordinate skill ordered to horsemanship because blacksmiths make bridles so horsemen can ride horses; whereas horsemen do not ride horses so that blacksmiths can make bridles.[698] Likewise, war is conducted for the good of the city, instead of cities existing in order to wage war. It is in this way that bridle making is referred to horsemanship, horsemanship falls under military science, and military science is ordered to the common good of the city. Thus, all these diverse works of the citizen participate in a shared political life that is directed towards the common good. Similarly, all the diverse hopes of the believer can participate in a unified religious life that is directed towards the final eschatological good.

Because secondary and primary goals can participate in one overall process, it is possible to intend more than one thing without dissipating intention:

> If [two things] be ordered to one another, it is evident ... that someone can intend many things simultaneously. For intention is not only of the ultimate end ... but also of an intermediary end. Someone intends, however, both the proximate and the last end simultaneously, such as in the preparing of medicine and bodily health.[699]

Thus, just as one can legitimately intend both bridle making and horsemanship as part of the same overall goal (insofar as the former is ordered to the latter), so one can legitimately hope for both daily bread and the coming of the Kingdom as part of the same overall process (insofar as the temporal good is ordered to the eschatological good). Something ordered or referred to a higher end, then, is at the service of, and not in opposition to, that higher goal.[700] In this way, secular hopes take part in ("participate") in eschatological hope.

Moreover, since God is the ultimate end of the human person, all human acts ought to be referred to God. As Aquinas states in the closing sentence of the treatise on distinctively human acts: "All that a human person is, all that he can do, and all that he possesses, must be ordered to God."[701] But just as all human action is referred to God, so all hope must likewise be ordered to God. What eschatological hope does, then, is gather in all secondary, temporal hopes and set them in the context of an eternal destiny. It thus gives them an importance they would not otherwise have possessed. The theological virtue of hope therefore adds dignity to the temporal project of constructing the human good *in via*. Gathered into the "great hope," it cannot be regarded as something ultimately insignificant, in the sense of bearing no relation to God as the final end. To the contrary, insofar as it participates in the primary goal of hope, it is caught up in the movement to God as the ultimate end.

Secular Hopes Constitute the Means of Eschatological Hope's Realization

Secondary hopes not only participate in the primary hope, but comprise the very movement that constitutes eschatological hope itself. This claim can be explored through a consideration of hope's essential nature as intention, that is, as a tending or moving to some end.[702] Unlike volition, which regards the end considered in itself, or enjoyment, which regards the end as achieved, intention considers the end "insofar as it is the term of anything that is ordered to it ... [that is, when] we will to attain it through something else."[703] More succinctly, intention is the will's movement to the end *as obtained through some means*.[704] Thus, insofar as eschatological hope intends eternal happiness with God, it must reach that end by means of something else. The specific means to the goal of eschatological hope are numerous and must be discerned through prayer, spiritual direction, and so on.[705] But the fact remains that eschatological hope has to be willed through something else, through some secondary objects of hope.

Citing Romans 8:24, Aquinas argues explicitly that eschatological hope is only approached through some action. One can be said to be "saved by hope," even though salvation is not yet attained:

> Someone is said, however, to already possess the end on account of the hope to acquire the end: whence ... the apostle says in Romans 8, "We are saved by hope." The hope of attaining the end, however, arises from someone being fittingly moved to the end, and drawing near it, which indeed happens through some action. Now someone is moved to and draws near the end of happiness through the operations of virtues.[706]

It is, therefore, something of an understatement to say, as Benedict says, that "our behavior is not indifferent" before God.[707] That litotes could be more directly expressed as follows: Human acts in the world constitute the way in which the person approaches the eschatological end. Consequently, not only do our secular hopes participate in eschatological hopes, but more fundamentally we only participate in eschatological hope in and through our secular hopes and actions. These "greater or lesser" hopes do not simply "keep us going day by day," as *Spe salvi* puts it.[708] They are the means by which we move towards the goal that eschatological hope intends; they are how our lives are gathered into and made worthy of union with God. Or, as Ratzinger stated in an earlier work, "The demands of truth, justice, and love upon our lives are eschatology's very own content."[709] Arguments such as these give substance to *Spe salvi*'s somewhat bare assertion that "all serious and upright human conduct is hope in action."[710]

There exists, then, a deep unity between eschatological and secular hope, so much so that it is better to think of one comprehensive hope whose primary goal envelops all secondary aims.[711] When the difference within this twofold finality was (for good reason) emphasized, the role of eschatological hope was understood primarily as sustaining secular hopes in light of their intrinsic limitations. In that context, eschatological hope saved secular hopes from the despair that follows from considering them without reference to God. But properly recognize the unity of eschatological and secular hope, and it becomes clear that the former plays more than a supporting role. Eschatological hope's reach extends throughout the whole range of human hopes as it orders, perfects, and sanctifies the totality of secular desires.

Crucially, those secular longings themselves comprise the very process whereby we move towards eternal happiness with God. For while it is true that the eschatological goal is beyond time—and thus differs vastly from secular goals—it is also true that, to recall Maritain, "what comes after time is prepared by time," and so is deeply interwoven within our ordinary, temporal hopes.[712] The movement towards eternal happiness, then, is coordinate with the desire for secular happiness, as the *Catechism of the Catholic Church* itself asserts:

> The virtue of hope responds to the aspiration to happiness which God has placed in the heart of every man; it takes up the hopes that inspire men's activities and purifies them so as to order them to the Kingdom of heaven.[713]

Secular hopes, then, participate in eschatological hope because they are ordered to the eschatological goal and constitute the very means by which the goal is attained. How, specifically, they constitute those means can be seen by exploring how they can prepare or dispose the person for God. For if secular hopes can truly participate in the desire for eternal life, they must correspond analogically with that eschatological desire. And the more this analogical correspondence is seen, the more Wolterstorff's objection—that Thomistic hope ignores "the struggle for justice within history"—fails.

How Secular Hopes Prepare the Person for God: Two Examples

Secular hopes prepare the person for God when they intend realities and values that are divine. When someone genuinely hopes for truth or goodness—that is, when someone seriously intends to achieve something true and good through some concrete means of action—that person reveals what he truly values, as distinct from what he says he values. But God is truth and love itself. Therefore, the person who chooses truth and love in the world is adhering to God by participating in essential attributes of divine life. And so, while eschatological hope does indeed make us capable of secular hopes,[714] secular hopes can themselves prepare us for God.[715] In ways such as this, *Spe salvi* intimates how authentic secular hopes dispose the person for God. This incipient claim finds scriptural grounding and systematic exposition in Aquinas's comments on the fourth commandment and on the fourth and fifth beatitudes.

The Fourth Commandment

Aquinas's reflections on the fourth commandment reveal an important correspondence between secular and eschatological hopes. Those reflections are found in his commentary on Ephesians 6:1, which reads as follows:

> Children, obey your parents in the Lord, for this is just. "Honor your father and mother"—which is the first commandment with a promise—"so that it may be well with you and you may live long upon the earth."[716]

Two preliminary comments about this text are in order. One, Aquinas understands this commandment to have significantly broad compass, as his comments in a question on almsgiving reveal: "All assistance to the neighbor is reduced to the precept concerning honor of parents."[717] Clearly, Aquinas is not talking about "family values" narrowly conceived. The range and importance of his extended application of the fourth commandment can be seen by the citation of Matthew 25:41–43 in the *sed contra* of that question on almsgiving (i.e., it includes caring for the hungry, the outsider, the ill, and so on).[718] Thus, Aquinas's claims about familial relations here bear upon wider social relations, especially those that concern the needs of the weak and marginalized.

The second preliminary comment about Aquinas's reflection on the fourth commandment concerns an objection to Aquinas's understanding of the relationship between law and hope. Aquinas argues that the effectiveness of the law depends upon the fact that the lawgiver is believed in and his promises hoped for. That is why, as mentioned, faith and hope are necessary preambles to the law. But here an objection arises. If secular behavior is related to eschatological hope only by the promise of reward, then an extrinsic and even mercenary connection seems to displace any intrinsic link between eschatological and secular hope.[719] I will use Aquinas's comments on the first promise of the commandments to address this objection. In order to assess how those comments might respond to that objection, one must see, first, why this commandment includes a promise and, second, what it promises.

God must explicitly attach a promise of reward[720] to this precept because, since it is natural for us to serve our parents, one might consequently think that such an act is not worthy in the eyes of God. Aquinas explains, "Lest someone believe that honor of parents be not meritorious because it is natural; for that reason he adds 'so that you may live long upon the earth.'"[721] In other words, God offers a promise of reward in this instance to show that just because an act is natural, it does not fall outside God's consideration. To the contrary, natural human acts—such as manifesting reverence and gratitude to one's parents—fall directly within divine providential care.

Turning to the promised reward itself, one sees concretely how secular longings correspond to eschatological hope. The reward has two components: "that you may live long on the earth" and "that it may be well with you." In the original context, this twofold promise referred to the temporal benefits of long, abundant life for the Israelites. But Aquinas maintains that in these words, "great goods were expressed in figurative language, namely, spiritual goods."[722] The identification of those spiritual goods is reached through an examination of the nature of gratitude in the light of Christian revelation.

> For one who is grateful for lesser benefits, deserves to receive greater ones. But we have the greatest of benefits from our parents: existence, rearing, and instruction. Therefore, when one is grateful for these, one is made worthy to receive greater benefits. And for that reason he says "that it may be well with you"; because, as 1 Timothy 4:8 says, "Piety is useful to all things, having the promise of life that is now and of the future."[723]

The greater goods that one may receive, then, include eternal life, as the citation of 1 Timothy indicates. In fact, Aquinas explicitly presents this as a possible interpretation in response to the objection that many who honor their parents die young:

> Or, it could refer to a spiritual meaning, that "thou may live long" in the land of the living. Psalm 142:10–11: "Your good spirit will lead me into the right land; on account of your name, O Lord, you will restore me to life."[724]

What is important here is not the validity of Aquinas's spiritual interpretation of scripture, but the value of its accompanying insight into the relationship between the secular and the eschatological. In claiming that gratitude concerning lesser gifts disposes one to receive greater gifts, his position bespeaks a correspondence between one's desire for natural goods and one's fittingness for the supernatural good.

For more specific reasons, gratefulness to parents can apply analogously to hope in God. This analogical understanding derives from the fact that the fourth commandment closely resembles the first commandment to worship God, "because God ought to be honored as the source of our existence, and because parents too are the source of our existence.... Therefore it is fitting that, after the commandments ordered to God, the first would be related our parents."[725] It is especially appropriate, then, that the natural act of honoring the two people from whom one received finite life manifests an attitude of gratefulness that prepares one to receive eternal life from the one who created all life. There exists, then, an intrinsic and intelligible connection between secular act and eschatological reward. The reward is analogically continuous in character with the act it rewards. In fact, the eschatological reward takes the natural dynamism of the act and moves it to its finality. Aquinas's comments on the fourth commandment, then, elaborate what it means for grace to perfect nature—that is, how the intrinsic quality of one's secular acts are taken up and transformed by God's grace.

But that transformation of nature by grace should not be considered seamless. Commandments, after all, proscribe those vicious actions that are all too often performed; otherwise there would be no need to proscribe them—or, in this case, they command virtuous actions that are frequently left undone. As Aquinas himself notes, the fourth commandment includes a reward for more pragmatic reasons than the ones explored above: "Because people, in other things they do, seek their own advantage; and because, from parents already old they expect no advantage, unless originating from God."[726] The comments above, then, about the correspondence between secular acts and eschatological hope, should not lead one to think that grace perfects nature easily. In fact, insofar as sin corrupts nature, the agency that redeems nature will be complex and cruciform. Therefore, the claim that "grace perfects nature" must acknowledge that Christ himself was made "perfect through sufferings" (Heb. 2:10) and that the perfection of secular hopes in a world marked by sin will involve suffering. Thus, secular hopes participate in eschatological hope not only because (1) they are ordered to and gathered into the eschatological goal and (2) they constitute the means by which the goal is attained, but also because (3) they can participate in the form of the paschal mystery, the dying and rising of Christ that is the heart of God's response to human suffering and sin.[727]

Something of that participation can be seen in Benedict's comments on the difficult context of many moral decisions. When someone chooses what is good, true, or just in the face of difficulty, that person places those higher goods above his or her comfort and security.[728] As those "symptoms of creeping privilege disappear,"[729] the nonnegotiable or absolute element in the claim of goodness or truth intimates some encounter with God's truth and love. This uncompromising commitment to truth or goodness constitutes a form of self-giving for others, a process of "allowing oneself to be drawn into [Christ's] *being for others*."[730] Thus, the one who suffers to realize these goods manifests a hope that participates in the form of Christ's cross and resurrection. The paschal form of hopes such as these can be seen in Aquinas's comments on the beatitudes, which reveal an intelligible and organic connection between act and reward.

The Fourth and Fifth Beatitudes

The beatitudes give a specifically Christian account of how actions relating to the good for the human person now, in particular with regards to justice and mercy, are intimately involved in the transcendence towards future life with God. Aquinas's reflections on the beatitudes, then, cannot be dismissed as arcane Thomistic pieties. To the contrary, he regards the Sermon on the Mount, which opens with the announcement of the beatitudes at the start of Matthew 5, as containing "the total formation of Christian life [because] in it the interior motion of the human person is perfectly ordered."[731] His comments thereon are thus central to his Christian moral vision. Indeed, Cajetan holds Aquinas's reflections on the beatitudes in such respect that his usually loquacious commentary gives way to the following laconic praise: "[They] are in need of frequent reading and consistent meditation, not exposition."[732]

For Aquinas, the beatitudes are the acts that flow from the theological virtues and the gifts of the Holy Spirit.[733] Each of these acts (being poor in spirit, mourning, being merciful, striving for justice, making peace, and so on) merits a particular reward. For example, those who mourn will be comforted, and those who show mercy will receive mercy.[734] Thus, all the acts of the beatitudes operate in the mode of hope, because they intend some future, difficult, yet possible, good.[735] As with the precepts of the law, the beatitudes derive something of their fundamental meaning from the reality of hope.

But the beatitudes differ from the precepts of the law in three important respects. One, they flow from the intrinsic habits and gifts infused by the Holy Spirit. They therefore contrast with the external act of obeying a legal precept.[736] Two, their acts are not only done in the mode of hope (as in the law, in which hope underlies all the precepts by way of preamble in the form of promise), but they also intensify hope as it draws close to its goal.[737] Three, the beatitudes also differ in degree, in that they more comprehensively manifest a direct, intelligible correspondence between act and hoped-for reward. Only two commandments were explicitly attached to a reward, whereas every beatitude directly corresponds to a specific reward.

The basic structure of the beatitudes is as follows. The seven beatitudes fall within three kinds of happiness—sensual, active, and contemplative—which correspond, respectively, to the obstacles, disposition, and beginning or essence of future happiness.[738] Thus, the first three beatitudes (being poor in spirit, being mild, and mourning) refer to one's sensual life, which, if desired as one's final goal, obstructs the way to true happiness; the fourth and fifth beatitudes (seeking justice, showing mercy) refer to the active life lived in relation to one's neighbors, which disposes[739] or prepares one for ultimate happiness; the last two beatitudes (being pure in heart and making peace) refer to the contemplative life in relation to God.[740] Since I am focusing here on the relationship between eschatological and secular hopes, I will concentrate on the two beatitudes that pertain to the active life in the world, that is, to one's relation to one's neighbors. But this focus should not obscure the fact that Aquinas sees the many beatitudes as aspects of the single goal of eternal life with God. Following Chrysostom, Aquinas recognizes that "all these rewards are one in reality, namely, eternal happiness; which the human intellect cannot grasp. And therefore it was necessary that it be described through various good things known to us, having observed the fittingness of the merits to which the promises are assigned."[741] In the beatitudes, then, one finds a more differentiated account of the ultimate end of eternal happiness than was discussed in general terms in the treatise on the last end of the human person (the first five questions of the *prima secundae*).

In the beatitudes, the reward corresponds to the act by counteracting the attraction of the false good that impedes the good act. For example, someone is impeded from acting justly or mercifully by an inordinate love of self that, from greed, wants more than its due or, from hardness of heart, screens out others' sorrow. "And for that reason the Lord assigns to these beatitudes those rewards on account of which persons forsake them."[742] Thus, since some forsake acting justly because they fear they will lose out, the reward for the just is to have their fill, which the sinful conditions of the world currently deny them. Likewise, since the merciless avoid the misery of strangers, God promises that the merciful, as they "enter into someone else's chaos" and risk being overwhelmed by another's problems, will be delivered from all misery.[743]

Aquinas's comments on the beatitudes, then, underscore the cruciform passage through which the "greater or lesser hopes" come to participate in "the great hope."[744] Whereas the fourth commandment presented a seamless continuation between secular act and eschatological reward, the beatitudes present a more complex connection. Their acts involve giving of self, at significant cost, for justice and goodness. The corresponding reward brings new life out of the sinful situation of misery and injustice. As acts performed in the modality of hope, they exhibit the intelligibility of human participation in the paschal mystery: that in giving one's life to what is good and true, one will find a life that is worth living. With reference to the fourth and fifth beatitudes that are especially relevant to this inquiry, a person who hopes to remove some of the injustice and misery in the world is, by that very process, disposing himself to God. For the extent to which a person shares in the living and dying of Christ, is the extent to which he or she can authentically hope to be raised with Christ. "For if we have been united with him in a death like his, we will certainly be united with him in a resurrection like his" (Rom. 6:5). Aquinas comments upon this text as follows:

> After he died, Christ rose; whence it is fitting that those who are conformed to his death through baptism would also be conformed to his resurrection through innocence of life. And this is what he says: "For if we have been united with him in a death like his," i.e., if we take on a likeness of his death in ourselves such that we are incorporated to it as a branch grafted onto a plant—almost as if we are inserted into the passion of Christ itself—"likewise too [we will be united] to his resurrection" … so that we might live innocently in the present and reach a similar glory in the future.[745]

Reading this Pauline text through the gospel passages examined above—since, according to *Dei Verbum*, the gospels have a "special preeminence … for they are the principal witness of the life and teaching of the incarnate Word"[746]—one can conclude the following: Just as someone shares in Christ's death through baptism—and, we might add, by meeting the costly obligations that baptism demands—so he or she will share in Christ's rising through leading a life that is innocent, among other things, of hardness of heart and injustice.

To be sure, the commitment to secular hopes does not bring about that eschatological fulfillment. But, as a dispositive cause, it sets the conditions for the realization of the effect. Just as the writings of the New Testament dispose the person to receive the grace of the Holy Spirit through their presentation of Christ;[747] or as purity of heart disposes one to see God by cleansing inordinate appetites;[748] or indeed as faith, by showing the goal, disposes one to hope; or as hope, by moving towards the goal, disposes one to charity's union with the goal,[749] so the commitment to justice and mercy in this world prepares one for a future happiness that transcends this world.

As in the discussion of the fourth commandment, the charge of a mercenary connection between act and reward fails.[750] It was seen above how gratefulness to the givers of one's finite life prepares one for union with the giver of eternal life. Here, a parallel claim arises: that compassion for the neighbors who make possible social life prepares one for the community of saints with whom one shares eternal life.[751] In both cases, the act/reward structure reveals an intelligible correspondence between what one does now and what one will receive in the future. The modality of hope that underlies this structure cannot be dismissed as extrinsic, since the hoped-for reward answers to the particular character of the act.[752] Indeed, the promise of reward manifests God's compassionate response to the human striving for the good, especially as it encounters difficulty and sin. It therefore completes the process of human growth towards a share in divine life. The brokenness or "cost" of that encounter is met by the future "reward" of unbroken happiness. In seeking the good in this life, one becomes worthy of belonging to God in the next.

Hope in the World: Not Resignation, but Re-Creation

Not Resignation ...

Hope's religious transcendence recognizes the depth of the difficulties that confront the attempt to live out Christian faith. In its cruciform realism, hope receives God's mercy and power to honestly admit and patiently endure the difficulties that distort the Christian vision of humanity. Hope may well begin with the experience of clinging to God's merciful power as it seeks a deliverance the world cannot offer. But that eschatological movement does not mean that hope is shot through with resignation and has nothing to offer the world. Christian hope is not baptized Stoicism.[753] It does not insulate the believer from the contingencies and vicissitudes of history. To the contrary, it immerses her in them. By keeping the humanistic potential of faith alive, hope moves the believer toward the love whereby that vision is realized. Because of this encounter with difficulty, the virtue of charity that ensues from this process, and the mercy that Aquinas names as one of its fruits or effects, are neither naïve nor arrogant. Therefore, to be a recipient of God's power and mercy in hope is to become empowered as an agent of that mercy in the world:[754]

> The Father of mercies and the God of all consolation ... consoles us in all our affliction, so that we may be able to console those who are in any affliction with the consolation with which we ourselves are consoled by God. (2 Cor. 1:3–4)

So while hope does indeed make the believer into a pilgrim, that pilgrim is not indifferent to others. David Tracy has breathed new life into the clichéd phrase, so often attached to the notion of pilgrimage, by altering its prepositions. It is not so much that Christians "are *in* the world but not *of* the world" as that they are "liberated *from* the world *for* the world."[755] This shift captures the renewed attention to the secular that conversion brings. Indeed, Matthew 25 presents the criterion of judgment for eschatological worthiness as precisely the commitment to such secular concerns of justice and mercy. For all the undeniable contrast between secular and eschatological hopes, there exists a deeper analogical participation.

The more one recognizes this participation, the less one's theology of hope can be mistaken for pessimistic resignation in the face of suffering. For example, *Spe salvi*'s closing discussion of the suffering that results from moral evil veers—contrary to the encyclical's intent—uncomfortably close to such a position. There, Benedict explores how meaning can be found in this suffering. For example, the suffering incurred by choosing the good reveals something about what it means to be authentically human. But caution is necessary here. To focus on the good effects that can result from suffering could create the impression that suffering itself is good, and not simply an opportunity to manifest the good. For example, the life of the Vietnamese martyr Paul Le-Bao-Tinh is held up as a model of how terrible suffering becomes "a hymn of praise."[756] But it seems the tradition has a more common way of responding to such hardships inflicted by the evil acts of others. The genre of lament expresses the prophetic "No" to this kind of suffering and so avoids the suspicion of a latent pessimism that, judging such suffering unavoidable, downplays the participation of secular hopes in eschatological hope. Some indication of this latent pessimism is suggested by the occasional unnuanced comment in *Spe salvi*. For example, when Benedict asserts that "the suffering of the innocent and mental suffering have, if anything, increased in recent decades," upon what evidence is he making this claim?[757] Similarly, while it is no doubt true that the "power of sin will continue to be a terrible presence," does not such homiletic brooding shortcut the political and cultural discernment of the variations in, and mitigations of, the inevitable influence of sin?[758]

In order to avoid this impression of undue pessimism with respect to secular hopes, one could rephrase the discussion of suffering as follows: It is not always a case of encouraging people to find meaning in it,[759] but rather of giving voice to their experience that it often has no meaning, and then assisting in the process that removes it. For beyond the meaningfulness of the noble and voluntary suffering that results from making a stand for the good, there lies the meaninglessness of the ordinary and involuntary suffering that results from being oppressed by the bad. It is one thing to willingly take vows to what St. Francis called "Lady Poverty,"[760] quite another to have an arranged marriage with her. Consequently, beyond the act of finding meaning in the optional suffering that purifies character lies the task of removing the imposed suffering that resists meaning and so often destroys character. And while it is true that much good can arise out of suffering caused by moral evil, it cannot be forgotten that it arises not from the suffering itself, but from the refusal to participate in the moral evil that caused it. Thus, any "hymn of praise" in the context of such suffering is to the goodness that is tested and proven by suffering, or to God's fidelity through suffering, not to the suffering itself.

Once this suffering is recognized as a surd that resists meaning, there is no need to project its unintelligibility onto God, as *Deus caritas est* seems to do, by positing a contradiction between God's justice, on the one hand, and God's love, which "turns against himself ... against his justice."[761] Rather, its unintelligibility resides exclusively within the human sin that causes injustice and misery. Consequently, the cross does not need to be asserted as an opaque paradox that "[culminates] that turning of God against himself."[762] Instead, it can be grasped as the transcendent intelligibility of God's loving response to human suffering that reverses the cycle of social decline, manifests the extent of God's love for the world, and heals human alienation from God.[763] As the subjective correlative to the objective reality of Christ's cross, the virtue of hope brings the believer to participate in that process. It moves faith's intellectual assent to this divine response, through difficulty, into the self-giving love that is the heart of this redemptive process.

... but Re-Creation

Now that the irreducibly secular dimensions of Aquinas's doctrine of hope are clear, one can respond to Moltmann's charge that it lacks any notion of re-creation, of "a new heaven and a new earth," of God's "making all things new" (Rev. 21:1, 5). Creatively extending Aquinas's position, one can argue that there exists a profound connection between the experience of hope and the recognition of createdness.[764]

Comparing the infusion of hope with the act of creation is not a fanciful exercise. Aquinas himself compares the relative excellence of the justification of the ungodly and creation, arguing that while creation is greater in terms of its mode of action (making something from nothing), justification excels in terms of what is made (eternal union with God).[765] *Mutatis mutandis*, one could say that the infusion of hope, insofar as it intends eternal union with God, similarly bears comparison with the act of creation, for the following reason. In the awareness of creation, there arises a sense of sheer gratitude for the fact that finite being came *ex nihilo*. At the heart of this sense of gratitude lies what Heidegger called the "wonder of all wonders": that there is something rather than nothing.[766] Analogously, in the infusion of hope, there emerges a sense of sheer gratitude for the fact that new life may come out of seemingly intractable personal and social difficulties. At the heart of this sense of gratitude lies the "amazing grace" of new life from the privation of death and sin.

To move from the recognition of createdness to the experience of hope is to undergo an intensification of the Christian experience of God from the One who creates existence from nothing, to the One who gives new life from death and sin.[767] In both the creation of all life and the re-creation of fallen life, God gives in excess of what is due: in creation, existence is given to what was nothing; in redemption, new life is given to what was damaged or lost. But the name for the giving of a gift beyond what is due is "mercy" (whereas "justice" names the giving of what is due).[768] Therefore, it is appropriate that the term "mercy" describes not only the experience of God in hope, but also the act of God in creation. For while creation, insofar as it is ordered and proportionate, reflects God's justice (since each part is given its due in the whole), insofar as it exists at all, it reflects God's mercy (since the bestowing of existence itself is not something owed). Hence, "the idea of mercy is, in a certain way, retained [in the act of creation], insofar as reality is brought from not existing to existing."[769] Mercy, then, underlies the act of creation, because creation is given through divine goodness, not owed by divine justice. Consequently, when Aquinas says that "at the deepest origin of any work of God appears mercy,"[770] we might paraphrase it by saying that God's mercy is woven into the very fabric of creation. And just as the recognition of the "merciful" act of creation conveys the radical transcendence of God, because God is acknowledged not as one thing alongside others, but as the source of existence, so the experience of the merciful infusion of hope similarly conveys the radical transcendence of God, because God brings about new life in a way that no finite helper could achieve, and sets the goal of union with Godself that transcends everything in creation.

Thus, just as creation reveals God's power and mercy—because it is God's external operation that is able to give existence itself (hence "power"[771]) and is therefore a gratuitous act that brings more than what could ever be due (hence "mercy")—so the hope that arises from the experience of salvation encounters the same divine attributes of power and mercy, but in a more intense and personal way. It sees as possible, through divine power, what previously seemed impossible. It therefore awakens gratitude for that unmerited divine gift. (In fact, precisely because grace brings the person into a new state of being that previously did not exist and certainly was not merited, it is analogically described as something created, that is, arising *ex nihilo*.[772]) This "journey of intensification"—from creation metaphysics to paschal dramatics—deepens the connection between secular and eschatological hopes, between the human good and religious transcendence. It thus fittingly conveys why the salvation of the world is called its re-creation. For God's redemptive action is the continuation and adaptation of God's creative action in the changed conditions of sin. In the words of Louis Bouyer:

> The redemption has meaning only as restoring and perfecting the creation.... [It] is simply creation attaining its end in spite of all; or better, it is creation triumphing over sin, which seemed to defeat it.[773]

There is no need, then, to choose between a hope focused on creation and a hope focused on redemption. There is no dichotomy between "incarnationalist" and "eschatological" Christian humanisms. On meeting the sin that marks human history, God's creative action becomes redemptive and therefore gives us hope that there is a providence that "shapes our ends / Rough-hew them how we will." The continuity between creation and hope is seen in the shared divine attributes of power and mercy that they both manifest, attributes which Aquinas explicitly links to divine providence.[774] The person's encounter with these attributes deepens in the transition from the recognition of creation to the reception of hope. The new life that results from the infusion of hope is so great that it is seen as part of a "new creation." And just as the awareness of createdness gives an extraordinary sense of wonder at a unique event that no one can possibly imagine, so the experience of hope raises powerful feelings of joy, trust, and confidence in an absolute future that no one can adequately grasp.[775] This subterranean connection between creation and hope conveys the existential resonance of, and gives systematic precision to, the relationship between the doctrines of creation and redemption.

Conclusion

Far from deflecting the person from the good here and now, Christian hope draws her toward it. By bringing persons into contact with the deepest moral Source, it protects their common good from totalitarian pretensions, removes the deleterious effects of despair, and sustains moral ideals in the face of difficulty. Conversely, the hope for the temporal good shares in the "great hope" for eschatological fulfillment. From the affirmation of ordinary life to the humanization of economic arrangements, secular hopes are enveloped, ordered, and perfected by the desire for eternal life. In fact, the very concern for justice and mercy here on earth prepares the person for life with God in the future. Christian hope is therefore the very opposite of resignation or indifference to the world. To the contrary, through its encounter with divine power and mercy, it gives some felt reality to the claim that God's fallen creation is being restored and made new.

Conclusion

THE HUMANISM OF HOPE

Any renewal of Christian humanism can only profit from more explicit recourse to the theological virtue of hope. As Aquinas's writings amply attest, the experience of hope sustains and integrates the twofold drive at the heart of any contemporary Christian humanism: to be closer to God and to be more compassionately human, not least, in the spirit of Paul VI's "new humanism," by helping those whose basic human needs are unmet. Christian hope thus unites within a single virtue what modern culture repeatedly drives apart: the desire for religious transcendence and the concern for the common good. Hope thus supports the enterprise of Christian humanism precisely at the point where it is most vulnerable to distortion from its cultural context in the modern West, namely, the failure to relate historical emancipation and religious salvation. By counteracting the perennial temptation to act as if God and humanity were competing causes, it avoids the false choice between a pessimistic Augustinianism that all but gives up on the world and an optimistic secularism that fails to see the world for what it is, as profoundly fallen but in the process of being redeemed by a power that transcends human agency.

This appeal to the virtue of hope should not be misconstrued as some placating, happy medium. Intelligible only in relation to faith and charity, it gives theological depth to an otherwise generic transcendence. For Christian hope takes up what faith believes and carries it through difficulty unto a deeper, transformed love. That passage, by definition, is not easy. It yields what Newman calls real, as distinct from notional, assent to the cruciform way and the eschatological horizon of Christian discipleship. By supporting the believer through finitude and sin, hope moves Christian faith to its fullest expression in love. For having been touched by God's power and mercy in hope, believers are empowered to become agents of God's mercy through their self-giving love for others who likewise encounter difficulty. Just as persons who receive hope lean on God's compassionate strength, which brings good out of their own suffering, so persons who receive charity cooperate with God's love, which brings good out of the evil around them. And so if the passage from faith to hope deepens the immersion in the Christian narrative from Incarnation to cross, then the passage from hope to charity further deepens that immersion from cross to resurrection, Christianity's founding and definitive event by which God brought new life from the sin that silenced the incarnate Word.

The enduring attraction of the Christian humanist tradition is that it seeks to bring all human culture into transforming conversation with God's revelation in Christ. But the more it recognizes the impediments to that aspiration, the more it must ground itself on hope. And the more it depends on this pivotal theological virtue, the deeper it is pulled into the Christian theological narrative. The basic structure of that narrative is a journey of intensification, sustained by hope, from the potency of faith to the actuality of charity; or, in a dogmatic register, a deepening personal resonance with the doctrines of Incarnation, cross, and resurrection; or, simply put, an ever closer patterning on the form of Christ. By bringing persons more thoroughly into the community of faith, hope, and love—and thereby into the distinctive traditions and social practices that constitute and sustain the church—the Christian humanist enterprise more effectively facilitates the conversation between gospel and culture. For it is only by its distinctiveness from the surrounding culture—that is, as announcing and embodying something about divine revelation that would otherwise remain unknown or inchoate—that a Christian humanism finally has relevance for that culture.[776]

A Christian humanism more explicitly grounded on hope thus takes up the challenge laid down by Tracey Rowland's *Culture and the Thomist Tradition: After Vatican II*. Synthesizing elements found in Radical Orthodoxy, Alisdair MacIntyre, and the Communio school of theology, Rowland's influential work seeks to remedy the Thomistic tradition's inadequate grasp of the significance of culture for moral formation. Its more culturally aware "post-modern Augustinian Thomism" persuasively argues that any theological engagement with modern culture must spring from specifically Christian "cult," that is, its distinctive complex of narratives, forms of life, and compelling, beautiful worship.

Accompanying this praiseworthy exhortation, however, is the wholesale dismissal of the culture of modernity. In this respect, Rowland's work, for all its insight, is symptomatic of an undiscriminating trend in contemporary theology. If one does not share this global rejection of modern culture and instead holds that there is something positive to learn from it (following the arguments of thinkers like Maritain, Taylor, and Boyle advanced in chapter 1), then one will be more receptive to the possibility, even desirability, of change in some aspects of Christian social practices and time-bound framings of its narrative.

The ability to handle such changes, however, entails the modification of Rowland's "Augustinian" reading of hope, which she correlates to the faculty of memory and, more tenuously, to the transcendental property of beauty.[777] No doubt this correlation offers suggestive avenues for thinking about hope in the culturally significant terms of narrative (because it accents memory) and worship (because it accents beauty). But this inchoate attempt to synthesize the Augustinian and Thomist traditions on hope suffers from a serious omission. The recognition of change and difficulty—which is so critical to Aquinas's account of hope—is silently passed over. Instead, by locating hope in the memory, this virtue conveniently dovetails with Rowland's antimodern sensibilities which, presumably, wish to revive memories of a purportedly golden age of Christendom, before the much-berated "nihilism" of modernity. Furthermore, by correlating hope with beauty, this virtue is uncomfortably fitted into a notion of aesthetic harmony that occludes conflict and struggle.[778] But without some notion of hope as pertaining to change and difficulty, it is hard to see how Rowland's own prescription for the Thomist tradition—to take history and culture more seriously—can succeed. Furthermore, it is hard to articulate a Christian notion of beauty that is "keyed into the historical drama," while at the same time overlooking what Aquinas actually says about hope, the virtue to which beauty is said to correlate.[779] For how can there be any drama, or for that matter any narrative at all, without the realities of change and difficulty that Aquinas believes hope to engage? Thus, if one wants to graft cultural specificity onto the Thomist tradition, then it would help to give a closer reading of what Thomas actually taught, along with a more nuanced evaluation of what modernity can positively offer, if that grafting is to take hold.

The Christian humanism that I wish to advance, precisely because it draws on Aquinas's understanding of hope, suggests an alternative direction for a less resolutely antimodern Thomistic notion of culture. Something of that differing sensibility can be gauged by the following two concluding reflections on where Catholic identity stands, in the words of Rowland's subtitle, "after Vatican II." The first sketches how a contemporary Christian humanism grounded on hope can speak to recent debates concerning the legacy of the council, that classic mid-twentieth-century ecclesial-sponsored flourishing of Christian humanism; the second offers a theological hermeneutic that distinguishes Christian humanism from another (depressingly common) response to the changes of modernity, religious fundamentalism.

Addressing the Conflict of Interpretation over Vatican II

Two recent articles by leading Catholic historians have addressed the issue of the interpretation of Vatican II. Both highlight the crucial influence of the idea of Christian humanism on the council. Focusing on the internal evidence of style and ecclesial debate, John O'Malley's "Vatican II: Did Anything Happen?" demonstrates the humanistic impulse behind the council's twofold aim of *ressourcement* (from the *ad fontes* motto of Renaissance humanism) and renewal (in its epideictic style, which invited the church to renew itself and to share in and guide humanity's striving for the common good).[780] Compared to previous juridical and dialectical council styles, that alone is evidence that "something happened."[781] In his earlier *Four Cultures of the West*, O'Malley judged the Second Vatican Council as "a moment of brilliance" for humanistic culture.

Focusing on the external evidence of historical and political context, Stephen Schloesser's "Against Forgetting: Memory, History, and Vatican II" underscores how the tumultuous change and suffering of the twentieth century generated an ethical imperative such that something "*had* to happen."[782]

> Situating the council historically can illuminate its deeply anxious concerns, its need to respond humanistically to the fragmentation of the world as well as to the brutal inhumanity its participants had eye-witnessed.[783]

Schloesser therefore cites the importance of the "challenge of late-modern humanisms" (baptized by Teilhard de Chardin, Henri de Lubac, and Karl Rahner) for interpreting Vatican II as the church's magnanimous response to these difficulties.

If the council owed a significant part of its inspiration to the Christian humanist vision, and if, as this book claims, hope is a crucial theological source for Christian humanism, then one should be able to detect the characteristic marks of hope on the thought and spirit of the council. Reading O'Malley's and Schloesser's articles, one is struck by how the key elements of their interpretation of the council correspond to the basic elements of hope in its classic Thomistic definition. Recall the formal definition of hope: the motion towards a future, difficult, yet possible good. Taking each of these components in turn, one finds significant correlation with the key elements of what, according to O'Malley and Schloesser, was going on at the council.

The virtue of hope pertains essentially to motion or *change*; as such, it is "preeminently the virtue of the *status viatoris*."[784] Even the most cursory look at the council shows the importance and novelty of its attempt to introduce the idea of change and temporality into the consciousness of the church. O'Malley's article addresses the growing denial of this fact in the myopic and patently false insistence that the council represents *only* continuity with the past. Schloesser catalogues the manifold ways in which the council demonstrably changed: from greater recognition of non-Catholics and non-Christians, to modernizing the church's stance on religious freedom, to recognizing its global, postcolonial nature, and so on. Underlying any particular change, though, is a qualitatively different change: the consciousness of change *per se*. This "embrace of temporality"[785] was forcefully defended by Bernard Lonergan in his article "The Transition from a Classicist World-View to Historical-Mindedness," to which O'Malley and Schloesser both appeal.[786] Thus, just as the virtue of hope makes the believer into a *viator*, so a council inspired by Christian humanism memorably called the community of faith a pilgrim people.

The second characteristic of hope is that its motion confronts *difficulty*. Likewise, the council, by facing the challenge of historical consciousness, confronted some of the painful changes in self-understanding that such a recognition entails (as O'Malley shows in the fraught nature of the intra-ecclesial debates during the council and subsequently over its legitimate interpretation). More fundamentally, according to Schloesser, the recognition of the terrible human suffering in the twentieth century generated the ethical impulse for the council to initiate (internally) a magnanimous shift in style and (externally) a greater openness to the modern world. The list of those traumatic events need not be repeated here, except to say that the coincidence of the Cuban missile crisis with the opening of the council had a certain appropriateness, coming in the midst of the most perilous episode of the Seventy-Five Year War (1914–1989),[787] in which the European empires collapsed as the global economy arose. At this most dangerous point in a process of enormous change, the council spoke not just to the church but to all of humanity, and, in its opening message, expressed the profound hopes for "peace between peoples" and "social justice ... so that man's life can become more human according to the standards of the gospel."[788] Thus, just as hope directly responds to difficulty, so a council inspired by Christian humanism squarely faced internal and external difficulties.

The final component of hope is the goal of a *possible good*. Hope may well regard what is future and difficult, but it would only move towards that good on the conviction that it is attainable. Likewise, the council, while soberly recognizing that its desired goods were future and difficult, nonetheless encouraged the typically humanist striving for the common good,[789] including, but by no means restricted to, the good of the earthly city. The council's conviction that such goods were possible was communicated, as O'Malley shows, in its magnanimous, epideictic style that summoned the church and humanity to strive for the good. The opening "Message to Humanity" concluded with the call to "build ... up a more just and brotherly city in this world" and ended with a prayer "that in the midst of this world there may radiate the light of our great hope in Jesus Christ, our only Savior."[790] Thus, appropriately enough, the council, inspired by the vision of Christian humanism, closed its opening message with an appeal to a Christologically grounded hope.

To the extent that this correlation between the virtue of hope and the spirit of this Christian humanist council is valid, it gives more historical substance to this book's systematic theological arguments that ground Christian humanism on hope. Moreover, it can calm fraught debates over the interpretation of Vatican II. As with any interpretation of historical events, the spectrum of readings ranges from "continuity" to "change." No doubt, prior ecclesio-political convictions tilt theologians to one side or the other of this axis. But, assuming there is a nonpolitical remainder in debates about the legitimate interpretation of Vatican II, then perhaps it is not too facile to suggest that those who emphasize "continuity" are talking about the council in terms of faith; and those who emphasize "change" are talking about the council in terms of hope. Thus, if one looks at the council through the lens of faith, then continuity is to be affirmed, because the council did not substantially alter any major article of Christian belief (even if major practices of the church were drastically revised, such as attitudes to non-Catholics and non-Christians). Thus, Avery Dulles (who has written a book on faith[791]) asserts (correctly, according to O'Malley) that the council did not change its "substantive teaching."[792]

Nonetheless, if one looks at the council through the lens of hope, then change is undeniable, because the council did substantially alter the ethos and habits of the church in its more expansive and magnanimous attempt to express its desire to live out its faith in the world; for example, the fact that the council was the first ever to address all of humanity, not just the church; or that there was a unique shift from a juridical-surveillance style (focusing on politics, or the "right"[793]) and from a dialectical-propositional style (focusing on doctrine, or the "true") to an epideictic style (focusing on ethics, or the "good").

Of course, one can overdo this reading. Faith undergoes development and hope alters not its ultimate object. Nonetheless, faith's center of gravity lies in the revelation of the apostolic era as expressed in past creeds. Thus, any reading of the council in terms of faith will rightly emphasize its continuity with the central doctrines of the Catholic tradition. Likewise, hope's center of gravity reaches to the future and thus essentially involves movement. Thus, any reading of the council in terms of hope may rightly emphasize its change from the preceding spirit of Catholic engagement with the modern world. Consequently, to the extent that one sees the Christian humanist influence upon the council, as O'Malley and Schloesser help one to see, one will be inclined to read the council not only through the lens of faith, but also through the lens of hope—since hope provides crucial grounds to the Christian humanist spirit that animated the council. One will therefore be in a position not only to recognize, but also to welcome, the change that the council dramatically effected, without thereby rejecting its underlying and substantial continuity in the faith.

This claim can be stated more simply: What happened in this episode of the historical life of the church is not dissimilar from what happens continually in the personal lives of believers. When a believer encounters serious change and difficulty in her life, she is really changed, even though her beliefs may remain the same. Likewise, when the church explicitly faced the historical consciousness and political trauma of the twentieth century, it emerged a radically changed church, even though its "substantive teaching" remained the same. However, that assertion of continuity must not obscure the reality of change. For when a believer undergoes some profound change (for example, an experience of personal loss), she may well hold her unchanged beliefs (for example, that Christ suffered for us) in radically changed ways (for example, not as substitutionary penal atonement that placates God's wrath and spares our suffering, but as the embodiment of God's mercy in which we participate). Likewise, when the church undergoes some profound change (for example, facing up to the sheer numbers of non-Christians), it may well reformulate its unchanged beliefs (for example, in the necessity of the church for salvation) in radically new ways (for example, not in the narrow and negative phrase *extra ecclesium nulla salus* but in the expansive and positive sixteenth chapter of *Lumen gentium*).[794]

Whatever the validity of this parallel between the personal and the ecclesial, the point remains that the council that self-consciously stood in the Christian humanist tradition clearly and centrally manifests the signature features of the theological virtue of hope. In doing so, it could draw on theological resources that enabled it to recognize and adjust to change, and thus become less susceptible to a self-defeating triumphalism or a self-enclosed antimodernism. Other religious movements of the twentieth century, however, refused to recognize and adjust to these changes. It is to them that I turn for the final cultural reflection on the significance of understanding a contemporary Christian humanism in terms of hope.

Fundamentalism: Substituting Security for Hope

These final reflections offer a Thomistic distinction that may help to clarify the significance of a contemporary Christian humanism in an age of religious fundamentalism. In his general discussion of the passion of hope, Aquinas distinguishes hope from security. That distinction, which Aquinas makes in passing, could be applied creatively to contemporary interpretations of religious fundamentalism. "Hope," he says, "considers the good to be sought; security regards an evil to be avoided."[795] This distinction captures the difference in ethos between a humanist Christianity and a fundamentalist Christianity. For each represents an opposite reaction to the same radical, unsettling changes in identity wrought by the transition to modernity. (As David Tracy and others have noted, fundamentalism is very much a modern phenomenon.[796]) In the face of these changes that threaten one's identity, the fundamentalist typically seeks security in order to avoid that "future evil," namely, the fear of change of identity and its accompanying difficulty. And if your identity is threatened, then there must be someone threatening it, mustn't there? So sociologists of religion, such as Martin Marty, find plenty of "oppositionalism" in fundamentalisms that gives them their negative cohesion as they battle enemies real or invented. By naming these "opposites," fundamentalists create a scapegoat, the criticism of which displaces the accurate analysis and realistic acceptance of the true "opponent," namely, the broad and deep currents of socioeconomic change that ineluctably erode the foundations of previously stable patterns of life.[797]

A Christian humanist, on the other hand, facing the same changes, can draw on resources that are not available to those who possess the security mindset. In the posture of hope—the movement toward a future, difficult, yet possible good—one internalizes change (since the good is future) and expects suffering (since the good is difficult). Hope, as opposed to security, therefore teaches one to live with profound change and its consequent difficulties. It is a trusting acceptance of providence—as opposed to a neurotic avoidance of history—anticipating, somehow, that out of the dislocation and pain of radically changed identities, new life may emerge.

Not that these reflections would persuade any fundamentalist. But at least they succinctly name the difference between a humanistic appropriation of Christian faith and a fundamentalist corruption of it. They might therefore help a sympathetic observer or a genuine inquirer to likewise draw that distinction, and thus to articulate reasons for rejecting the argument that humanism and Christianity do not belong together.[798] For there are many who, seeing the actions performed in the name of religion, reject the religious enterprise altogether. The relevance of this distinction between hope and security, then, is to make plain the contrasting theological grounds of authentic and inauthentic appeals to religion. It thus captures explicitly what most people know intuitively: that participating in the enterprise of hope differs vastly from becoming enthralled to the mindset of security.

Select Bibliography

Thomas Aquinas

Unless otherwise indicated, I have used Enrique Alarcón's *Corpus thomisticum* web site (http://www.corpusthomisticum.org/) for the following works:
Compendium theologiae
Quaestiones disputatae De potentia
Quaestiones disputatae De virtutibus, quaestio 4 (i.e., *De spe*).
Quaestiones disputatae De veritate
Scriptum super Libros Sententiarum III
Summa contra gentiles
Summa theologiae
Otherwise, I have used the following printed editions:
Expositio libri Posteriorum Analyticorum. Leonine edition, vol. 1/2. Rome: Commisio Leonina; Paris: Vrin, 1989.
Faith, Reason and Theology: Questions I–IV of His Commentary on the "De Trinitate" of Boethius. Translated by Armand A. Maurer. Toronto: Pontifical Institute of Mediaeval Studies, 1987.
Lectura super Evangelium S. Matthaei. Rome: Marietti, 1951.
Summa theologica. Translated by the Fathers of the English Dominican Province. 5 vols. Allen, TX: Christian Classics, 1981.
In Epistolam I ad Corinthios. In *Opera omnia*, Parma edition, vol. 13. New York: Musurgia, 1949.
In Epistolam ad Ephesios. In *Opera omnia*, Parma edition, vol. 13. New York: Musurgia, 1949.
In Epistolam ad Hebraeos. In *Opera omnia*, Parma edition, vol. 13. New York: Musurgia, 1949.
In Epistolam ad Romanos. In *Opera Omnia*, Parma edition, vol. 13. New York: Musurgia, 1949.
In Epistolam I ad Timotheum. In *Opera omnia*, Parma edition, vol. 13. New York: Musurgia, 1949.
In Psalmos Davidis expositio. In *Opera omnia*, Vivès edition, vol. 18. Paris: Vivès, 1876.
Summa Contra Gentiles, Book III: Providence, Part II. Translated by Vernon Bourke. Notre Dame, IN: University of Notre Dame Press, 1975.
Sentencia Libri De Anima. In *Opera omnia*, Leonine edition, vol. 45/1. Rome: Commisio Leonina; Paris: Vrin, 1984.
Sententia Libri Ethicorum. In *Opera omnia*, Leonine edition, vol. 47/1. Rome: Ad Sanctae Sabinae, 1969.

Other Literature

Abbey, Ruth. *Charles Taylor*. Princeton, NJ: Princeton University Press, 2000.
Alves, Rubem A. *A Theology of Human Hope*. New York: Corpus, 1969.
Aristotle. *The Basic Works of Aristotle*. Edited by Richard McKeon. New York: Random House, 1941.

———. *The Complete Works of Aristotle: The Revised Oxford Translation*. Edited by Jonathan Barnes. Princeton, NJ: Princeton University Press, 1984.

Augustine. *The Enchiridion on Faith, Hope, and Love*. Edited by Henry Paolucci. Translated by J. F. Shaw. Washington, DC: Regnery Gateway, 1961.

Basse, Michael. *Certitudo Spei: Thomas von Aquins Begründung der Hoffnungsgewissheit und ihre Rezeption*. Göttingen: Vandenhoeck & Ruprecht, 1993.

Bequette, John P. *Christian Humanism: Creation, Redemption, and Reintegration*. Lanham, MD: University Press of America, 2004.

Benedict XVI. *Deus caritas est*. Official English translation: http://www.vatican.va/holy_father/benedict_xvi/encyclicals/documents/hf_ben-xvi_enc_20051225_deus-caritas-est_en.html.

———. *Spe salvi*. Official English translation: http://www.vatican.va/holy_father/benedict_xvi/encyclicals/documents/hf_ben-xvi_enc_20071130_spe-salvi_en.html

———. *See also* Ratzinger, Joseph.

Bernard, Charles André. *Théologie de l'espérance selon Saint Thomas d'Aquin*. Paris: J. Vrin, 1961.

Bhargava, Rajeev. *Secularism and Its Critics*. New York: Oxford University Press, 1998.

Bougerol, Jacques Guy. *La théologie de l'espérance aux XIIe et XIIIe siècles*. Paris: Études Augustiniennes, 1985.

Bouyer, Louis. *Christian Humanism*. Westminster, MD: Newman Press, 1959.

Bowlin, John R. *Contingency and Fortune in Aquinas's Ethics*. New York: Cambridge University Press, 1999.

Boyle, Nicholas. " 'Art,' Literature, Theology: Learning from Germany." In *Higher Learning and Catholic Traditions*, edited by Lawrence Sullivan, 87–111. Notre Dame, IN: University of Notre Dame Press, 2001.

———. *Sacred and Secular Scriptures: A Catholic Approach to Literature*. Notre Dame, IN: University of Notre Dame Press, 2004.

———. *Who Are We Now? Christian Humanism and the Global Market from Hegel to Heaney*. Notre Dame, IN: University of Notre Dame Press, 1998.

Bradley, Denis J. M. *Aquinas on the Twofold Human Good: Reason and Human Happiness in Aquinas's Moral Science*. Washington, DC: Catholic University of America Press, 1997.

Brown, Stephen F. "The Theological Virtue of Faith: An Invitation to an Ecclesial Life of Truth (IIa IIae, qq. 1–16)." In *The Ethics of Aquinas*, edited by Stephen J. Pope, 222–31. Washington, DC: Georgetown University Press, 2002.

Buckley, Michael J. *The Catholic University as Promise and Project: Reflections in a Jesuit Idiom*. Washington, DC: Georgetown University Press, 1998.

———. *Denying and Disclosing God: The Ambiguous Progress of Modern Atheism*. New Haven, CT: Yale University Press, 2004.

Burrell, David B. *Freedom and Creation in Three Traditions*. Notre Dame, IN: University of Notre Dame Press, 1993.

———. *Knowing the Unknowable God: Ibn-Sina, Maimonides, Aquinas*. Notre Dame, IN: University of Notre Dame Press, 1986.

Capps, Walter H. *Time Invades the Cathedral: Tension in the School of Hope.* Philadelphia: Fortress Press, 1972.
Cessario, Romanus. *Christian Faith and the Theological Life.* Washington, DC: Catholic University of America Press, 1996.
———. "The Theological Virtue of Hope (IIa IIae, qq. 17–22)." In *The Ethics of Aquinas*, edited by Stephen J. Pope, 232–43. Washington, DC: Georgetown University Press, 2002.
Charles, Pierre. "Spes Christi II: Equisse de l'histoire d'une doctrine." *Nouvelle Revue Theologique* 10 (1937): 1057–75.
Clarke, W. Norris. *Explorations in Metaphysics: Being—God—Person.* Notre Dame, IN: University of Notre Dame Press, 1994.
———. *The One and the Many: A Contemporary Thomistic Metaphysics.* Notre Dame, IN: University of Notre Dame Press, 2001.
Conlon, W. M. "The Certitude of Hope." *The Thomist* 10 (1947): 75–119, 226–52.
Daley, Brian. *The Hope of the Early Church: A Handbook of Patristic Eschatology.* Cambridge: Cambridge University Press, 1991.
Dawson, Christopher. "Christianity and the Humanist Tradition." *Dublin Review* 226 (1952): 1–11.
———. *The Historic Reality of Christian Culture: A Way to the Renewal of Human Life.* New York: Harper, 1960.
———. "Notes on True Humanism by J. Maritain." Department of Special Collections, O'Shaughnessy-Frey Library, University of St. Thomas, 1938–1939: box 7, folder 53.
———. *Religion and the Modern State.* New York: Sheed & Ward, 1936.
———. *Religion and the Rise of Western Culture.* Garden City, NY: Doubleday, 1958.
De Letter, P. "Hope and Charity in St. Thomas." *The Thomist* 13 (1950): 204–48, 325–52.
Dell'Olio, Andrew J. "Divine Goodness and Human Goodness: The Relationship between the Natural and the Theological Virtues in the *Summa theologiae* of Thomas Aquinas and Its Implications for Contemporary Moral Thought." PhD dissertation, Columbia University, 1994. Ann Arbor, MI: University Microfilms International, 1995.
Dupré, Louis K. "Hope and Transcendence." In *The God Experience: Essays in Hope*, edited by Joseph P. Whelan, 217–25. New York: Newman Press, 1971.
———. *Passage to Modernity: An Essay in the Hermeneutics of Nature and Culture.* New Haven: Yale University Press, 1993.
Engelhard, G. "Hoffnung." In *Lexikon für Theologie und Kirche*, 5:412–24. Freiburg im Breisgau: Herder, 1993–2001.
Feingold, Lawrence. *The Natural Desire to See God according to St. Thomas Aquinas and His Interpreters.* Rome: Apollinare studi, 2001.
Flannery, Austin, ed. *Vatican Council II: The Basic Sixteen Documents.* Northport, NY: Costello, 1996.
Franklin, R. W., and Joseph M. Shaw. *The Case for Christian Humanism.* Grand Rapids, MI: Eerdmans, 1991.

Fries, Albert. "Hoffnung und Heilsgewissheit bei Thomas von Aquino." *Studia Moralia* 7 (1969): 215–37.
Garrigou-Lagrange, Réginald. "La confiance en Dieu." *La vie spirituelle* 43 (1935): 225–36.
———. *De virtutibus theologicis: Commentarius in Summam theologicam S. Thomae, Ia IIae, q. 62, 65, 68, et IIa IIae q. 1–46*. Turin: R. Berruti, 1949.
Gauthier, René Antoine. *Magnanimité: L'idéal de la grandeur dans la philosophie païenne et dans la théologie chrétienne*. Paris: J. Vrin, 1951.
Geffré, Claude. *Humanism and Christianity*. New York: Herder and Herder, 1973.
Glenn, Mary Michael. "The Thomistic and Scotistic Concepts of Hope." *The Thomist* 20 (1957): 27–74.
Greer, Rowan A. *Christian Life and Christian Hope: Raids on the Inarticulate*. New York: Crossroad, 2001.
Guardini, Romano. *The Word of God on Faith, Hope, and Charity*. Chicago: Regnery, 1963.
Gustafson, James M. "The Conditions of Hope: Reflections on Human Experience." *Continuum* 7 (1970): 535–45.
Harent, S. "Espérance." In *Dictionnaire de Théologie Catholique*, 5:606–75. Paris: Letouzey et Ané, 1930–1950.
Hayes, Zachary. *A Vision of the Future: A Study of Christian Eschatology*. Collegeville, MN: Liturgical Press, 1990.
Hermans, Francis. *Histoire doctrinale de l'humanisme chrétien*. 4 vols. Tournai: Casterman, 1948.
Hill, William J. "Hope." In *Summa Theologiae*, vol. 33, *Hope, 2a–2ae, 17–22*, edited by William Hill, 123–79. New York: Blackfriars / McGraw–Hill, 1966.
Hollenbach, David. "The Catholic University under the Sign of the Cross: Christian Humanism in a Broken World." In *Finding God in All Things: Essays in Honor of Michael J. Buckley, S.J.*, edited by Michael Himes and Stephen Pope, 279–98. New York: Crossroads, 1996.
Kasper, Walter. "Christian Humanism." In *Proceedings of the Twenty-Seventh Annual Convention*, 1–17. New York: Catholic Theological Society of America, 1972.
Kaufman, Gordon D. *In Face of Mystery: A Constructive Theology*. Cambridge, MA: Harvard University Press, 1993.
Keenan, James F. *The Works of Mercy: The Heart of Catholicism*. Lanham, MD: Rowman & Littlefield, 2005.
Kent, Bonnie. "Habits and Virtues (Ia IIae, qq. 49–70)." In *The Ethics of Aquinas*, edited by Stephen J. Pope, 116–30. Washington, DC: Georgetown University Press, 2002.
Kerr, Fergus. *After Aquinas: Versions of Thomism*. Malden, MA: Blackwell, 2002.
———. *Immortal Longings: Versions of Transcending Humanity*. Notre Dame, IN: University of Notre Dame Press, 1997.
Komonchak, Joseph. *Foundations in Ecclesiology*. Supplementary issue of the journal *Lonergan Workshop*, vol. 11. Boston: Boston College, 1995.
Kristeller, Paul Oskar. *Renaissance Thought: The Classic, Scholastic, and Humanistic Strains*. New York: Harper, 1961.

Lash, Nicholas. *A Matter of Hope: A Theologian's Reflections on the Thought of Karl Marx*. Notre Dame, IN: University of Notre Dame Press, 1982.
Letter, P. de. "Hope and Charity in St. Thomas." *The Thomist* 13 (1950): 204–48, 325–52.
Lindbeck, George. "Discovering Thomas (4): Hope and the *Sola fide*." *Una sancta* 25, no. 1 (1968): 66–73.
Lonergan, Bernard. *Insight: A Study of Human Understanding*. Toronto: University of Toronto Press, 1992.
———. "The Natural Desire to See God." In Bernard Lonergan, *Collection*, edited by Frederick E. Crowe and Robert M. Doran, 81–91. Toronto: University of Toronto Press, 1967.
Lubac, Henri de. *Catholicism: Christ and the Common Destiny of Man*. London: Burns & Oates, 1962.
Macquarrie, John. *Christian Hope*. New York: Seabury Press, 1978.
Maritain, Jacques. *Integral Humanism: Temporal and Spiritual Problems of a New Christendom*. New York: Scribner, 1968.
———. *The Range of Reason*. New York: Scribner, 1952.
———. *St. Thomas Aquinas*. New York: Meridian Books, 1958.
Marty, Martin E., and R. Scott Appleby. *Accounting for Fundamentalisms: The Dynamic Character of Movements*. Chicago: University of Chicago Press, 1994.
Massa, Mark. *Catholics and American Culture: Fulton Sheen, Dorothy Day, and the Notre Dame Football Team*. New York: Crossroad, 1999.
Mathewes, Charles T. *A Theology of Public Life*. Cambridge: Cambridge University Press, 2007.
Merkt, Joseph. "The Discovery of the Genetic Development of Thomas Aquinas' Theology of Hope and Its Relevance for a Theology of the Future." In *Rising from History: U.S. Catholic Theology Looks to the Future* (The Annual Publication of the College Theology Society, vol. 30 [1984]), edited by Robert J. Daly, 103–23. Lanham, MD: University Press of America, 1987.
———. *Sacra Doctrina and Christian Eschatology: A Test Case for a Study of Method and Content in the Writings of Thomas Aquinas*. PhD dissertation, Catholic University of America, 1982. Ann Arbor, MI: University Microfilms, 1983.
Merriell, D. Juvenal. *To the Image of the Trinity: A Study in the Development of Aquinas' Teaching*. Toronto: Pontifical Institute of Mediaeval Studies, 1990.
Middendorf, Heinrich. *Über die Hoffnung*. Würzburg: Konrad Triltsch Verlag, 1937.
Mollard, Georges. "Le Problème de l'unité de l'espérance." *Revue Thomiste* 40 (1935):196–210.
Moltmann, Jürgen. "Christian Hope: Messianic or Transcendent? A Theological Discussion with Joachim of Fiore and Thomas Aquinas." *Horizons* 12, no. 2 (1985): 328–48.
———. "Theology as Eschatology." In *The Future of Hope: Theology as Eschatology*, edited by Frederick Herzog, 1–50. New York: Herder and Herder, 1970.

———. *Theology of Hope: On the Ground and the Implications of a Christian Eschatology*. Translated by James W. Leitch. Minneapolis: Fortress Press, 1967.

Moule, C. F. D. *The Meaning of Hope: A Biblical Exposition with Concordance*. London: Highway Press, 1953.

Muntzel, Philip Alan. "Hope and the Moral Life: A Study in Theological Ethics." PhD dissertation, Yale University, 1984. Ann Arbor, MI: University Microfilms, 1985.

Murray, John Courtney. *Bridging the Sacred and the Secular: Selected Writings of John Courtney Murray, S.J.* Edited by J. Leon Hooper. Washington, DC: Georgetown University Press, 1994.

———. "The Problem of State Religion." *Theological Studies* 12, no. 2 (1951): 155–78.

———. "Towards a Theology of the Layman." *Theological Studies* 5, no.1 (1944): 43–75.

———. *We Hold These Truths: Catholic Reflections on the American Proposition*. Kansas City, MO: Sheed and Ward, 1988.

Niebuhr, H. Richard. "Reflections on Faith, Hope and Love." *Journal of Religious Ethics* 2 (1974): 151–56.

O'Collins, Gerald. "Spes Quaerens Intellectum." *Interpretation* 22, no. 1 (1968): 36–52.

O'Connor, William R. *The Eternal Quest: The Teaching of St. Thomas Aquinas on the Natural Desire for God*. New York: Longmans, Green, 1947.

Oliver, Bernard. *Christian Hope*. Translated by Philip S. Watson. New York: Harper and Row, 1969.

O'Malley, John W. *Four Cultures of the West*. Cambridge, MA: Harvard University Press, 2004.

———. *Praise and Blame in Renaissance Rome: Rhetoric, Doctrine, and Reform in the Sacred Orators of the Papal Court, c. 1450–1521*. Durham, NC: Duke University Press, 1979.

———. "Vatican II: Did Anything Happen?" *Theological Studies* 67 (2006): 3–33.

Ozmont, Steven E. "*Homo viator*: Luther and the Late Medieval Theology." In *The Reformation in Medieval Perspective*, edited by Steven Ozment, 142–54. Chicago: Quadrangle Books, 1971.

Penta, Clement Della. *Hope and Society: A Thomistic Study of Social Optimism and Pessimism, a Study in Social Philosophy*. Washington, DC: Catholic University of America Press, 1942.

Peter, Carl. "Metaphysical Finalism or Christian Eschatology?" *Thomist* 38 (1974): 125–45.

Pieper, Josef. *Faith, Hope, Love*. San Francisco: Ignatius Press, 1997.

———. *Hope and History: Five Salzburg Lectures*. San Francisco: Ignatius Press, 1994.

———. *On Hope*. San Francisco: Ignatius Press, 1986.

Pinckaers, Servais. "La nature vertueuse de l'espérance." *Revue Thomiste* 54 (1958): 405–42, 623–44.

———. *Le renouveau de la morale: Études pour une morale fidèle à ses sources et sa missions présente.* Tournai: Casterman, 1964.
Pope, Stephen, ed. *The Ethics of Aquinas.* Washington, DC: Georgetown University Press, 2002.
Radcliffe, Timothy. *Sing a New Song: The Christian Vocation.* Springfield, IL: Templegate, 1999.
Rahner, Karl. *Foundations of Christian Faith: An Introduction to the Idea of Christianity.* New York: Crossroad, 1995.
———. "Immanent and Transcendent Consummation of the World." In *Theological Investigations*, vol. 10, translated by David Bourke, 273–89. London: Darton, Longman and Todd, 1973.
———. "On the Theology of Hope." In *Theological Investigations*, vol. 10, translated by David Bourke, 242–59. London: Darton, Longman and Todd, 1973.
———. *The Practice of Faith: A Handbook of Contemporary Spirituality.* Edited by Karl Lehmann and Albert Raffelt. New York: Crossroad, 1986.
———. "The Theological Problems Entailed in the Idea of the 'New Earth.' " In *Theological Investigations*, vol. 10, translated by David Bourke, 260–72. London: Darton, Longman and Todd, 1973.
Ramirez, S. M. "Hope." *New Catholic Encyclopedia*, 2nd ed., 7:92–102. Detroit: Gale, 2003.
Ratzinger, Joseph. *Church, Ecumenism, and Politics: New Essays in Ecclesiology.* New York: Crossroad, 1988.
———. *Eschatology, Death, and Eternal Life.* Washington, DC: Catholic University of America Press, 1988.
———. "On Hope." *Communio: International Catholic Review* 12 (Spring 1985): 71–84.
———. *The Yes of Jesus Christ: Exercises in Faith, Hope, and Love.* New York: Crossroad, 2005.
———. *See also* Benedict XVI.
Redhead, Mark. *Charles Taylor: Thinking and Living Deep Diversity.* New York: Rowan & Littlefield, 2002.
Ricoeur, Paul. "Hope and the Structure of Philosophical Systems." In *Philosophy and Christian Theology = Proceedings of the American Catholic Theological Society* 44 (1970): 55–69.
Ross, W. D. *Aristotle.* New York: Methuen, 1949.
Rowland, Tracey. *Culture and the Thomist Tradition: After Vatican II.* New York: Routledge, 2003.
Schloesser, Stephen. "Against Forgetting: Memory, History, Vatican II." *Theological Studies* 67 (2006): 275–319.
———. *Jazz Age Catholicism: Mystic Modernism in Postwar Paris, 1919–1933.* Toronto: University of Toronto Press, 2005.
Schockenhoff, Eberhard. *Bonum Hominis: Die Anthropologischen und Theologischen Grundlagen der Tugendethik des Thomas von Aquin.* Mainz: Matthias-Grünewald-Verlag, 1987.

———. "The Theological Virtue of Charity (IIa IIae, qq. 23–46)." Translated by Grant Kaplan and Frederick G. Lawrence. In *The Ethics of Aquinas*, edited by Stephen J. Pope, 244–58. Washington, DC: Georgetown University Press, 2002.

Schumacher, Bernard N. *A Philosophy of Hope: Josef Pieper and the Contemporary Debate on Hope*. Translated by D. C. Schindler. New York: Fordham University Press, 2003.

Schwartz, Daniel. *Aquinas on Friendship*. New York: Oxford University Press, 2007.

Sherwin, Michael S. *"By Knowledge and by Love": Charity's Relationship to Knowledge in the Theology of St. Thomas Aquinas and Its Implications for Charity's Status as a Virtue*. Washington, DC: Catholic University of America Press, 2005.

Sokolowski, Robert. *Christian Faith & Human Understanding: Studies on the Eucharist, Trinity, and the Human Person*. Washington, DC: Catholic University of America Press, 2006.

———. *The God of Faith and Reason: Foundations of Christian Theology*. Washington, DC: Catholic University of America Press, 1995.

Southern, Richard W. *Medieval Humanism*. New York: Harper & Row, 1970.

Tanner, Kathryn. *God and Creation in Christian Theology: Tyranny or Empowerment?* Oxford: Blackwell, 1988.

Taylor, Charles. *A Catholic Modernity? Charles Taylor's Marianist Award Lecture*. Oxford: Oxford University Press, 1996.

———. "Comments and Replies." *Inquiry: An Interdisciplinary Journal of Philosophy* 34 (1991): 237–54.

———. *The Ethics of Authenticity*. Cambridge, MA: Harvard University Press, 1992.

———. "Humanismus und moderne Identität." In *Der Mensch in den Modernen Wissenschaften*, edited by Krzysztof Michalski, 117–70. Stuttgart: Klett-Cotta, 1985.

———. "Iris Murdoch and Moral Philosophy." In *Iris Murdoch and the Search for Human Goodness*, edited by Mario Antonaccio and William Schweiker, 3–28. Chicago, IL: University of Chicago Press, 1996.

———. *Modern Social Imaginaries*. Durham: Duke University Press, 2004.

———. "Modes of Secularism." In *Secularism and Its Critics*, edited by Rajeev Bhargava, 31–53. New York: Oxford University Press, 1998.

———. "A Philosopher's Postscript: Engaging the Citadel of Secular Reason." In *Reason and the Reasons of Faith*, edited by Paul Griffiths and Reinhard Hütter, 339–53. New York: T&T Clark, 2005.

———. *Philosophical Arguments*. Cambridge, MA: Harvard University Press, 1995.

———. "Reply and Re-articulation." In *Philosophy in an Age of Pluralism: The Philosophy of Charles Taylor in Question*, edited by James Tully and Daniel M. Weinstock, 213–57. Cambridge: Cambridge University Press, 1994.

———. *A Secular Age*. Cambridge, MA: Harvard University Press, 2007.

———. *Sources of the Self: The Making of Modern Identity*. Cambridge, MA: Harvard University Press, 1989.

———. *Varieties of Religion Today: William James Revisited.* Cambridge, MA: Harvard University Press, 2002.

Tilly, J. le. "Appendice II. Renseignements Techniques." In *Somme Théologique. L'Espérance. 2a-2ae, Questions 17–22,* 2nd ed., edited by J. le Tilly, 193–257. Paris: Desclée, 1950.

———. "L'espérance dans la vie chrétienne." *La vie spirituelle* 30 (1932): 123–35.

Torrell, Jean-Pierre. *Saint Thomas Aquinas.* Vol. 1, *The Person and His Work.* Translated by Robert Royal. Washington, DC: Catholic University of America Press, 1996.

———. *Saint Thomas Aquinas.* Vol. 2, *Spiritual Master.* Translated by Robert Royal. Washington, DC: Catholic University of America Press, 2003.

Tracy, David. *On Naming the Present: Reflections on God, Hermeneutics, and Church.* Maryknoll, NY: Orbis, 1994.

———. *Plurality and Ambiguity: Hermeneutics, Religion, Hope.* Chicago: University of Chicago Press, 1994.

Tully, James, and Daniel M. Weinstock, eds. *Philosophy in an Age of Pluralism: The Philosophy of Charles Taylor in Question.* Cambridge: Cambridge University Press, 1994.

Utz, Arthur Fridolin. "Die ethische Wertung der christlichen Hoffnung." *Zeitschrift für katholische Theologie* 68 (1944): 28–39.

———, with Brigitta von Galen. "Kommentar." In *Die Hoffnung: Theologische Summe II–II, Fragen 17–22,* 93–187. Freiburg: Herder, 1988.

Velde, Rudi te. *Aquinas on God: The "Divine Science" of the Summa Theologiae.* Burlington, VT: Ashgate, 2006.

Wadell, Paul J. *The Primacy of Love: An Introduction to the Ethics of Thomas Aquinas.* New York: Paulist Press, 1992.

Weeks, L. "Can Saint Thomas's *Summa Theologiae* Speak to Moltmann's Theology of Hope?" *The Thomist* 33 (1969): 215–28.

White, Victor. *Holy Teaching: The Idea of Theology according to St. Thomas Aquinas.* London: Blackfriars, 1958.

Wippel, John F. *The Metaphysical Thought of Thomas Aquinas: From Finite Being to Uncreated Being.* Washington, DC: Catholic University of American Press, 2000.

Wolterstorff, Nicholas. "Seeking Justice in Hope." In *The Future of Hope: Christian Tradition amid Modernity and Postmodernity,* edited by Miroslav Wolf and William Katerberg, 77–100. Grand Rapids, MI: Eerdmans, 2004.

Zimara, Coelestin. *Das Wesen der Hoffnung in Natur und Übernatur.* Paderborn: Verlag Ferdinand Schoningh, 1933.

Notes

1   For a brief presentation of the classic statements of atheism in the nineteenth and early twentieth century, see Michael J. Buckley, "God as the Anti-Human," in *Denying and Disclosing God: The Ambiguous Process of Modern Atheism* (New Haven: Yale University Press, 2004), 70–98.

2   *Gaudium et spes* §1, in Austin Flannery, ed., *Vatican II: The Basic Sixteen Documents* (Northport, NY: Costello, 1996), 163. As John O'Malley (*Four Cultures of the West* [Cambridge, MA: Harvard University Press, 2004], 245–46, n. 37) and others have pointed out, this text alludes to Terence's maxim, spoken by Chremes, in *Heautontimorumenos* I.i.77: "Homo sum; humani nihil a me alienum puto." Augustine notes how this line was received with great applause in the theater, and he cites it during the course of an argument urging the universality of human love that transcends familial and business connections: "The union of human minds naturally stirs the love of all human beings so that each human being in it feels that he is a neighbor of any other" (letter 155, to Macedonius, in *The Works of Saint Augustine: Letters 100–155*, II/2, ed. Boniface Ramsey, trans. Roland Teske [Hyde Park, NY: New City Press, 2003], 407–15, at 414). Such was its popularity that it became a commonplace, especially in Stoic philosophy and European humanism, invoked by Cicero, Seneca, Vico, Pope, Voltaire, and others, as Jonathan Z. Smith notes in his overview of the use of this term in philosophical reflection, "Nothing Alien is Human to Me," *Religion* 26 (1996): 297–309, esp. 297–300. For a less sanguine view, though, which interprets the phrase as a reminder of human limits and weaknesses, see Louis Bouyer, *Christian Humanism*, trans. A. V. Littledale (Westminster, MD: Newman, 1959), 103. In the context of Terence's play, Chremes delivers this maxim during the course of his solicitous inquiries to a distressed neighbor, although it is not unlikely that the line is used ironically to establish his character as a busybody.

3   *Gaudium et spes* §22, in Flannery, ed., *Vatican II*, 185.

4   Hans-Georg Gadamer, *Truth and Method*, 2nd rev. ed., translation revised by Joel Weinsheimer and Donald Marshall (New York: Crossroad, 1989), 306–7, 369–79.

5   On the notion of a "creative appropriation" of Thomistic thought, as distinct from mere repetition, see Clarke, *The One and the Many*, 1–2.

6   For a comprehensive genetic study of Aquinas's doctrine of hope, see Joseph Merkt, *Sacra doctrina and Christian Eschatology* (Washington, DC: Catholic University of America, 1983). For a study particularly rich on the spirituality of Aquinas's doctrine of hope, see Charles Bernard, *Théologie de l'espérance selon Saint Thomas d'Aquin* (Paris: Vrin, 1961). On hope's certainty, see Walter M. Conlon, "The Certitude of Hope," *The Thomist* 10 (1947): 75–119; 226–52. For a sympathetic critique of Aquinas's view of hope as foundational for the moral life, see Philip Alan Muntzel, "Hope and

the Moral Life: A Study in Theological Ethics" (PhD dissertation, Yale University, 1984), which focuses on the psychological factors involved in hope, especially in light of Gabriel Marcel's philosophy.

7   For a study of John of the Cross's more affective, spiritual approach, see André Bord, *Mémoire et Espérance chez Jean de La Croix* (Paris: Beauchesne, 1971). For Karl Rahner's existentialist reformulation, see "On the Theology of Hope," *Theological Investigations*, vol. 10, trans. David Bourke (London: Darton, Longman & Todd, 1973), 242–59.

8   This summary draws on Paul Kristeller, *Renaissance Thought: The Classic, Scholastic, and Humanistic Strains* (New York: Harper, 1961), esp. 3–23, 100–103, and 110–11; and O'Malley, *Four Cultures*, 127–77.

9   For the historical background of the rivalry between humanism and scholasticism in the Italian Renaissance (often subsequently exaggerated for polemical reasons) and for evidence of their often peaceful coexistence at that time, see Kristeller, *Renaissance Thought*, esp. 113–17.

10 Michael J. Buckley, "Humanism and Jesuit Theology," in *Catholic University as Promise and Project: Reflections in a Jesuit Idiom* (Washington, DC: Georgetown University Press, 1998), 74–102.

11 In Irenaeus's original formulation, from the preface to *Contra haereses* 5 (*Patrologia graeca* 7:1120): "Verbum Dei, Iesum Christum Dominum nostrum: qui propter immensam suam dilectionem factus est quod sumus nos, uti nos perficeret esse quod est ipse." See also Thomas Aquinas, *Summa theologiae* (hereafter *ST*), III.1.2, quoting (pseudo-) Augustine: "Factus est Deus homo, ut homo fieret Deus." Unless otherwise indicated, the Latin text used is from Enrique Alarcón's *Corpus thomisticum* web site (http://www.corpusthomisticum.org/) and, unless indicated, translations are, with the exception of chapter 3 and the first section of chapter 4, my own.

12 Irenaeus, *Contra haereses* 4.20.7 (*Patrologia graeca* 7:1037): "Gloria enim Dei vivens homo." For examples of Renaissance elaborations of the connection between the doctrine of the Incarnation and the dignity of the human person, see John O'Malley, *Praise and Blame in Renaissance Rome: Rhetoric, Doctrine, and Reform in the Sacred Orators of the Papal Court, c. 1450–1521* (Durham: Duke, 1979), esp. 144–52.

13 The full sentence reads, "Gloria enim Dei vivens homo: vita autem hominis visio Dei." *Contra haereses* 4.20.7 (*Patrologia graeca* 7:1037).

14 *ST* II-II.23.1.

15 *ST* I.1.8, ad 2: "gratia non tollat naturam, sed perficiat." This maxim will be discussed in chapter 3, below.

16 For a recent example, see Tracey Rowland, *Culture and the Thomist Tradition: After Vatican II* (New York: Routledge, 2003). I discuss this book briefly in the conclusion.

17 These temporal foci do not, of course, exclude other foci. Murray, for example, played a crucial role in introducing one of the most radical changes of Vatican II, the notion of religious liberty; and Boyle and Taylor give historical accounts of contemporary identity, both of which lament ahistorical accounts that ignore the past. Thus Boyle: "The loss of a sense of

the past, the collapsing of all significance into the present ... is one of the most paralyzing features of the socio-economic system that has developed since 1945." Nicholas Boyle, *Who Are We Now? Christian Humanism and the Global Market from Hegel to Heaney* (Notre Dame, IN: University of Notre Dame Press, 1988), 83. And Taylor, towards the end of *A Secular Age*, cautions that his story "has no place for unproblematic breaks with a past which is simply left behind us.... The story of how we got here is inextricably bound up with our account of where we are." Charles Taylor, *A Secular Age* (Cambridge, MA: Harvard University Press, 2007), 772. But the historical aspects of Boyle's and Taylor's works seek to understand the forces of those past events in the context of the perplexing transitions of the present, so as to assist decisions about the future.

18 See Christopher Dawson, "Christianity and the Humanist Tradition," *Dublin Review* 226 (Winter 1952): 1–11, especially the penultimate section, "The Humanist Decision of the Apostolic Church."

19 Christopher Dawson, *Religion and the Rise of Western Culture* (New York: Image, 1958), 224.

20 Dawson, however, clearly recognized the need for the "re-interpretation of the tradition of Christian culture in terms of the new knowledge [of nature and man and history]" (*Religion and the Rise of Western Culture*, 230); he even described "Christian Culture as a Culture of Hope," the title of an essay collected in *The Historic Reality of Christian Culture: A Way to the Renewal of Human Life* (New York: Harper, 1960), 60–67. But even in that essay, his accent on the past comes out as he concludes that "we find ourselves back in the same situation as that which the Christians encountered during the decline of the ancient world" (67) and therefore presumably called to rebuild what they once built, namely, Christendom.

21 For a criticism of Dawson's idealized view of the past, see Hugh Trevor-Roper, "Review of Dawson, *Religion and the Rise of Western Culture*," *New Statesman*, March 11, 1950, 276–77. For an extended critique of Dawson's historiography, see Hayden White, "Religion, Culture, and Western Civilization in Christopher Dawsons's Idea of History," *English Miscellany* 9 (1958): 247–87, esp. 276–87. White concludes that Dawson's cardinal error is to "hypostasize Roman Catholic Christianity as an eternal archetype ... [and to see that] any deviation from it is not because of the institution's inadequacies, but the fault of those who abandon it.... It constitutes a return to the myth of the golden age" (ibid., 286). Note also Dawson's uncritical support for the nationalists in the Spanish civil war in their fight for "the recovery of a Christian Spain" against the "new enemy of Christendom," i.e., communism. Quoted in Stephen Carter, "The 'Historical Solution' versus the 'Philosophical Solution': The Political Commentary of Christopher Dawson and Jacques Maritain, 1927–1939," *Journal of the History of Ideas* 69, no. 1 (January 2008): 93–115, at 105.

22 John Courtney Murray, "Towards a Theology of the Layman," *Theological Studies* 5, no. 1 (March 1944): 43–75, at 62.

23 John Courtney Murray, "The Problem of State Religion," *Theological Studies* 12, no. 2 (June 1951): 155–78, at 163.

24 John Courtney Murray, *We Hold These Truths: Catholic Reflections on the American Proposition* (Kansas City, MO: Sheed and Ward), 43.
25 Murray, *We Hold These Truths*, 53.
26 Murray, *We Hold These Truths*, ix–x.
27 Mark Massa, *Catholics and American Culture* (New York: Crossroads, 1999).
28 Boyle, *Who Are We Now?* 9.
29 Boyle, *Who Are We Now?* 64.
30 For an expression of the function of regulative ideals in the context of Catholic universities, see Michael Buckley, *The Catholic University as Promise and Project: Reflections in a Jesuit Idiom* (Washington, DC: Georgetown University Press, 1988), especially xvii–xxii.
31 Boyle, *Who Are We Now?* 93.
32 See, for example, his discussion of Christopher Dawson, T. S. Eliot, Hilaire Belloc, and Action Française in *A Secular Age*, 733; and of Maritain in ibid., 744.
33 See his discussion of Charles Péguy and Gerard Manley Hopkins, *A Secular Age*, 752–58. Incidentally, the final paragraph of section 4 (*A Secular Age*, 755) summarizes Taylor's understanding of the development in forms of Christian life.
34 Taylor, *A Secular Age*, 766.
35 For a fascinating complication to my oversimplified temporal foci, see Dawson's unpublished review of Maritain's *Integral Humanism*, "Notes on True Humanism by J. Maritain," 1938–1939, box 7, folder 53, held at the Department of Special Collections, O'Shaughnessy-Frey Library, University of St. Thomas, in which Dawson argues that Maritain "does not really get to grips with the essential problem of humanism itself" since he ignores the actual historical culture of humanism from the fourteenth to the nineteenth century (Petrarch to Hegel). In Dawson's opinion, "the real theme of [Maritain's] book is not, as its title would suggest, the problem of the preservation or rectification of the humanist tradition, bur rather the restoration of medieval Christendom edited and adapted to modern needs. His thesis is essentially that of the Catholic Romantics of a century ago, viz. [...] that Europe took the wrong turning in the 15th century misled by the mirage of humanism and that it must now return to the ideals of mediaeval Christendom interpreted in a wider spirit and freed from the local and temporal limitations of the Middle Ages" (p. 3 of 3 in the second and larger of the two handwritten manuscripts). Dawson's criticism seems fair enough insofar as Maritain uses the term without giving full consideration to its historical meaning, although it does seem to understate the radical nature of the newness of Maritain's "*new* Christendom." In any case, Dawson's disagreement with Maritain reveals the differing uses of the term humanism—historical and systematic—mentioned in the introduction of this book. (Quotations are used courtesy of the Department of Special Collections, University of St. Thomas, St. Paul, MN.)
36 Maritain, *Integral Humanism: Temporal and Spiritual Problems of a New Christendom*, trans. Joseph W. Evans (New York: Charles Scribner's Sons, 1936), 139–41, at 139.

37 Maritain, *Integral Humanism*, 141.
38 Maritain, *Integral Humanism*, 140.
39 Maritain, *Integral Humanism*, 209.
40 Jacques Maritain, *St. Thomas Aquinas* (Cleveland, OH: Meridian, 1958), 16. Maritain is here quoting his own *Antimoderne* (1922).
41 Maritain, *St. Thomas Aquinas*, 11.
42 Stephen Schloesser, *Jazz Age Catholicism: Mystic Modernism in Postwar Paris, 1919–1933* (Toronto: University of Toronto Press, 2005).
43 This is the title of Schloesser's chapter 3: "Mystic Realism: A Faith that Faced the Facts."
44 Maritain, *Integral Humanism*, 162–63.
45 Maritain, *Integral Humanism*, 168.
46 Maritain, *Integral Humanism*, 119.
47 For a critique of the political application of Maritain's social philosophy in the context of Chile, see William Cavanaugh, *Torture and the Eucharist: Theology, Politics, and the Body of Christ* (Oxford: Blackwell, 1998), especially chapter 4, "A Distinction of Planes," 151–202. Cavanaugh argues that Maritain's distinction between secular and sacred planes, and the consequent emphasis on the interiority of religious life, although meant to free the church from party politics and to order the temporal to the spiritual, in fact dissolved the very social, ecclesial practices that could have resisted political abuse.
48 Quoted in James Heft's introductory essay in *A Catholic Modernity? Charles Taylor's Marianist Award Lecture*, ed. James Heft (New York: Oxford University, 1999), 3, which, in turn, is quoting from Adam Begley, "The *Mensch* of Montreal," *Lingua Franca*, May/June 1993, 39, which, in turn, cites (without reference) the "blurb" on the book (presumably the dust jacket, which I have been unable to obtain).
49 Alan Wolfe, "Review of *Sources of the Self*," *Contemporary Sociology* 19, no. 4 (July 1990): 627–28, at 627.
50 David Martin, *Tablet* 261.8719, December 1, 2007, 23.
51 Nicholas Boyle, *Goethe: The Poet and His Age*, vol. 1, *The Poetry of Desire, 1749 to 1790* (Oxford: Clarendon, 1991); and *Goethe: The Poet and His Age*, vol. 2, *Revolution and Renunciation, 1790–1803* (Oxford: Clarendon, 2000).
52 Eamon Duffy, *Tablet* 252.8262, December 19 and 26, 1998, 1706.
53 Nicholas Lash, review of *Who Are We Now?* in *Priests and People* 13, no. 4 (April 1999): 165–167, at 165.
54 Fergus Kerr, "The Real Presence in Literature," *Tablet* 258.8568, December 18 and 25, 2004, 36.
55 Rowan Williams, *Lost Icons: Reflections on Cultural Bereavement* (Edinburgh: T&T Clark, 2000), 8 n. 1.
56 Rowan Williams, review of *Who Are We Now?* in *Tablet* 253.8291 (July 17, 1999): 990.
57 My thanks to John Milbank for his permission to refer to our electronic discussion.
58 "The alternative [to trying to preserve fortress nation states] is to take the idea that we are all citizens of the world *seriously*. A book that spells this

out beautifully (by a great Catholic thinker, by the way) is Nicholas Boyle's book *Who Are We Now?* http://www.filozofia.pl/czat2/hilary_putnam.php3 (accessed August 20, 2008). This web page is currently unavailable. I can supply a copy of the text upon request.

59 Stanley Hauerwas, "The Christian Difference: Or Surviving Postmodernism," in *Anabaptists and Postmodernity*, ed. Susan and Gerald Biesecker-Mast (Telford, PA: Pandora, 2000), 41–59, at 41.

60 With some revisions, this paragraph and the section on Boyle in the first part of this article have been previously published in my note, "Nicholas Boyle's Christian Humanism: An Overview and Critique by a Systematic Theologian," *Heythrop Journal* 45, no. 2 (April 2004): 233–242. Permission to republish granted by Blackwell.

61 This is less so in Taylor's case. Nevertheless, the responses the two figures have elicited do not directly engage their Christian humanism. For articles on Taylor, see the footnotes in the section on Taylor, below. Also, the third footnote in Michael L. Morgan, "Religion, History, and Moral Discourse," in *Philosophy in an Age of Pluralism: The Philosophy of Charles Taylor in Question*, ed. James Tully (Cambridge: Cambridge University Press, 1994), 49–66, gives a reasonably full list of articles and reviews on Taylor. For book-length appropriations see L. Gregory Jones, *Transformed Judgment: Toward a Trinitarian Account of the Moral Life* (Notre Dame, IN: University of Notre Dame Press, 1990); and David Hollenbach, *The Common Good and Christian Ethics* (Cambridge: Cambridge University Press, 2002).

62 With some exceptions, e.g., chaps. 5 and 6 of Michael Buckley's *Catholic University*; and John Bequette, *Christian Humanism: Creation, Redemption, and Reintegration* (Lanham, MD: University Press of America, 2004). Beyond systematic theologians, David Hollenbach and William Schweiker are influential examples of the appropriation of the idea of Christian humanism in theological ethics. For Hollenbach, see "The Catholic University under the Sign of the Cross: Christian Humanism in a Broken World," in *Finding God in All Things: Essays in Honor of Michael J. Buckley, S.J.*, ed. Michael Himes and Stephen Pope (New York: Crossroads, 1996), 279–298. For Schweiker, see "Distinctive Love: Gratitude for Life and Theological Humanism," in *Humanity Before God* (Minneapolis: Fortress, 2006), 91–117. For a biographical appropriation of the idea from the Reformed tradition, see John de Gruchy, *Confessions of a Christian Humanist* (Minneapolis: Fortress Press, 2006). In the context of liberal arts education, see R. William Franklin and Joseph Shaw, *The Case for Christian Humanism* (Grand Rapids, MI: Eerdmans, 1991); and the accompanying reader, *Readings in Christian Humanism*, ed. Joseph Shaw (Minneapolis: Augsburg, 1982).

63 Charles Taylor, "Humanismus und moderne Identität," in *Der Mensch in den modernen Wissenschaften*, ed. Krzysztof Michalski (Stuggart: Klett-Cotta, 1985), 117–170, at 117. The translations are my own.

64 Taylor, *Catholic Modernity?* 19.

65 Taylor, *Catholic Modernity?* 123. Taylor's general allegiance to Christian humanism is opposed to a form of Christianity that, reacting against a

hostile secular climate, simply opposes God's commands to any human moral source.

66 In addition to those instances cited above, another example of his rejection of secular humanism can be found in his review of Martha Nussbaum's *The Fragility of Goodness: Luck and Ethics in Greek Tragedy and Philosophy*, in *Canadian Journal of Philosophy* 18, no. 4 (December 1988): 805–814. He appreciates "her commitment to a kind of all-inclusive humanism" (811), and her reading of Aristotle as giving a "principled defense of … ethics as the *human* good, that is, the good which is peculiar to us humans; something therefore which we can only grasp from within the human form of life; which we therefore can't get to by transcending the human viewpoint" (810). But he qualifies that appreciation by insisting on Plato's "aspiration to transcendence" without which "we will never understand ourselves" (812). "The transcendent can be seen as endorsing or affirming the value of ordinary human attention and concern, as has undoubtedly been the case with the Judaeo-Christian tradition, with decisive consequences for our whole moral outlook" (813).

67 Charles Taylor, *Sources of the Self: The Making of Modern Identity* (Cambridge, MA: Harvard University Press, 1989), 318. In this passage, examples of religious antihumanism are "much evangelical religion today, or … figures like Cardinal Ratzinger." The accuracy of these particular identifications is not relevant to this inquiry, although my conclusion will offer some reflections on Pope Benedict's theology of hope that suggest Taylor might now agree more with Ratzinger's position than he did then.

68 Taylor, *Sources*, 521. Earlier in the book, Taylor puts it as follows: "[Being] dedicated to the cause of God … includes an affirming of life, which incorporates what I have called ordinary life. What differentiates God from humans in this respect is the fullness, the force of the affirmation—something humans can't match on their own, but which they can participate in by following God…. In the Christian case, the key notion is that of agape, or charity, God's affirming love for the world (John 3:16), which humans through receiving can then give in turn…. [It] is something beyond morality, as it were, viz., participation in God's affirming power" (270). Taylor repeats this theme of divine affirmation in a later essay responding to the secular humanist Quentin Skinner. " 'The death of God,' says Skinner, 'leaves us with an opportunity, perhaps even a duty, to affirm the value of our humanity more fully than ever before.' … The issue is: what kind of affirmation can one make?… I have a hunch that there is a scale of affirmation of humanity by God which cannot be matched by humans rejecting God." Charles Taylor, "Reply and Re-articulation," in *Philosophy in an Age of Pluralism: The Philosophy of Charles Taylor in Question*, ed. James Tully and Daniel Weinstock (Cambridge: Cambridge University Press, 1994), 213–57, at 225–26.

69 For the bibliographical reference, see n. 48 above. For a discussion of these themes in *A Secular Age*, see chap. 15, "The Immanent Frame," esp. 569–70.

70 Taylor, "Humanismus," 118.

71 Taylor, "Humanismus," 118.

72 Taylor, "Humanismus," 118. According to Taylor, Dostoyevsky captured aspects of both responses. On the one hand, he laid bare the atheistic tendency in modern culture's self-affirmation. On the other, he did not deny modern aspirations, believing instead that their striving for transfiguration will not be abandoned, but, to the contrary, is the foundation for the renewed realization that we create only in partnership with God.
73 Taylor, "Humanismus," 166 (drawing on Titus 3:4.).
74 Taylor, *Sources*, 521.
75 Taylor, *Catholic Modernity?* 35. The last two sentences of this quotation are reproduced verbatim in *A Secular Age*, 703.
76 Taylor, *Catholic Modernity?* 16.
77 Taylor, *Catholic Modernity?* 21.
78 Taylor, *Sources*, 518, where Taylor explores how a theistic perspective may provide "the moral sources which might sustain our rather massive professed commitments in benevolence and justice."
79 Boyle, *Who Are We Now?* 9.
80 Boyle, *Who Are We Now?* 89.
81 Boyle, *Who Are We Now?* 6–7.
82 One of the most influential figures in Catholic theology on this point is Bernard Lonergan. The first sentence of *Method in Theology* (Toronto: University of Toronto Press, 1971) states that "theology mediates between a cultural matrix and the significance and role of religion in that matrix" (xi). For a recent survey of the relationship between theology and culture in the context of postmodernity, see Kathryn Tanner, *Theories of Culture: A New Agenda for Theology* (Minneapolis: Fortress, 1997). From a Catholic perspective, see Michael Gallagher, *Clashing Symbols: An Introduction to Faith and Culture* (New York: Paulist, 2003).
83 Aiden Nichols, *Christendom Awake: On Re-energising the Church in Culture* (Grand Rapids, MI: Eerdmans, 1999).
84 Taylor, *A Secular Age*, 29.
85 The "we" refers to the people of the modern (i.e., post-Enlightenment) West, especially the North Atlantic region. In Taylor's later works, *Modern Social Imaginaries* and *A Secular Age*, he explores "multiple modernities," that is, the various ways in which modernity has taken root in different cultural and historical contexts.
86 Taylor, *Sources*, x. The other two sources of modern selfhood are expressive individualism and inwardness, which means "the sense of ourselves as beings with inner depths, and the connected notion that we are 'selves.'" For a Thomistic critique of expressive individualism, see Stephen Pope, "Expressive Individualism and True Self-love: A Thomistic Perspective," *Journal of Religion* 71, no. 3 (July 1991): 384–399. For an Augustinian critique of Taylor's account of inwardness, see Stanley Hauerwas and David Matzko McCarthy, "The Sources of Charles Taylor," *Religious Studies Review* 18, no. 4 (October 1992): 286–289.
87 Taylor, *Catholic Modernity*, 22. For a criticism of the potential shortcomings of an uncritical affirmation of ordinary life, see Jean Bethke Elshtain, "The risks and responsibilities of affirming ordinary life," in *Philosophy of Charles Taylor*, 67–82.

88 Taylor, *Sources*, 218.
89 Charles Taylor, *The Ethics of Authenticity* (Cambridge, MA: Harvard University Press, 1991).
90 Because of modernity's individualism (e.g., the emphasis on autonomy and self-exploration), it appeals to the notion of rights; because of its egalitarianism, it applies these rights universally. Taylor, *Sources*, 305.
91 The work was originally presented as the Massey Lectures of the Canadian Broadcasting Company in 1991 under the title "The Malaise of Modernity" and subsequently published in Canada under the same title (Concord, ON: Anansi, 1992).
92 "As long as the order of things embodies an ontic logos, then ideas and valuations are also seen as located in the world, and not just in subjects. Indeed, their privileged locus is in the cosmos, or perhaps beyond it, in the realm of Ideas in which both the world and soul participate." Taylor, *Sources*, 186. In contrast, "modernity comes with the destruction of traditional horizons, of belief in the sacred, of old notions of hierarchy; it comes with the disenchantment of the world." Taylor, *Catholic Modernity?* 106. This situation was memorably described in the last lines of Alexandre Koyré's study of sixteenth- and seventeenth-century conceptions of the universe, *From the Closed World to the Infinite Universe* (Baltimore, MD: John Hopkins, 1957): "The infinite Universe of the New Cosmology, infinite in Duration as well as in Extension, in which eternal matter in accordance with eternal and necessary laws moves endlessly and aimlessly in eternal space, inherited all the ontological attributes of Divinity. Yet only those—all the others the departed God took away with Him" (276). For a brief and lucid contemporary theological response to the distressed sensibility this may occasion, see David Burrell's *Knowing the Unknowable God: Ibn-Sina, Maimonides, Aquinas* (Notre Dame, IN: University of Notre Dame Press, 1986), chap. 1, "Picturing the Connection," 5–18, esp. the section "From Picturing the Connection to Articulating the Distinction," 14–18. For a comprehensive historical treatment of this problem in its cultural setting, see Louis Dupré, *Passage to Modernity: An Essay in the Hermeneutics of Nature and Culture* (New Haven: Yale University Press, 1993), which examines the fragmentation of the premodern "felt synthesis" of "thinking, being and acting" (6).
93 Taylor, *Sources*, 13.
94 Taylor, *Sources*, 17.
95 Or nigh impossible, in Alisdair MacIntyre's more pessimistic analysis at the opening of *After Virtue: A Study in Moral Theory* (London: Duckworth, 1981). Taylor also suggests less cosmic reasons for this "malaise of modernity," namely, modernity's pluralism and its resulting liberalism, which values procedural rights over substantial goods, thereby making it harder for the broader culture to articulate its common good.
96 Charles Taylor, *Philosophical Arguments* (Cambridge, MA: Harvard University Press, 1995), 225.
97 Taylor, *Catholic Modernity?* 107.
98 Taylor, *Sources*, 18.
99 Taylor, *Sources*, 31.
100 Taylor, *Sources*, 18–19.

101 Charles Taylor, "Modes of Secularism," in *Secularism and Its Critics*, ed. Rajeev Bhargava (New York: Oxford University Press, 1998), 31–53, at 36. Taylor distinguishes this type of secularism from those that seek to maintain public order in religiously diverse societies and are not intrinsically hostile to theological commitments. This latter form of secularism Taylor supports. See also Charles Taylor, "Liberal Politics and the Public Sphere," in his *Philosophical Arguments*, 257–87, especially 267–272. In his latest work, *A Secular Age*, Taylor offers a more differentiated, threefold distinction in the meaning of secularity (discussed below).

102 In that case, we would be "living beyond our means." Taylor, *Sources*, 517. He suggests earlier that a "theistic source would be a far greater moral source than the belief in the dignity of disengaged reason or the goodness of nature. Whereas faith may be questioned as to its truth, dignity and nature are also called into question in respect of their adequacy if true" (517).

103 Taylor, *Sources*, 342.

104 Taylor, *Sources*, 342.

105 Taylor, *Sources*, 521.

106 Taylor, *Catholic Modernity?* 35.

107 Taylor, *Catholic Modernity?* 20.

108 Taylor, *Catholic Modernity?* 24.

109 Taylor, *Catholic Modernity?* 28.

110 Taylor explores these instances of transcendence in *A Secular Age*. On beauty, see the discussions of Hopkins and Péguy, 755. On limit situations, see his discussion of death, 720–27. On political reconciliation, see 706–7.

111 Taylor, *A Secular Age*, 726.

112 Boyle, *Who Are We Now?* 116.

113 Boyle, *Who Are We Now?* 40–41.

114 Boyle, *Who Are We Now?* 41.

115 Boyle, *Who Are We Now?* 251.

116 Timothy Radcliffe, *Sing a New Song: The Christian Vocation* (Springfield, IL: Templegate, 1999).

117 For Boyle's comments on creaturely status, see, e.g., *Who Are We Now?* 93 and 198.

118 Boyle, *Who Are We Now?* 9.

119 Boyle, *Who Are We Now?* 321.

120 A fuller historical account would obviously have to nuance this summary oversimplification by registering the emergence of fascism as a serious political force after the crisis of liberal capitalism from 1929.

121 Boyle, *Who Are We Now?* 46.

122 See, for example, Taylor, *A Secular Age*, 649; or idem, *A Catholic Modernity?* 14: "Redemption happens through Incarnation, the weaving of God's life into human lives." For Boyle, see his comments on Hopkins, *Who Are We Now?* 301–3.

123 Whereas chapter 1 discussed Maritain's and Murray's Christian humanisms in terms of their historical and sociological contexts, the present chapter discusses them in terms of their systematic theological foundations.

124 Boyle, *Who Are We Now?* 292.

125 Boyle, *Who Are We Now?* 303.
126 Boyle, *Who Are We Now?* 309–10.
127 Seamus Heaney, *The Haw Lantern* (London: Faber and Faber, 1987), 12–13.
128 Boyle, *Who Are We Now?* 311. The original reference is to Diogenes the Cynic; the episode with the lamp is recorded in Diogenes Laertes, *Lives of the Philosophers* 4.41.
129 Boyle has explored this theme in greater detail in a subsequent book, *Sacred and Secular Scriptures: A Catholic Approach to Literature* (Notre Dame, IN: University of Notre Dame Press, 2005), in which he argues that sacred literature, despite its overlap and connection with secular literature, alone possesses the authority to pronounce commandments (see chap. 9, "A Catholic Approach to Literature"). While recognizing the value of these arguments, I have found the notion of theological virtue a more helpful concept with which to discuss the theological grounds of Christian humanism because of its humanistic emphasis on the good (as distinct from a juridical emphasis on the right and on commandments). Also, following Aquinas, I understand the notions of law and obligation to derive their intelligibility from the broader framework of virtue and desire. Finally, Aquinas argues that law itself presupposes faith and hope, since a law is only effective if the lawgiver is believed and his promises (and threats) hoped for (and feared). See, for example, *ST* II-II.22.1.
130 By natural virtues are meant those moral virtues proportionate to the human person prior to the supernatural gift of charity. No dichotomy between nature and supernature is intended, as will become clear below in chapter 3's elaboration of some general principles of Aquinas's theology.
131 E.g., in his comments on the shared theological stem of the different branches of humane studies (*Who Are We Now?* 6–7), or in his criticism of W. B. Yeats (ibid., 306–9).
132 See his criticisms of Goethe and Eliot in *Who Are We Now?* 294–99.
133 E.g., 1 Cor. 13:13; 1 Thess. 1:3; Augustine's *Enchridion*; Aquinas's *Summa theologiae, secunda secundae*, qq. 1–46; and his final work, *Compendium theologiae*. For a modern example of the importance of the theological virtues for a Christian presentation of a graced humanism, see the programmatic reflections on faith, hope, and love in the concluding chapter of Bernard Lonergan, *Insight: A Study of Human Understanding* (Toronto: University of Toronto Press, 1992), esp. sections 3 and 5 on "The Heuristic Structure of the Solution," 718–725, 740–750.
134 This comment is from his lecture at Boston College's Lonergan Workshop (March 31, 2000) and is recalled from memory. I believe it was in response to Nicholas Lash's review of *Who Are We Now?* in *Priests and People* 13, no. 4 (April 1999): 165–167.
135 Taylor, *Sources*, 342.
136 In a response to a secular critic who ridiculed his suggestion that God is a crucial moral source, Taylor clearly stated that his position was only a "tentative hunch," not an argument. Charles Taylor, "Comments and Replies," *Inquiry: An Interdisciplinary Journal of Philosophy* 34 (1991):

237–54, at 240. The expression recurs in another, later reply to the same critic: "I have a *hunch* that there is a scale of affirmation of humanity by God which cannot be matched by humans rejecting God" (emphasis added). "Reply and Re-articulation," 225–26. But Taylor's plea that it is only a hunch contradicts the evidence in *Sources* and *Catholic Modernity?* Even *A Secular Age*, which, as I show later, gives more justification for this hunch as a form of "anticipatory confidence," still uses the term, e.g., at 550 and, in the plural, 609.

137 Taylor raises, but does not pursue, this age-old question of whether meaningful moral action requires, at least implicitly, belief in God. For an earlier example in *Sources* of Taylor's touching on this issue, see the brief mention of the argument "that one or another ontology is in fact the only adequate basis for our moral responses.... A thesis of this kind was invoked by Dostoyevsky and discussed by Leszek Koakowski in a recent work [*Religion* (London: Fontana, 1982)]: 'If God does not exist, then everything is permitted.' ... I will probably not be able to venture very far out on this terrain in the following." *Sources*, 10. For a sympathetic extension of Taylor's tentative suggestions, see Andrew J. Dell'Olio, "God, the Self, and the Ethics of Virtue," *Philosophy and Theology* 11, no. 1 (1998): 47–70.

138 Taylor, *Sources*, 490.

139 Taylor, *Sources*, 518. See also idem, *A Secular Age*, 609.

140 Taylor, *Sources*, 517.

141 Taylor, *Sources*, 517.

142 Taylor, *Sources*, 518.

143 Taylor, *Sources*, 520. The original text reads "without any dimension or radical hope," which I presume is an error for "without any dimension of radical hope."

144 Referring to Taylor's account of Christianity's "central promise of a divine affirmation of the human." Taylor, *Sources*, 521.

145 Fergus Kerr, *Immortal Longings: Versions of Transcending Humanity* (Notre Dame, IN: University of Notre Dame Press, 1997), ix. Kerr is thinking particularly of Taylor's "astonishing, and disappointing [failure to] question [Isaiah] Berlin's conception of Christian theology as involving a deterministic teleological metaphysics" (154–155).

146 Russell Hittinger, *Review of Metaphysics* 44, no. 1 (September 1990): 111–30, at 126. Hittinger continues: "It remains to be seen whether he can formulate the kind of philosophy he has in mind unless he fastens upon a religious tradition that articulates its devotion to the good in a language of being" (130).

147 Charles Taylor's *Varieties of Religion Today: William James Revisited* (Cambridge, MA: Harvard University Press, 2002) confirms both his religious humanism and its thin theological foundation. In that work, he loosely places William James, for whom he has the greatest respect as a religious thinker, in the tradition of devout humanism. "There are modes of devotion in which we try to come closer to God, or center our lives on him, where we proceed in a fashion that trusts and builds on our own inner élan, our own desire to approach God. We see examples ... in some of the major

figures in what Henri Bremond has called 'l'humanisme dévot' in the French seventeenth century, such as St. François de Sales, or in Jesuit spirituality." Taylor, *Varieties*, 15–16. The major concern of that book, however, is not James's religious humanism, but the sociology of secularization. Taylor cites Henri Bremond, *Histoire littéraire du sentiment religieux en France* (Paris: Armand Colin, 1967). It should be noted that Taylor qualifies James's "devout humanism" as individualist and anarchic. "His model is more George Fox the Quaker than it is François de Sales." Taylor, *Varieties*, 18.

148 "But it is through the particularities [of living religious traditions] that they animate our lives.... The route of Nathan the Wise is the road to post-Enlightenment banalities, which lose their transforming power very quickly." Taylor, "Reply and Re-articulation," 229.
149 Taylor, *Catholic Modernity?* 13.
150 Tully, ed., *Philosophy of Charles Taylor*, 48.
151 Bernard Williams, "Republican and Galilean," *New York Review of Books*, November 8, 1990, 45–47.
152 Williams, "Republican and Galilean," 47.
153 Mark Redhead, *Charles Taylor: Thinking and Living Deep Diversity* (New York: Rowan and Littlefield, 2002), 192.
154 Redhead, *Charles Taylor*, 202.
155 For Taylor, such "foundational" arguments do not provide "basic reasons" so much as articulate a "fuller, more vivid, or clearer, better defined understanding of what the good is," and thus "not only [help] us know what to do but also know what we want to be, and even more crucially make us love the good." Charles Taylor, "Iris Murdoch and Moral Philosophy," in *Iris Murdoch and the Search for Human Goodness*, ed. Mario Antonaccio and William Schweiker (Chicago, IL: University of Chicago Press, 1996), 3–28, at 15–18. Thus, the kind of argumentation involved is not a disproof of an exclusive humanist position, but rather an appreciation for what is good in the "secular citadel" alongside an attempt to alter and broaden the horizon within which shared human realities are experienced and interpreted. On this point, see Taylor's discussion of "superseding transitions" as more "articulative" than "argumentative" in "A Philosopher's Postscript: Engaging the Citadel of Secular Reason," in *Reason and the Reasons of Faith*, ed. Paul Griffiths and Reinhard Hütter (New York: T&T Clark, 2005), 339–53.
156 Taylor, *A Secular Age*, 3.
157 Taylor, *A Secular Age*, 15–20. See also 632 for his comments on the problematic nature of this distinction, especially when conceived formally as a distinction between natural and supernatural, which, Taylor believes, sets the condition for the possibility of setting nature apart as an autonomous realm (542).
158 Taylor, *A Secular Age*, 640. See also 548–49: "the question really is whether [transcendence] is only threat, or doesn't also offer a promise"; and 510: "this whole book is an attempt to study the fate in the modern West of religious faith in a strong sense. This strong sense I define ... by a double

criterion: the belief in transcendent reality, on one hand, and the connected aspiration to a transformation which goes beyond ordinary human flourishing on the other."

159 Taylor, *A Secular Age*, 693–703.
160 Taylor, *A Secular Age*, 645.
161 Taylor, *A Secular Age*, 644.
162 Taylor, *A Secular Age*, 17–20. See also 151.
163 For example, the final chapter "Conversions," especially 768–70, or the discussion of the meaning of suffering in Christian doctrine, 654–56, which talks less about God's affirmation of the human and more about a future transformation of the tension of human hope in God.
164 In addition to the instances already mentioned, see Taylor, *A Secular Age*, 44; on time, 56–58; on eschatological judgment and responsibility, 67; on the apparently competing demands to love God and affirm ordinary life, 80–84; on Renaissance Italian and later Dutch painting, 144–45; on the basic novelty of Axial Age religion as introducing the tension between "transcendental and mundane orders," 793 n. 13, quoting Shmuel Eisenstadt, ed., *The Origin and Diversity of Axial Age Civilizations* (Albany, NY: State University of New York Press, 1986), 1; providential deism's equation of God's will with human flourishing found in design, and the consequent emergence of a purely immanent notion of human flourishing, 263–66 and 542–43; but nonetheless the endurance of the "désir d'éternité," 530; on modern attempts to find a *via media* between "the transformation and the immanence perspectives," 431; in the discussion of Henri Bremond's "humanisme devout" and Jansenists, 510; chap. 15 on the "cross-pressures" experienced within the "immanent frame" between the conscious, exclusive focus on the human good and submerged yet enduring lure of transcendence; chap. 17, esp. sections i and ii "Humanism and 'Transcendence' " and "Against Mutilation" (618–56); on the attempt of some exclusive humanists (e.g., Martha Nussbaum and Luc Ferry) to allow for transcendence, but only "immanent" or "horizontal" transcendence, not "external" or "vertical" transcendence, 625 and 677. Examples could be multiplied.
165 Charles Taylor, "Iris Murdoch and Moral Philosophy," in *Iris Murdoch and the Search for Human Goodness* (Chicago: University of Chicago, 1996), 3–28, at 27.
166 Taylor, *A Secular Age*, 708–9.
167 From the final paragraph on 151, beginning "The portrait of the early ..." until the end of the first full paragraph on 153, ending "... branded as an imperfection"; excluding the first two sentences of the first full paragraph on 152, "But perhaps ..." to "... supposedly achieved," which are in Charles Taylor, *Modern Social Imaginaries* (Durham, NC: Duke University Press, 2004). This added section begins with a long quotation from Francis Oakley, *Kingship* (Oxford: Blackwell, 2006), who is not cited in *Modern Social Imaginaries*, and thus presumably generated this new insight for Taylor. In an e-mail to the author (January 1, 2010), Taylor said that this addition did not signal a significant theological shift in his position. The

reader will have to decide whether this addition carries the significance I attribute to it.

168 The term "felt synthesis" is from Louis Dupré, *Passage to Modernity* (New Haven: Yale University Press, 1993). Taylor cites this work in a long footnote in *Modern Social Imaginaries*, 203 n. 4.
169 Taylor, *A Secular Age*, 706–7.
170 *ST* II-II.16.1, ad 2, emphasis added.
171 *ST* II-II.174.6.
172 Maritain, *Integral Humanism*, 72.
173 Maritain, *Integral Humanism*, 206.
174 Anthropocentricism also finds its roots in Catholic rationalist theology, in which "God becomes an idea" instead of a vivifying principle. Maritain, *Integral Humanism*, 32.
175 Maritain, *Integral Humanism*, 25, emphasis in original.
176 Maritain, *Integral Humanism*, 26.
177 Maritain, *Integral Humanism*, 15, emphasis in original.
178 Jacques Maritain, *Range of Reason* (New York: Charles Scribner's Sons, 1953), 195.
179 Maritain, *Integral Humanism*, 27.
180 Maritain, *Integral Humanism*, 43. For the phrase "socio-temporal realization of the Gospel" that is inserted in this quotation, see ibid., 7.
181 Maritain, *Integral Humanism*, 123. A succinct account of what Maritain considers the essential difference between medieval and modern Christendom is given in *Range of Reason*, 192–95.
182 Maritain, *Range of Reason*, 94.
183 Maritain, *Integral Humanism*, 102.
184 Maritain, *Range of Reason*, 101, referring to his own work, *Integral Humanism*.
185 Maritain, *Integral Humanism*, 74.
186 Maritain, *Integral Humanism*, 292–93. With Maritain's distinctions in mind, one can now appreciate more fully Boyle's claim that "the tradition of Catholic humanism ... is ... inspired by the belief that all areas of human life must be reached by the good news and can be bearers of it, and that that is in the nature of the good news itself." *Who Are We Now?* 9.
187 Maritain, *Integral Humanism*, 125.
188 Maritain, *Integral Humanism*, 6.
189 Maritain, *Integral Humanism*, 90.
190 A more precise distinction might be drawn by exchanging the word "temporal" for "secular," since temporal things cannot be sufficiently distinguished from spiritual things. Maritain adds an appendix, "The Structure of Action," in order to systematize this relationship.
191 Maritain, *Integral Humanism*, 254. But this work was written before the awareness that nation states are not as self-contained as they once were. For example, in the section on "The Ages of Christian History" (242–44), there is no mention of a "global age." Also, Maritain's *Man and the State*, published in 1951, is understandably overshadowed by oppositions between East and West.

192 John Courtney Murray, "Is it Basket Weaving? The Question of Christianity and Human Values," in *We Hold These Truths: Catholic Reflections on the American Proposition* (Kansas City: Sheed and Ward, 1988), 175–196, at 176. The quotation from Pius XII is from his reply to the address of a Liberian politician in 1951.

193 Murray, "Is it Basket Weaving?" 176. Murray goes on to say that the expression of this doctrine may "vary from age to age." But this awareness of temporality is not accompanied by a sense of the practical nature of the foundation of Christian humanism.

194 This quotation is from a different essay published in the same year, "Towards a Christian Humanism: Aspects of the Theology of Education," in *Bridging the Sacred and the Secular: Selected Writings of John Courtney Murray, S.J.*, ed. J. Leon Hooper (Washington, DC: Georgetown University Press, 1994), 124–132, at 130.

195 Murray, "Towards a Christian Humanism: Aspects of the Theology of Education," 127.

196 "The Construction of a Christian Culture," in *Bridging the Sacred and the Secular*, 101–123, here at 109. Murray adds that alongside this pride, there must be humility, because man realizes he is fully dependent on God. For similar appeals to the doctrinal basis of Christian humanism, see Murray's unpublished lectures at the Jewish Theological Seminary, February–March 1942, esp. lecture 2, paragraph 25: "[W]e see in the fact of the Incarnation God's affirmation of the validity of all things human. He assumed a human nature [...] and by that assumption all human nature was ennobled." My thanks to Joseph Komonchak for sharing his transcription of these lectures with me. The original typescript is held at the Woodstock Theological Center Library, Georgetown University.

197 Murray, "Towards a Christian Humanism," 128.

198 Murray, "Towards a Christian Humanism," 126, emphasis added.

199 Murray, "The Construction of a Christian Culture," 106. The second principle is the doctrine of the Trinity; the third, the redemption.

200 Murray, "The Construction of a Christian Culture," 102.

201 In the final section of "The Construction of a Christian Culture," 118–23. Towards the end of that section, at 123, Murray discusses the "location" of the Christian humanist. "The Christian humanist has a vantage point from which to view the world and understand his work in it. He stands on Calvary.... From Calvary one can truly see the earth in its full reality.... The highest and holiest task of the Christian humanist [is] to share something of the sufferings of the sons of men, to seek some measure of union with their age-long crucifixion—that thus made over into the image of the Son of Man crucified on Calvary, he may have some share in the world's redemption, Man's passage into the possession of God."

202 Murray, "Towards a Christian Humanism," 129.

203 Murray, "Towards a Christian Humanism," 131. See also Taylor, *A Secular Age*, 656.

204 Murray concludes one of his early speeches with some searching questions that call for "living arguments" for a Christian culture—that is, believers

who incarnate Christian humanism and are its final proof. This passage conveys something of the "difficult task" of Christian humanism. "The secularist proposes to test the truth of our premise by the product we turn out. He is not being unfair when he says to our product: 'I shall judge the validity of your Christianity by the type of manhood it has wrought in you. Let us see. Are you at peace with yourself? Have you resolved in yourself the interior conflict that tears me apart? Are you able to resist the attraction of matter, and to save yourself from immersion in it? Do you understand this world? Are you able to see a meaning in its history?' " Murray, "Towards a Christian Humanism," 132.

205 Murray, "Is it Basket Weaving?" 193–196, esp. 195–96.
206 Murray, "The Construction of a Christian Culture," 107. See also his comments later in the essay, at 108: "Man, since he is capable of divinity, is capable also, and for the first time, of full humanity. Old Aristotle saw truly: a man cannot and will not be perfectly human unless somehow he becomes divine."
207 Taylor, "Humanismus," 117.
208 *ST* I-II.67.3, ad 2.
209 Thus, the figures examined so far understand humanism as involving a crucial practical component. Taylor's definition links humanism to a "practical philosophy." Boyle states at the opening of *Who Are We Now?* that "I believe we have choices, and that it matters that we should choose the paths most likely to lead to justice and peace" (4). Maritain's *Integral Humanism* is centrally preoccupied with the sociotemporal work of the Christian, and Murray is likewise concerned with "The Construction of a Christian Culture."
210 See "The Search for a New Humanism: The University and the Concern for Justice," in Buckley, *Catholic University*, 105–128. Paul VI in turn is following the use of the term in *Gaudium et spes*: "We are witnessing the birth of a new humanism, where people are defined before all else by their responsibility to their sisters and brothers and at the court of history" (§55).
211 Buckley, *Catholic University*, 76.
212 Buckley, *Catholic University*, 118.
213 Buckley, *Catholic University*, 119.
214 Buckley, *Catholic University*, 119–20.
215 In addition to the references cited above in chapter 1, see also Taylor, "Iris Murdoch and Moral Philosophy," 5, 21.
216 Boyle, *Who Are We Now?* 86.
217 Boyle, *Who Are We Now?* 179. For example, the inability to imagine a future political arrangement that surpasses the nation state. For a discussion of Hegel's secularizing of theology, see Martin Henry, "G. W. F. Hegel: A Secularized Theologian?" *Irish Theological Quarterly* 70, no. 3 (2005): 195–214.
218 On modern philosophy's treatment of God as a guarantee in a philosophical system, see James Collins, *God in Modern Philosophy* (Chicago: H. Regnery, 1959), especially the section "God and Functionalism," 378–83. For more sympathetic views on the role of hope in Kant's philosophy that

see it as more central to his work, see Allen Wood, *Kant's Moral Religion* (Ithaca: Cornell University Press, 1970); and Michael Despland, *Kant on History and Religion* (Montreal: McGill-Queen's University Press, 1973). I am grateful to an anonymous referee at *Theological Studies* for this point.

219 These two phrases are italicized to indicate that they are part of a definition. They are not exact quotations from Aquinas. The textual warrant for the generic features of hope (as the movement towards a future, difficult, yet possible good) can be found in Aquinas's treatment of hope as a passion in *ST* I-II.40.1. The textual warrant for the specifically theological features of hope (as involving eternal happiness through God's help) can be found in Aquinas's citation of Peter Lombard and 2 Timothy in *ST* II-II.18.4, s.c.: "*spes est certa expectatio futurae beatitudinis*, sicut Magister dicit, 26 dist. III *Sent*. [26, 1 (Quaracchi II, 670)] quod potest accipi ex hoc quod dicitur *2 ad Tim*. 1:12, *Scio cui credidi, et certus sum quia potens est depositum meum servare.*"

220 "[Spes] attingit [Deum] sicut primam causam efficientem, inquantum eius auxilio innititur, et sicut ultimam causam finalem, inquantum in eius fruitione beatitudinem expectat" (*ST* II-II.17.5).

221 See *ST* II-II.23.5, ad 2: "Caritate diligitur Deus propter seipsum"; whereas hope loves God as one's own future good. This point can also be seen in charity and hope's opposing vices: hatred is against God in Godself, whereas despair is against God as God is participated by us. See *ST* II-II.20.3.

222 "Inquantum ergo speramus aliquid ut possibile nobis per divinum auxilium, spes nostra attingit ad ipsum Deum, cuius auxilio innititur" (*ST* II-II.17.1).

223 Rowan Greer, *Christian Hope and Christian Life: Raids on the Inarticulate* (New York: Crossroads, 2001).

224 Greer, *Christian Hope*, 8.

225 An etymological association also made by Moltmann in a Christological context: "The *missio* of Jesus becomes intelligible only by the *promissio*." Jürgen Moltman, *Theology of Hope: On the Ground and the Implications of a Christian Eschatology*, trans. James Leitch (Fortress, Minneapolis, 1993), 203.

226 Greer, *Christian Hope*, 7.

227 Greer, *Christian Hope*, 170–71.

228 Gordon Kaufman, *In Face of Mystery: A Constructive Theology* (Cambridge, MA : Harvard University Press, 1993), xi.

229 Kaufman, *In Face of Mystery*, 381.

230 Kaufman, *In Face of Mystery*, 458.

231 *Quaestiones disputatae De potentia* (hereafter *De pot*.), q. 6, a. 9, ad 10: "spei non proprie attribuitur miracula facere; spes enim ordinatur ad aliquid consequendum, unde est solum de aeternis. Fides autem est de aeternis et temporalibus; unde potest se extendere ad facienda." According to Jean-Pierre Torrell, *De Potentia* was written around 1265–66; see *Saint Thomas Aquinas*, vol. 1, *The Person and His Work*, trans. Robert Royal (Washington, DC: Catholic University of America Press, 1996), 335.

232 *De pot*. q. 6, a. 9, ad 11: "obiectum spei est arduum consequendum, non autem arduum faciendum."

233 Jürgen Moltmann, "Theology as Eschatology," in *The Future of Hope: Theology as Eschatology*, ed. Frederick Herzog (New York: Herder and Herder, 1970), 1–50, at 13 n. 19.
234 Jürgen Moltmann, "Christian Hope: Messianic or Transcendent? A Theological Discussion with Joachim of Fiore and Thomas Aquinas," *Horizons* 12, no. 2 (1985): 328–348, at 329. See also his description of Aquinas's understanding of the relationship between nature and grace as a "dichotomy" at 343, including n. 38.
235 Moltmann, "Christian Hope," 328–348, at 333. For a brief discussion and criticism of Moltmann's account of hope, with alternative accounts by other theologians, see Zachary Hayes, "History and Eschatology," in *A Vision of the Future: A Study of Christian Eschatology* (Collegeville, MN: Liturgical Press, 1990), 126–53.
236 Nicholas Wolterstorff, "Seeking Justice in Hope," in *The Future of Hope: Christian Tradition amid Modernity and Postmodernity*, ed. Miroslav Wolf and William Katerberg (Grand Rapids, MI: Eerdmans, 2004), 77–100.
237 Wolterstorff, "Seeking Justice," 79.
238 "It is not my main aim here to engage in Aquinas exegesis, but rather to have a before us a *type* of view. Nevertheless, I think I had better protect my flanks against the charge of those who will claim that I have misinterpreted Aquinas." Wolterstorff, "Seeking Justice," 80.
239 *ST* II-II.17.5, obj. 1.
240 *ST* II-II.17.2.
241 The reference is to Aquinas's claim that secondary hopes can be referred to the principal end. As an example, he cites *ST* II-II.17.2, ad 2: "We ought not to pray to God for any other goods things, except as ordered to eternal happiness. Hence hope principally concerns eternal happiness; other things for which we pray to God, hope regards secondarily as ordered to eternal happiness."
242 Wolterstorff, "Seeking Justice," 81.
243 The inadequacies of Wolterstorff's argument from silence will be shown in the next chapter and chapter six. For now, it is sufficient to note the tenor of Aquinas's understanding of the relationship between the theological and moral virtues in the following question, "Whether Christians are bound to obey the secular power?": "Faith in Christ is the foundation and cause of justice.... Therefore faith in Christ does not remove the order of justice but rather strengthens it" (*ST* II-II.104.6).
244 On this, see Bernard Lonergan's contrast between common-sense eclecticism and theory in *Insight*, 442–45. For a historical analysis of patristic eschatology, see Brian Daley, *The Hope of the Early Church* (Cambridge: Cambridge University Press, 1991).
245 "Metaphysical" pertains to the study of being *qua* being; "philosophical" to the study of a particular aspect of being (in this case, the human person) in terms of its underlying nature and its relation to other aspects of being; and "theological" to the ordered reflection on Christian faith.
246 Following David Burrell's formulation that Creator and creation are not competing causes. See "On the Relations between the Two Actors," in

Freedom and Creation in Three Traditions (Notre Dame, IN: University of Notre Dame Press, 1993), 95–140.

247 For secondary sources I rely principally on W. Norris Clarke, Jean-Pierre Torrell, John Wippel, Bernard Lonergan, William O'Connor, Rudi te Velde, and D. Juvenal Merriell. Because of the summary nature of this chapter (and of the first section of chapter 4 "From Grace to Virtue") quotations from Aquinas are from the translation by the Fathers of the English Dominican Province in *Summa theologica* (Allen, TX: Christian Classics, 1981).

248 Technically, creatures participate in the *similitudo*, not *essentia*, of God, as Rudi te Velde points out in *Aquinas on God: The "Divine Science" of the "Summa theologiae"* (Burlington, VT: Ashgate, 2006), 146 n. 49, referencing Aquinas, *In librum Beati Dionysii De divinis nominibus exposition*, cap. 2, lect. 3, n. 158. But for sake of simplicity and stylistic variation, this chapter will occasionally use the shorthand "participation in God" for "participation in the likeness of God," even though the former is accurate only when talking about grace.

249 *ST* I.1.7. See also the prologue to question 2.

250 To identify God as the source of being presupposes that God's existence has been demonstrated or accepted on faith. But such a demonstration is beyond the scope of this inquiry. For an inquiry that follows the proper philosophical order of procedure, and for a more detailed examination of the several meanings of the term "participation," including the important difference between participation in *esse commune* and *esse subsistens*, see John F. Wippel, *The Metaphysical Thought of Thomas Aquinas: From Finite Being to Uncreated Being* (Washington, DC: Catholic University of America Press, 2000), 94–131 and 590–592.

251 Te Velde, *Aquinas on God*, 142.

252 W. Norris Clarke, *The One and the Many: A Contemporary Thomistic Metaphysics* (Notre Dame, IN: University of Notre Dame Press, 2001), 72. Wippel formulates the question as follows: "How is one to account for the fact that many different beings do indeed exist, and yet that each of them in some way shares in the perfection of being?" *Metaphysical Thought*, 95.

253 W. Norris Clarke, *Explorations in Metaphysics: Being—God—Person* (Notre Dame, IN: University of Notre Dame Press, 1994), 93. Wippel quotes Aquinas's definition of participation in *De Hebdomadibus*: "When something receives in particular fashion that which belongs to another in universal (or total) fashion, the former is said to participate in the latter." *Metaphysical Thought*, 96. A participating being thus shares partially in, but is not identical with, the perfect thing itself.

254 *ST* I.4.3.

255 The likeness is called "analogical" at the end of same the *respondeo* (*ST* I.4.3), which also makes clear why Aquinas's so-called "analogy of being" cannot be charged with "ontotheology." "Therefore if there is an agent not contained in any genus, its effects will still more distantly reproduce the form of the agent [than an agent that is in the same species or genus as its effect], not, that is, so as to participate in the likeness of the agent's form according to the same specific or generic formality, but only according to

some sort of analogy [*sed secundum aliqualem analogiam*]; as existence is common to all. *In this way* all created things, so far as they are beings, are like God as the first and universal principle of all being" (emphasis added). For a recent discussion of Aquinas's purported ontotheology, see Jean Luc Marion's change of mind in exempting Aquinas from that charge in the preface to *God without Being* (Chicago: University of Chicago Press, 1991), which is the English edition of his *Dieu sans l'être: Hors-texte* (Paris: Librairie Arthème Fayard, 1982).

256 The likeness, however, is not symmetrical. "Although it may be admitted that creatures are in some sort like God, it must nowise be admitted that God is like creatures; because, as Dionysius says 'A mutual likeness may be found between things of the same order, but not between a cause and that which is caused.' For we say that a statue is like a man, but not conversely" (*ST* I.4.3, ad 4). The likeness is strictly one of analogy: "Likeness of creatures to God is not affirmed on account of agreement in form according to the formality of the same genus or species, but solely according to analogy, inasmuch as God is essential being, whereas other things are beings by participation" (*ST* I.4.3, ad 3). For a good discussion of why being is not a common denominator under which both God and creation fall, see Te Velde, *Aquinas on God*, 85–90.

257 *ST* I.13.5.
258 *ST* I.3, *proemium*.
259 *ST* I.3.5.
260 "That God is not in any genus, as reducible to it as its principle, is clear from this, that a principle reducible to any genus does not extend beyond that genus.... But God is the principle of all being. Therefore He is not contained in any genus as its principle" (*ST* I.3.5). Again: God "is first in respect of all being, outside [*extra*] of every genus" (*ST* I.3.6, ad 2). Or: "God is not related to creatures as though belonging to a different *genus*, but as transcending every *genus*, and as the principle of all *genera*" (*ST* I.4.3, ad 2).
261 *ST* I.7.1, ad 3. "Apart from" (*removatur*) conveys God's transcendence from creation, not creation's separation from God.
262 "emanationem totius entis a causa universali, quae est Deus ... designamus nomine *creationis*" (*ST* I.45.1). Creation, then, is a specific term that should be distinguished from *emanatio*, which is defined by Deferrari as "a general term for something proceeding from a principle."
263 Clarke express this notion of the composition of existence with essence as follows: "Every real being, save perhaps one, must be constituted by a real metaphysical composition ... or complementary polarity of two correlative metaphysical co-principles within the unity of one being; namely, (1) an act of existence, by which it actually exists, is actively present in the universe of beings; and (2) a limiting essence, by which it exists in this or that particular mode or manner of existing, as this or that particular being and not some other." *One and Many*, 80.
264 Why? Because whatever is created cannot, *ipso facto*, be an infinite, underived act of existence, for to be created is to receive existence from

another. To be uncreated, on the other hand, is to be pure act without any potency, that is, without any need for some agent to actualize its existence. Consequently, for God to create anything else, some factor must distinguish what God creates from Godself. (For if there were no distinguishing factor, then Creator and created would be identical—and then one is back in the impossible position of God creating God.) So what God creates must be distinguished from the infinite God by some limiting factor (for something cannot be different from the infinite by some additional factor)—and hence whatever is created must be a finite essence.

265 On the unique nature of this distinction, see Robert Sokolowski, *The God of Faith and Reason: Foundations of Christian Theology* (Washington, DC: Catholic University of America Press, 1995), esp. 31–40; David Burrell, *Knowing the Unknowable God: Ibn-Sina, Maimonides, Aquinas* (Notre Dame, IN: University of Notre Dame Press, 1986), esp. 17–34; and Kathryn Tanner, *God and Creation in Christian Theology: Tyranny or Empowerment?* (Oxford: Blackwell, 1988), esp. 42–48.

266 Tanner, *God and Creation*, 46.

267 *ST* I.45.5.

268 *ST* I.8.1. For more argumentation as to why the idea of creation involves being sustained in being by God, see *ST* I.104.1: "Now every creature may be compared to God, as the air is to the sun which enlightens it. For as the sun possesses light by its nature, and as the air is enlightened by sharing the sun's nature; so God alone is Being by virtue of His own essence, since His Essence is His existence; whereas every creature has being by participation, so that its essence is not its existence. Therefore, as Augustine says (*Gen ad lit.* iv. 12): 'If the ruling power of God were withdrawn from His creatures, their nature would at once cease, and all nature would collapse.' " Thus, Aquinas answers the question "Whether God can annihilate anything?" in the affirmative, as follows: "That God gives existence to a creature depends on His will; nor does He preserve things in existence otherwise than by continually pouring out existence into them, as we have said. Therefore, just as before things existed, God was free not to give them existence, and not to make them; so after they have been made, He is free not to continue their existence; and thus they would cease to exist; and this would be to annihilate them" (*ST* I.104.3). In Te Velde's words: "Creation is not like the past origin of a thing's physical existence; it is the permanent condition of any form of existence in the world." *Aquinas on God*, 126.

269 Thus, the perfection in which all else participates is existence. And although "existence is common to all" (*ST* I.4.3), it does not follow that it is some sort of lowest common denominator. To the contrary, "existence is the most perfect of all things, for it is compared to all things as that by which they are made actual; for nothing has actuality except so far as it exists. Hence existence is that which actuates all things, even their forms" (*ST* I.4.1, ad 3; see also *De pot.* q. 7, a. 2, ad 9). Existence, then, is the crucial term in the Thomistic metaphysic of participation. Clarke explains Aquinas's understanding of existence as follows: "The principle of existence must be a *maximum*, an all-encompassing plentitude, with essences serving as limiting,

diversifying principles within the fullness of existence itself, diversifying being by limiting it in different ways from within, partially negating the fullness of being by diverse, limited modes of existing.... Essences are thus not something positive added on to a minimum base of existence, but rather intrinsic limiting or restrictive principles particularizing and finitizing each act of existence that is not the total plenitude of pure unrestricted existence." *One and Many*, 83. Again, in fewer (but less precise) words: "the essence is like the restrictive channel along which flows and expresses itself the encapsulated energy of the act of existence." *One and Many*, 151.

270 *ST* I.8.1.
271 An efficient cause, according to Clarke, is "that which contributes positively to the being of another by its action: it is the agent that makes something to be, brings it into being, in whole or in part." *One and Many*, 187. At the start of the treatise on creation, Aquinas shows the link between participation and causation: "It must be said that every being in any way existing is from God. For whatever is found in anything by participation, must be caused in it by that to which it belongs essentially" (*ST* I.44.1). Or, more tersely, in the reply to objection 1 in the same article: "from the fact that a thing has being by participation it follows that it is caused."
272 It must be remembered, though, that God does not communicate his essence in the procession of creatures, only his likeness; otherwise pantheism would result. On this, see Wippel, *Metaphysical Thought*, 120; and Te Velde, *Aquinas on God*, 146 n. 49.
273 This point is most obvious in the discussion of the omnipresence of God in relation to bodies: "God fills every place; not indeed like a body, for a body is said to fill place inasmuch as it excludes the co-presence of another body; whereas by God being in a place, others are not thereby excluded from it; indeed, by the very fact that He gives being to the things that fill every place, He Himself fills every place" (*ST* I.8.2).
274 Te Velde, *Aquinas on God*, 139–40.
275 I owe this winsome phrase to Michael Buckley.
276 *ST* I.5.1.
277 *ST* I.5.1.
278 "God is existence itself, of itself subsistent. Consequently, He must contain within Himself the whole perfection of being .... Now all created perfections are included in the perfection of being; for things are perfect, precisely so far as they have being after some fashion. It follows therefore that the perfection of no one thing is wanting to God" (*ST* I.4.2).
279 This does not mean that God is only good because creation desires God. "Before" creation, God desires God; i.e., in this case, the desiring subject and desired object are identical. On goodness as relational term (similar to truth), see *Quaestiones disputatae De veritate* (hereafter *De ver.*), q. 1, a.1.
280 *ST* I.4.2.
281 *ST* I.6.1.
282 *ST* I.6.1.
283 Te Velde, *Aquinas on God*, 80–81.
284 *ST* I.44.4.

285 This conclusion is also reached through a consideration of the divine government of the world. "The end of things corresponds to its beginning.... [And] since the beginning of all things is something outside the universe, namely, God, it is clear from what has been expounded above (*ST* I.44.1 and 2) that we must conclude that the end of all things is some extrinsic good. This can be proved by reason. For it is clear that good has the nature of an end; wherefore, a particular end of anything consists in some particular good; while the universal end of all things is the Universal Good; which is good of itself by virtue of its essence, which is the very essence of goodness; whereas a particular good is good by participation. Now it is manifest that in the whole created universe there is not a good which is not such by participation. Wherefore that good which is the end of the whole universe must be a good outside the universe" (*ST* I.103.2).

286 *ST* I.6.2.

287 Although being is prior to goodness in *ratio*, because the intellect first must conceive something as actual before it can attribute goodness to it (*ST* I.5.2).

288 It should be remembered, though, that distinguishing two different causes in God is an accommodation to our understanding. The distinction has only mental reality and is not really true of God. Thus, the diverse understandings of God as efficient and final cause do not entail any difference in God. For "the first principle of all things is one in reality. But this does not prevent us from mentally considering many things in Him, some of which come into our mind before others" (*ST* I.44.4, ad 4).

289 This intrinsic dynamic orientation to the end does not necessarily imply any conscious explicit intending of the end.

290 *ST* I.93.6. This theme of the human person as the image of God will be considered in more detail later.

291 This distinction between the end as the thing itself and the end as its use or acquisition is from *ST* I-II.1.8.

292 Indeed, both types of question (*an sit* and *quid sit*) arise naturally, requiring neither acquired habit nor divine grace. "Hence, since the questions are natural, the desire they manifest must also be natural. There exists, then, a desire that is natural to intellect, that arises from the mere fact that we possess intellects." Bernard Lonergan, "The Natural Desire to See God," in *Collection*, ed. Frederick Crowe and Robert Doran (Toronto: University of Toronto Press, 1988), 81–91, at 81.

293 *ST* I.3, *proemium*.

294 *ST* I.12.1.

295 *ST* I-II.3.8.

296 It should be noted that Aquinas rules out the option that this natural desire can (in principle) remain unfulfilled: from reason, because "if the intellect of the rational creature could not reach (*pertingere*) so far as to the first cause of things, the natural desire would remain void" (*ST* I.12.1); and from faith, because "if we suppose that the created intellect could never see God, it would either never attain to (*obtinebit*) beatitude, or its beatitude would consist in something else belonging to God" (ibid.).

297 "Happiness is the perfect good, which lulls the appetite altogether; else it would not be the last end, if something yet remained to be desired" (*ST* I-II.2.8).
298 *ST* I-II.5.8.
299 This paragraph summarizes the argument of *ST* I-II.2.6–7.
300 On the distinction between the end itself (the object of happiness) and the attainment of the end (the subject's possession of happiness), see *ST* I-II.1.8 and *ST* I-II.2.7.
301 Further arguments for the inadequacy of any good of the soul are made in *ST* I-II.3.6, such as the inability of speculative science to go beyond where knowledge of sensibles leads.
302 *ST* I-II.2.8, ad 1. It should be noted, however, that although the object of beatitude lies outside the soul, happiness itself nonetheless *belongs* to the soul, since man attains the desired object through the soul's highest operation. Thus, the supreme good may be described, formally, as the use of man's highest function to attain the highest object; materially, as the intellectual vision of the divine essence, from which delight flows.
303 *ST* I.93.4.
304 Obviously, this "need" is a hypothetical necessity; that is, if the human person is to fulfill his or her natural desire for God, then God's grace is required. In using the term "need," I follow Aquinas's phrasing of the question (*ST* I-II.109, *De necessitate gratiae*). Framing the issue of grace in terms of need, however, raises difficult problems, not least whether God becomes morally bound to give grace since God made humans desire an end exceeding their natural abilities. For an overview of the twentieth-century controversies over grace in Catholic theology, see Fergus Kerr, "Quarrels About Grace," in *After Aquinas: Versions of Thomism* (Oxford: Blackwells, 2002), 134–48. Perhaps this antinomy can only be avoided by starting not from the natural human desire for God, but from God's desire to freely give Godself. In this more Rahnerian/Scotistic approach, God's bringing into existence what is not God (i.e., creation) culminates in the human person, who is created with the obediential potency to receive God's self-communication. For a recent and very detailed exploration of this theme, see Lawrence Feingold, *The Natural Desire to See God according to St. Thomas and His Interpreters* (Rome: Apollinare Studi, 2001).
305 *ST* I.12.4.
306 In Lonergan's terms: Human understanding "is by the reception in the intellect of an intelligible form or species proportionate to the object that is understood.... It can be had naturally only with respect to material things; for we can understand directly and properly only what first we can imagine, and so the proportionate object of our intellects in this life is said to be the *quidditas rei materialis*." *Collection*, 82.
307 *ST* I.12.11.
308 *ST* I.12.2.
309 *ST* I.12.2.
310 In Lonergan's terms: "Proper knowledge is an act of understanding in virtue of a form proportionate to the object; hence proper of knowledge of God

must be in virtue of an infinite form, in virtue of God Himself; such knowledge is beyond the natural proportion of any possible finite substance and so is strictly supernatural." *Collection*, 83.

311 *ST* I-II.5.5. The following is a good summary of the limited reach of the natural knowledge of God. It occurs in the reply to the objection that the existence of the infinite God cannot be proved from his finite effects, because there exists no proportion between the finite and infinite. "From effects not proportionate to the cause, no perfect knowledge of that cause can be obtained. Yet from every effect the existence of the cause can be clearly demonstrated, and so we can demonstrate the existence of God from His effects; though from them we cannot perfectly know God as He is in His essence" (*ST* I.2.2, ad 3). Thus, in the so-called attributes of God (such as simplicity, perfection, goodness, and infinity), God's infinite nature remains unknown to finite minds. Each attribute is simply the negation of a limitation. It affirms not what God is, but only what God is not. "Now because we cannot know what God is, but rather what He is not, we have no means for considering how God is, but rather how He is not" (*ST* I.3, prologue). So to call God "infinite" and "simple" does not presume any understanding of God's infinitude and simplicity; it simply denies the predication of finitude and composition to God.

312 This is a reformulation of Lonergan's expression of the "paradox." *Collection*, 84. For a recent discussion of this paradox, see Te Velde, *Aquinas on God*, 154–60. For a similar formulation of this paradox in the context of a discussion of the possibility of proofs for God's existence, see Denys Turner, *Faith, Reason, and the Existence of God* (Cambridge: Cambridge University Press, 2004), 261: "Reason opens up ... into the mystery which lies unutterably beyond it, for it can, out of fidelity to its own native impulse, ask the question which it knows it could not answer, the asking being within its powers, the answering being in principle beyond them."

313 The following paragraphs draw on William O'Connor, *The Eternal Quest: The Teaching of St. Thomas Aquinas on the Natural Desire for God* (New York: London, 1947).

314 O'Connor, *Eternal Quest*, 151. O'Connor also tackles the related question, "How can there exist a finite desire for an infinite good?" His response is that the lack of proportion between finite intelligence and God is not absolute, because every creature is related to God as effect to cause. And so once finite intelligence knows the existence of the divine cause, there arises naturally the tendency to know God's nature. See ibid., 150–52.

315 Except indirectly, insofar as it desires the perfection of the intellect. "To say, then, that the will naturally desires the vision of God after His existence is known is far from saying that the will is naturally tending towards the vision of God as the one and only object that constitutes its beatitude. To tend towards knowing an object is not the same as tending towards an object already known.... [Only] when we shall see God as He is, then for the first time will the created will experience a necessary surging of its nature towards Him as its final end and true beatitude. [For now,] we may speak

... of a necessary tendency of the will towards a knowledge of the still unknown essence of God." O'Connor, *Eternal Quest*, 164–65.
316 *ST* I-II.5.8.
317 O'Connor, *Eternal Quest*, 135 and 140. "Many writers fail to distinguish what St. Thomas has to say of [1] the natural desire for happiness from what he says of [2] the natural desire for the vision of God. St. Thomas himself kept these two natural desires clearly distinct, but they have been, as it were, fused into one whenever he is made to speak of a natural desire for the beatific vision." Ibid., 141.
318 *ST* I-II.5.8.
319 Variations on this phrase can be found throughout *ST*. For example: "Every movement of the will must be preceded by apprehension" (*ST* I.82.4, ad 3); "The will tends to its object, according as it is proposed by the reason" (*ST* I-II.19.10); and *ST* I-II.9.1 ("Whether the will is moved by the intellect?" especially the last line of the *respondeo*: "The intellect moves the will, as presenting its object to it."
320 The classic instance of this being Augustine's *Confessions* and its description of the "restless heart." In Thomistic terms, this point could be expressed positively as follows: the will possesses a natural movement towards God by default, since no participated good satisfies its longing.
321 The notion of the restless heart, or, to coin a phrase, the *volens negativa*, could also be described more positively as a "general and confused" desire for God. "To know that God exists in a general and confused way is implanted in us by nature, inasmuch as God is man's beatitude. For man naturally desires happiness, and what is naturally desired by man must be naturally known by him. This, however, is not to know absolutely that God exists; just as to know that someone is approaching is not the same as to know that Peter is approaching, even though it is Peter who is approaching; for many there are who imagine that man's perfect good which is happiness, consists in riches, and others in pleasures, and others in something else" (*ST* I.2.1, ad 1). Thus, in O'Connor's terms, one can distinguish between claiming (1) that true beatitude is the result of the fulfillment of the natural desire for the vision of God, and (2) that this beatitude is the actual object of the will's natural desire. *Eternal Quest*, 166.
322 Stanley Hauerwas, *The Peaceable Kingdom: A Primer in Christian Ethics* (Notre Dame, IN: University of Notre Dame Press, 1983), 58.
323 *ST* I-II.114.2.
324 *De ver.* q. 29, a. 5: "ipse est principium quodammodo omnis gratiae secundum humanitatem, sicut Deus est principium omnis esse: unde, sicut in Deo omnis essendi perfectio adunatur, ita in Christo omnis gratiae plenitudo et virtutis invenitur, per quam non solum ipse possit in gratiae opus, sed etiam alios in gratiam adducere. Et per hoc habet capitis rationem."
325 For these three meanings of grace, see *ST* I-II.110.1.
326 Here quoting 1 John 4:10 and 19.
327 *ST* I-II.110.2.
328 *ST* I-II.112.1. See 2 Pet. 1:4. Aquinas distinguishes several stages that lead up to this term. Thus, grace heals the soul and causes it to desire the good;

it implements the good; it causes the persevering in the good, and, finally, the attainment of glory (*ST* I-II.111.3). Alternatively, and more extensively, the effects of grace are analyzed in the final two questions of the treatise on grace: question 113—the justification of the ungodly as the effect of operative grace; and 114—merit (of eternal life) as the effect of cooperative grace. Grace itself is also be distinguished between sanctifying and gratuitous, operative and cooperative, prevenient and subsequent (*ST* I-II.111).

329 "The operations of God whereby He moves us to good pertain to grace" (*ST* I-II.111.2, s.c.).
330 *ST* I-II.113.10.
331 *ST* I-II.111.3, s.c.
332 *ST* I.23.1, ad 3. In distinction from mercy, the ordering of all things to their proper due is justice (*ST* I.21).
333 "For grace is not a term of movement, as happiness is; rather is it the principle of the movement that tends towards happiness" (*ST* I-II.5.7, ad 3).
334 For historical analysis of this principle, see J. B. Beumer, "Gratia supponit naturam. Zur Geschichte eines theologischen Prinzips," *Gregorianum* 20 (1939): 381–406, 535–52; and Bernhard Stoeckle, *Gratia supponit naturam: Geschichte und Analyse eines theologischen Axioms* (Rome: Herder, 1962).
335 *ST* I.2.2, ad 1.
336 See *ST* I-II.110.2, "Whether grace is a quality of the soul?"
337 Torrell, *Aquinas*, 2:181.
338 *ST* I.1.8, ad 2.
339 *ST* I-II.89.6.
340 *Faith, Reason, Theology: Questions I–IV of his Commentary on the De Trinitate of Boethius*, trans. Armand Maurer (Toronto: Pontifical Institute of Mediaeval Studies, 1987), 48–49.
341 *ST* I.1.8, ad 2.
342 This transposition, though, requires some qualification, since the intellect is less damaged by sin than the will is. Thus, with respect to his intellect, a person "does not need a new light added to his natural light, in order to know the truth in all things, but only in some that surpass his natural knowledge" (*ST* I-II.109.1), whereas with regards to the will, "man, in the state of corrupt nature, falls short of what he could do by his nature, so that he is unable to fulfill it by his own natural powers" (*ST* I-II.109.2). The intellectual shortcoming is a limitation of the intellect's natural capabilities, whereas the volitional shortcoming is an impediment resulting from the distortion of the will's natural capabilities. Perhaps this explains why the perfective action of grace upon the intellect and will is described with the following different modulations: "The effect of grace ... both perfects the intellect by the gift of wisdom, and softens the affections by the fire of charity" (*ST* I-II.79.3).
343 *ST* I-II.113.3.
344 *Summa contra gentiles: Book Three: Providence. Part II*, trans. Vernon J. Bourke (Notre Dame, IN: University of Notre Dame Press, 1975), 260 (chap. 159, par. 2).

345 Ibid., 261.
346 The relationship between grace and freedom becomes more complex when one considers that, according to Aquinas, God opens the eyes of some—and only some—who have willfully closed them. While it is true that "out of the abundance of His goodness, He offers His help in advance, even to those who put an impediment in the way of grace ... in order that the working of His power may be evident," it is also true that "He does not assist with His help all who impede grace, so that that they may be turned away from evil and towards the good, but only some, in whom He desires His mercy to appear, so that the order of justice may be manifested in the other cases." The unanswerable question is, Why are some turned but not others? God does "come to the assistance of ... some, while He ... permits others [to sin]—there is no reason to ask why He converts the former and not the latter. For this depends on His will alone; just as it resulted from His simple will that, while all things were made from nothing, some were made of higher degree than others." Ibid., 263–64 (chap. 161, par. 1 and 2). This is a difficult problem that, thankfully, falls outside the scope of this inquiry.
347 Te Velde, *Aquinas on God*, 150.
348 *ST* I.12.5.
349 *ST* I.8.3.
350 *ST* I-II.109.6.
351 *ST* I.109.6.
352 *ST* I-II.109.3, ad 1.
353 *ST* I-II.110.1.
354 *ST* I-II.109.3, ad 1.
355 *ST* I-II.110.1.
356 This paraphrase draws directly on Karl Rahner, *Foundations of Christian Faith: An Introduction to the Idea of Christianity*, trans. William Dych (New York: Crossroad, 1995), 131: "A person who opens himself to his transcendental experience of the holy mystery at all has the experience that this mystery is not only an infinitely distant horizon ... [but also] a hidden closeness, a forgiving intimacy, his real home"; and, indirectly, on various phrases: "Hence there is really only one question, whether this God wanted to be merely the eternally distant one, or ... the innermost center of our existence in free grace and in self-communication" (p. 12); "God is present for man in his absolute transcendentality not only as the absolute, always distant, radically remote term and source of his transcendence which man always grasps only asymptotically, but ... is present in the mode of closeness" (p. 119); and "the spirit's transcendental movement ... is borne by God himself in his self-communication in such a way that this movement has its term and its source not in the holy mystery as eternally distant ... but rather in the God of absolute closeness and immediacy" (p. 129).
357 These paragraphs draw on D. Juvenal Merriell, *To the Image of the Trinity: A Study in the Development of Aquinas's Teaching* (Toronto: Pontifical Institute of Mediaeval Studies, 1990), esp. 241–245.
358 *ST* I.43.3.
359 *ST* I.45.7. See also *ST* I.93.6.

360 See Phil. 2:5: "Let the same mind be in you that was in Christ Jesus."
361 *ST* III.23.2 ad 3.
362 "Nothing is distant from [God] as if it could be without God in itself. But things are said to be distant from God by the unlikeness to Him in nature or grace" (*ST* I.8.1, ad 3).
363 Merriell, *Image of the Trinity*, 245.
364 Merriell, *Image of the Trinity*, 241. But note Merriell's exegetical caution that Aquinas "never makes any explicit connection between the indwelling of the Trinity and the image of the Trinity, although in the *Summa* we are almost justified in assuming such a connection because there is such a close resemblance in the analysis of both the image and the indwelling." Ibid., 242.
365 On Aquinas's humanistic spirit from a philosophical perspective, see Richard W. Southern's essay, "Medieval Humanism": "The two *Summae* of Thomas Aquinas mark the highest point of medieval humanism.... The dignity of human nature is not simply a poetic vision; it has become a central truth of philosophy.... Man was important because he was the link between the created universe and the divine intelligence. He alone in the world of nature could understand nature. He alone in nature could understand the nature of God. He alone could use and perfect nature in accordance with the will of God and thus achieve his full nobility." *Medieval Humanism and Other Studies* (Oxford: Basil Blackwell, 1970), 49–50. See also Gerard Verbeke, "Man as a 'Frontier' according to Aquinas," in *Aquinas and Problems of His Time*, ed. G. Verbeke and D Verhelst (The Hague: Leuven University Press, 1976).
366 *Summa contra gentiles* (hereafter *SCG*), III, c. 69.
367 *ST* I.23.8.
368 *ST* I.22.3. See also *SCG* III, c. 70: "It is clear that a single effect is not attributed to its natural cause and to God, as if one part was from God and the other from the natural agent; it is completely from the one and the other (*totus ab utroque*), but differently. A little in the way in which a single effect is attributed entirely to the instrument and entirely to the principle cause." Quoted in Jean-Pierre Torrell, *Saint Thomas Aquinas*, vol. 2, *Spiritual Master*, trans. Robert Royal (Washington, DC: Catholic University of America Press, 2003), 239.
369 As Robert Sokolowski argues in *Christian Faith and Human Understanding: Studies on the Eucharist, Trinity, and the Human Person* (Washington, DC: Catholic University of America Press, 2006), summarized and critiqued in my review, "Robert Sokolowski, *Christian Faith and Human Understanding: Studies on the Eucharist, Trinity, and the Human Person*," *National Catholic Bioethics Center Quarterly* 7, no. 2 (Summer 2007): 17–20.
370 Torrell, *Aquinas*, 2:327. For Moltmann's objections, see p. 45–46 above.
371 Both these texts are taken from the prologue to the *Compendium theologiae* (hereafter *Comp. theol.*): "apostolus, I Cor. 13:13 in fide, spe et caritate, quasi in quibusdam salutis nostrae compendiosis capitulis, totam *praesentis vitae* perfectionem consistere docuit, dicens: 'nunc autem manent fides, spes,

caritas.' Consistit enim humana salus in veritatis cognitione ...; in debiti finis intentione ...; in iustitiae observatione." Emphasis added.

372 "As from the essence of the soul flows its powers, which are the principles of deeds, so likewise the virtues, whereby the powers are moved to act, flow into the powers of the soul from grace" (*ST* I-II.110.4, ad 1). See also *ST* I-II.110.3, ad 1: "the act of faith working through love is the first act in which sanctifying grace is shown."

373 *ST* I-II.110.3.

374 In the treatise on grace, Aquinas omits mention of hope. "Grace, as it is prior to virtue, has a subject prior to the powers of the soul, so that it is in the essence of the soul. For as man in his intellective power participates in the Divine knowledge through the virtue of faith, and in his power of the will participates in the Divine love through the virtue of charity, so also in the nature of the soul does he participate in the Divine Nature, after the manner of a likeness, through a certain regeneration or re-creation" (*ST* I-II.110.4).

375 *ST* I-II.6, *proemium*.

376 "After the general consideration of virtues and vices and other things relating to moral matters [*prima secundae*], it is necessary to consider singular things in particular, because universal moral lessons are less useful than [a consideration of] actions, which are in the particulars" (*ST* II-II, *proemium*).

377 The natural virtues are those moral and intellectual virtues acquired by human effort and within the proportionate range of human nature. For an alternative designation of the moral virtues, see Aquinas's labeling of the four cardinal virtues as social or political virtues in *ST* I-II.61.5.

378 *ST* I.81.2, which this paragraph summarizes.

379 This paragraph draws, for the most part, on *ST* I-II.23.2 and 4.

380 There is no contrary to anger, for there can be no *arduous* good that is present, for once present, it is no longer arduous.

381 *ST* I-II.40.1.

382 *ST* I-II.25.1.

383 On the "saute brusque" between mere desire and real hope, Gauthier has written: "Entre le désir du bien futur et la joie du bien possédé, s'étend le monde de l'effort et de la lutte, et c'est par l'espérance que nous pénétrons en ce monde nouveau." René Gauthier, *Magnanimité: L'idéal de la grandeur dans la philosophie païenne et dans la théologie chrétienne* (Paris: Vrin, 1951), 331. The difficulty, then, is not simply something negative, but derives also from the greatness of the goal, as Gauthier notes in his exploration of the relationship between magnanimity and hope.

384 *ST* I-II.24.1. See also *ST* I-II.56.4.

385 *ST* I.82.5, ad 2.

386 *ST* I-II.45.4.

387 *ST* II-II.25.5, ad 2. The role and significance of the bodily feelings in the theological life is not dissimilar to the role and significance of pleasure in Aristotle's *Ethics*. There, the importance of pleasure is initially minimized, but, after its ordering principles have been examined, it can assume its

proper, important function as that which attends the operation of virtue. Likewise, the passions are not discussed initially in the treatise on grace, but they are mentioned towards the end of the treatise on the theological virtues, in the section on the effects of charity. As with the naturally acquired virtues, bodily effects indicate the presence and fruition of a theological virtue.

388   *ST* I-II.40.6. As held in common with dumb animals, see *ST* I-II.40.3. On its object as sensible, see *ST* II-II.18.1, ad 1: "The object of the irascible is the arduous sensible. The object of the virtue of hope, however, is the arduous intelligible, or rather what exists above the intellect." But there is of course a nontheological hope that is distinctive to man, insofar as it shares in human reason, e.g., I-II.40.2, and *Scriptum super Libros Sententiarum III* (hereafter *In III Sent.*), d. 26, q. 1, a. 5: "spes in parte sensitiva nominat quamdam passionem materialem, in parte autem intellective simplicem operationem voluntatis immaterialiter tendentis in aliquod arduum." But as will be shown later in this chapter, hope does not become virtuous until it relies on divine help.

389   Following Aquinas's definition in *ST* I-II.55.4.

390   Aristotle, *Ethics* 2.6, 1106a22–23, quoted from *The Basic Works of Aristotle*, ed. Richard McKeon (New York: Random House, 1941), 957. Aristotle continues in the same section to define virtue as "a state of character concerned with choice, lying in a mean, i.e. the mean relative to us, this being determined by a rational principle, and by that principle by which the man of practical wisdom would determine it" (1106b36–1107a2).

391   Josef Pieper, *On Hope*, trans. Mary Frances McCarthy (San Francisco: Ignatius Press, 1986), 35.

392   A habit is a "firm disposition, difficult to change" (*ST* I-II.54.4, ad 1). For a more explicit consideration of the nature of virtue, see *ST* I-II.55, "The Essence of Virtue," especially article 4, which accepts Augustine's definition of virtue as "a good quality of the mind, by which one lives rightly, of which no one can make bad use, and which God works in us, without us." Aquinas restricts the final clause—"God works in us, without us"—to the infused virtues.

393   See *ST* I-II.62.3: "virtutes theologicae hoc modo ordinant hominem ad beatitudinem supernaturalem, *sicut* per naturalem inclinationem ordinatur homo in finem sibi connaturalem" (emphasis added).

394   *ST* I-II.62.1, citing the critical passage from 2 Pet. 1:4: "Through Christ we are made sharers in the divine nature." See also *ST* I-II.5.3 and 5.

395   *ST* I-II.63.1. As mentioned, the theological virtues are extrinsic as regards the agency by which they are attained, not the subject in which they are held.

396   *ST* I-II.51.4.

397   *ST* I-II.62.2.

398   *ST* I-II.62.2, ad 1.

399   *ST* I-II.62.1.

400   The formula "in nobis sine nobis" is the last clause in Augustine's definition of virtue, quoted by Aquinas in *ST* I-II.55.4.

401 *ST* I-II.62.1.
402 *ST* I-II.64.1 and 2. In more colloquial terms, one may describe the mean as the point at which a certain moral act is "just right," i.e., when it accurately and fittingly responds to the particulars of a given situation.
403 A similar structure holds for the intellectual virtues, in which judgments are ruled by the reality that is judged. Thus, judgments are deemed good insofar as they are true, that is, as they conform to the measure set by the thing considered (see *ST* I-II.64.3). A true proposition corresponds to the reality considered, while a false affirmation exceeds the reality, and a false denial falls short. The difference between the mean of moral and intellectual virtues is summarized as follows: in moral virtues, "insofar as the appetite is ruled by reason; … [in intellectual virtues] insofar as our intellectual is measured by the thing" (*ST* I-II.64.4, obj. 2).
404 *ST* II-II.17.5, ad 2.
405 *ST* I-II.64.4, ad 3.
406 *ST* I-II.64.4.
407 *Quaestiones disputatae De virtutibus* (hereafter *De spe*), q. 4, 1, obj. 7: "theologicae virtutis non est esse in medio, sed in extremo, secundum illud Deut., VI, 5: *diliges dominum Deum tuum ex toto corde tuo*."
408 *ST* I-II.64.4.
409 "Fides autem ostendit [finem], spes facit tendere in eum, caritas unit." Aquinas, *In Epistolam I ad Timotheum* (hereafter *In ad I Tim.*), cap. 1, lect. 2, in *Opera Omnia*, Parma ed. (New York: Musurgia, 1949), 13:587.
410 *ST* I-II.62.3.
411 *ST* I-II.62.3.
412 *ST* I-II.62.3. *Credibilia*, translated here as "things worthy of belief," is sometimes translated as "the articles of faith."
413 On faith's act as perfecting the intellect, see *ST* II-II.4.4 and 5.
414 *ST* I-II.66.6, obj. 1.
415 *ST* I-II.62.3. For a more detailed account, see P. de Letter, "Hope and Charity," *The Thomist* 13 (1950): 204–48, 325–52.
416 I.e., *ST* I-II.62.3. The *prima secundae*, as stated in the prologue immediately before I-II.6, treats moral matters in general. See also the prologue to the *secunda secundae*: "Post communem considerationem de virtutibus et vitiis et aliis ad materiam moralem pertinentibus [i.e., in the *prima secundae*], necesse est considerare singula in speciali [i.e., in the *secunda secundae*]."
417 *ST* I-II.64.4. See also *De spe* 1: "formale obiectum spei est auxilium divinae potestatis et pietatis, propter quod tendit motus spei in bona sperata."
418 Although one could interpret *magnitudinem* more loosely as referring to God's magnanimity or greatness of compassion that forgives sins. Perhaps this explains why Aquinas describes the object of hope as God's majesty (*De spe* 4, obj. 13), since majesty conveys both the great distance between God and the *viator*, and the graceful condescension of a compassionate power that can bridge that distance.
419 "Non autem potest esse superabundantia spei ex parte Dei, cuius bonitas est infinita" (*ST* I-II.64.4, ad 3).

420 "fides habet Deum pro objecto, inquantum est prima veritas; spes vero, inquantum est summa largitas vel majestas; caritas autem, inquantum est summa bonitas" (*In III Sent.* d. 23, q. 1 a. 5, arg. 4).

421 "idem secundum rem est objectum omnium virtutum theologicarum, sed differt secundum rationem ... inquantum est altissimum arduum, est objectum spei" (*In III Sent.* d. 26, q. 2, a. 3, solutio 1, ad 1).

422 "certitudo spei causatur ex liberalitate divina ordinante nos in finem" (*In III Sent.* d. 26, q. 2, a. 4).

423 *De pot.* q. 6, a. 9, ad 12. See also *De virtutibus in communi*, q. 1, a. 12, arg. 10 for a reference simply to *sublimitas* as the aspect under which hope regards God.

424 *ST* II-II.4.1.

425 On their shared object: "virtus aliqua dicitur theologica ex hoc quod habet Deum pro obiecto cui inhaeret" (*ST* II-II.17.6); and on their different aspects: "Deus secundum aliam et aliam rationem est obiectum harum virtutem" (*ST* II.II.17.6, ad 1).

426 Paraphrasing *ST* II-II.1.1: "cuiuslibet cognoscitivi habitus obiectum duo habet, scilicet id quod materialiter cognoscitur, quod est sicut materiale obiectum; et id per quod cognoscitur, quod est formalis ratio obiecti." This distinction finds slightly different expression in *ST* II-II.5.1: "in obiecto fidei est aliquid quasi formale, scilicet veritas prima super omnem naturalem cognitionem creaturae existens; et aliquid materiale, sicut id cui assentimus inhaerendo primae veritati." An analogy with a different cognitive habit illustrates this distinction: in geometry, the material object is the conclusion, while the formal object is the demonstration.

427 *ST* II-II.4.5, ad 2.

428 *ST* II-II.1.9, ad 5.

429 *ST* II-II.1.1, obj. 1.

430 *ST* II.II.1.1.

431 *ST* II-II.1.6, ad 1.

432 "Et secundum ista distinguuntur articuli fidei" (*ST*, II-II.1.6, ad 1). Whereas other things in scripture, which simply manifest these principle objects, do not warrant distinct articles.

433 "Actus autem credentis non terminatur ad enuntiabile, sed ad rem, non enim formamus enuntiabilia nisi ut per ea de rebus cognitionem habeamus, sicut in scientia, ita et in fide" (*ST* II-II.1.2, ad 2). Articles are necessary, though, because "cognita sunt in cognoscente secundum modum cognoscentis" (*ST*, II-II.1.2) and the mode of human knowing is through synthesis and analysis.

434 It should also be noted that this is not an immediate or mechanical assent. The pedagogy involved in approaching God as revealer is analogous to any pupil learning from a teacher: "quod homo perveniat ad perfectam visionem beatitudinis praeexigitur quod credat Deo tanquam discipulus magistro docenti" (*ST* II-II.2.3). Thus, as Aquinas says earlier in the *respondeo*, "Huius autem disciplinae fit homo particeps non statim, sed successive, secundum modum suae naturae." For an amplification of this idea through a study of the concept of *sacra doctrina* as a process of God's teaching us,

see Victor White, *Holy Teaching: The Idea of Theology according to St. Thomas Aquinas* (London: Blackfriars, 1958).
435 *ST* II-II.3.2, obj. 1.
436 This twofold root of all the articles of the creed is mentioned in the course of a discussion on "Whether the articles of faith have increased in the course of time?" (*ST* II-II.1.7), to which the basic answer is that while the number of articles has grown, they are all nonetheless contained implicitly in certain primary matters of faith. In the next question, Aquinas equates these *prima credibilia* with the articles of faith and insists that one is bound to believe them; see "Quantum ergo ad prima credibilia, quae sunt articuli fidei, tenetur homo explicite credere" (*ST* II-II.2.5).
437 Following *In ad I Tim.*: "Fides autem ostendit [finem], spes facit tendere in eum, caritas unit," in *Opera Omnia*, Parma ed., 13:587.
438 *ST* II-II.1.7.
439 *ST* II-II.1.8, being a loose translation to accent the twofold nature of the *prima credibilia*.
440 *ST* I-II.65.4. In the *secunda secundae*, which gives a more differentiated account of faith's act, the topic is given two questions. The first deals with faith's internal act. The second (and much shorter) deals with faith's external act—confession—which is not treated here.
441 *ST* II-II.2.1.
442 *ST* I-II.67.3.
443 *ST* II-II.2.1, ad 3. In science, assent is compelled, but consideration is free; in faith both assent and consideration are free; whereas opinion has no firm assent and is therefore not from a perfect act of will and thus cannot be meritorious (*ST* II.II.2.9, ad 2). See also *ST* II-II.1.4 for a comparison of the two types of assent: "Assentit autem alicui intellectus dupliciter. Uno modo, quia ad hoc movetur ab ipso obiecto, quod est vel per seipsum cognitum, sicut patet in principiis primis, quorum est intellectus; vel est per aliud cognitum, sicut patet de conclusionibus, quarum est scientia. Alia modo intellectus assentit alicui non quia sufficienter moveatur ab obiecto proprio, sed per quandam electionem voluntarie declinans in unam partem magis quam in aliam. Et si quidem hoc fit cum dubitatione et formidine alterius partis, erit opinio, si autem fit cum certitudine absque tali formidine, erit fides."
444 Because "voluntas movet intellectum et alias vires animae in finem. Et secundum hoc ponitur actus fidei credere in Deum" (*ST* II-II.2.2, ad 4).
445 *ST* II-II.2.9. This account of faith's act comes in the question, "Whether to believe is meritorious?" Hence the emphasis on actions proceeding from free will moved with grace by God—the criteria for merit.
446 *ST* II-II.4.1.
447 *ST* II-II.4.2. In a slightly later text, which explains why unformed and formed faith are not distinct virtues, further confirmation is offered for why faith is primarily in the intellect: "habitus diversificatur secundum illud quod per se ad habitum pertinet. Cum autem fides sit perfectio intellectus, illud per se ad fidem pertinet quod pertinet ad intellectum, quod autem pertinet ad voluntatem non per se pertinet ad fidem, ita quod per hoc

diversificari possit habitus fidei" (*ST* II-II.4.4). Therefore, the distinction between formed and unformed regards the will, "idest secundum caritatem," for which reason unformed and formed faith are not different habits.
448 *ST* II-II.4.4.
449 "Et sumitur argumentum pro argumenti effectu, per argumentum enim intellectus inducitur ad adhaerendum alicui vero; unde ipsa firma adhaesio intellectus ad veritatem fidei non apparentem vocatur hic argumentum. Unde alia littera habet convictio, quia scilicet per auctoritatem divinam intellectus credentis convincitur ad assentiendum his quae non videt" (*ST* II-II.4.1). In this way, it differs from opinion, suspicion, and doubt, all of which lack conviction.
450 *ST* II-II.4.1, emphasis added.
451 Faith may be understood as concerning the good in two ways. One, truth, to which faith is ordered, is the good of the intellect. And so, in directing the intellect to the truth, faith is about the good (*ST* II-II.4.5, ad 2). Two, when faith is formed by charity, it is ordered to the good insofar as the good is the object of the will: "Verum est bonum intellectus, cum sit eius perfectio. Et ideo inquantum per fidem intellectus determinatur ad verum, fides habet ordinem in bonum quoddam. Sed ulterius, inquantum fides formatur per caritatem, habet etiam ordinem ad bonum secundum quod est voluntatis obiectum" (*ST* II-II.4.5, ad 1). This second relationship to the good gives faith its distinctively volitional component. The relationship between the intellectual and volitional components of faith may be described as follows: Although the will crucially brings the intellect to assent, it is still the intellect that assents to the truth, not the will. Otherwise, one could assent to anything as long as one willed it. And so to believe is, in the first instance, about that intellectual assent, howsoever it be moved to assent. The key distinction, then, is between what constitutes an act and what causes it. Faith is *constituted* as an act of the intellect, but is *caused* by the will (as moved by God). For example: imagine a situation in which someone hears a rumor (but has no evidence) that his friend has gossiped maliciously about a personal difficulty that he had confided in him. He is then reassured by his friend that the rumor is false and he consequently believes that no malicious gossip passed his friend's mouth. What constitutes this act is an intellectual assent based on belief (possessing the evidence of opinion). But the cause for this act is the will's trust in the friend (possessing a conviction similar to knowledge). Returning to Aquinas's text, one can see the relationship between faith's intellectual and volitional components through a consideration of the sin of unbelief. A sinful act has a "duplex principium.... [1] primum et universale, quod imperat omnes actus peccatorum, et hoc principium est voluntas, quia omne peccatum est voluntarium. [2] Aliud ... proprium et proximum, quod elicit peccati actum.... Dissentire autem, qui est proprius actus infidelitatis, est actus intellectus, sed moti a voluntate, sicut et assentire. Et ideo infidelitas, sicut et fides, est quidem in intellectu sicut in proximo subiecto, in voluntate autem sicut primo motivo. Et hoc modo dicitur omne peccatum esse in voluntate" (*ST*, II-II.10.2). Hence, the

summary in the response to the second objection: "The cause of infidelity is in will, but infidelity itself is in intellect."
452 *ST* II-II.4.1.
453 "veritas prima est obiectum fidei secundum quod ipsa non visa.... Et secundum hoc oportet quod ipsa veritas prima se habeat ad actum fidei per modum finis secundum rationem rei non visae. Quod pertinet ad rationem rei speratae" (*ST* II-II.4.1).
454 *ST* II-II.4.1.
455 *ST* II-II.4.1.
456 *ST* I-II.66.6, ad 1. Here, a contrast is drawn with a virtue of the intellect, prudence, which does moderate the appetitive motion.
457 *ST* I-II.62.3.
458 Servais Pinckaers, *Le renouveau de la morale: Études pour une morale fidèle à ses sources et à sa mission présente* (La Sart-Huy: Casterman, 1964), 231–32, revising his earlier opinion that the use of formal and material object in *De spe* suggests a development from the *Summa theologiae*, in "La nature vertueuse de l'espérance," *Revue Thomiste* 54 (1958): 405–42, 623–44, at 634.
459 *ST* II-II.17.4. See also *ST* II-II.17.6, ad 3, which also reflects this twofold causality: "spes facit tendere in Deum sicut in quoddam bonum finale adipiscendum, et sicut in quoddam adiutorium efficax ad subveniendum."
460 *ST* II-II.17.5 ("Whether hope is a theological virtue?") succinctly states hope's twofold attaining of God: "spes habet rationem virtutis ex hoc quod attingit supremam regulam humanorum actuum; quam attingit et sicut primam causam efficientem, inquantum eius auxilio innititur; et sicut ultimam causam finalem, inquantum in eius fruitione beatitudinem expectat."
461 By way of contrast, faith's material object was, at its most basic level, "God's existence and providence," and its formal object was "God as revealing."
462 *ST* II-II.17.1.
463 Just as, for example, a coat is good when it attains the proper measure, i.e., when it fits, and fails to attain its proper measure when it is too long or too short.
464 As a remote and exceding measure. Reason is the proximate and proportionate rule of human acts, and to attain reason is the character of humanly acquired virtue.
465 *ST* II-II.17.1. Contrast Aquinas's arguments in *In III Sent.* d. 26, q. 2, a. 1 and 2, which derive the theological virtuousness of hope solely from its transcendent goal. By the time of the *Summa theologiae*, however, Aquinas begins the treatise on hope by arguing that it is precisely the reliance on God's help that makes hope a virtue (*ST* II-II.17.1). On that basis, the next article can argue that hope must ultimately intend eternal happiness, since the effect of relying on God's infinite help must be proportionate to its cause. The key breakthrough in this development between the *Sentences* commentary and the *secunda secundae* is made in *De spe*. Drawing explicitly on the twofold nature of faith, this text clarifies the twofold nature

of hope by distinguishing help from goal, and then grounds hope's virtuousness on its reliance on divine help (*De spe* 1). The *secunda secundae* differs from *De spe* by refining the terms used to describe the twofold relation to God as goal/helper (from material/formal object to final/efficient cause). As will be seen in chapter 5, this means that the connection between hope and faith need no longer be made extrinsically through the use of parallel terms drawn from Aristotelian causality, but rather can be made on biblical grounds by the shared appeal to Hebrews 11:6 (which is not cited in this role in either *In Sent.* or *De spe*). Incidentally, the dependence of hope's future-oriented final cause on the efficient cause of God's help in the present undercuts Moltmann's criticism that Aquinas's notion of hope is dominated by a nonbiblical notion of final causality, as Merkt notes in *Sacra Doctrina and Christian Eschatology*, 351–52.

466 Since a thing's efficient cause is that which is responsible, in part, for its existence as this or that thing; it is the agent that produces the effect, hence, *efficient* cause.

467 One might ask why hoping, through God's power, to commit genocide is not therefore a virtue. *ST* II-II.17.1, obj. 1 makes the same type of objection, arguing that hope can be used badly because the passion of hope has a mean and extremes. The reply to this objection argues that in the passions the mean of virtue consists in attaining right reason, just as hope is virtuous when it attains the fitting rule, i.e., God. Therefore, when hope is virtuous (i.e., when it attains God), it cannot simultaneously intend what is contrary to its rule (i.e., something evil). Similarly, when a passion is virtuous (i.e., when it attains the mean set by reason), it cannot simultaneously intend what is contrary to its rule (i.e., an unreasonable act). Thus, a believer cannot virtuously hope for anything bad any more than a soldier can courageously flee a just war; and so hope, like any other virtue, cannot be used badly. See also *De spe* 1, ad 1: "quod spes secundum quod inhaeret divino auxilio, non potest se ad malum habere; nullus enim potest nimis de Deo sperare. Sed quod aliquis male speret, hoc contingit quia non inhaeret Deo, sed suae virtuti, vel falsae opinioni; puta cum praesumit se salvandum etiam in peccatis perseverans."

468 When dealing with things that fall under human power, faith and hope are not virtuous (*ST* I-II.62.3, ad 2). For a detailed account of the varying degrees of virtuousness in hope, ranging from the passion to the theological virtue, as well as an account of hope's relationship to the virtue of magnanimity, see Jacques-Guy Bougerol, *La théologie de l'espérance aux XIIe et XIIIe siècles* (Paris: Études augustiniennes, 1985), 278–86.

469 And, indeed, a vice: "spes habet rationem virtutis ex hoc ipso quod homo inhaeret auxilio divinae potestatis ad consequendum vitam aeternam. Si enim aliquis inniteretur humano auxilio, vel suo vel alterius, ad consequendum perfectum bonum absque auxilio divino, esset hoc vitiosum" (*De spe* 1).

470 If, however, one hoped to pass the exam through God's help, then it would be a virtue.

471 *ST* II-II.17.1, ad 3: "ille qui sperat est quidem imperfectus secundum considerationem ad id quod sperat obtinere quod nondum habet, sed est perfectus quantum ad hoc quod iam attingit propriam regulam, scilicet Deum, cuius auxilio innititur." See also *De spe* 1, ad 4: "Spes, secundum quod refertur ad materiale objectum [i.e., future goal], est dispositio imperfecti, quia quod speratur, nondum habetur; sed secundum quod respicit objectum formale, scilicet auxilium divinum, sic est dispositio perfecti; in hoc enim consistit perfectio hominis ut Deo inhaereat."

472 *ST* II-II.17.2. Incidentally, the resurrection of the body is not hope's proper object. Hope "non respicit gloriam corporis sicut principale obiectum, sed potius fruitionem divinam" (*ST* II-II.18.2, ad 1), here speaking about Christ. Responding to the objection that there is hope in heaven (an objection based on the claim that the saints hope for the glory of their bodies), it is argued that "cum spes sit virtus theologica habens Deum pro obiecto, principale obiectum spei est gloria animae, quae in fruitione divina consistit, non autem gloria corporis. Gloria etiam corporis, etsi habeat rationem ardui per comparationem ad naturam humanam, non habet tamen rationem ardui habenti gloriam animae. Tum quia gloria corporis est minimum quiddam in comparatione ad gloriam animae. Tum etiam quia habens gloriam animae habet iam sufficienter causam gloriae corporis" (*ST* II-II.18.2, ad 4).

473 "Indirectly" reflexive, because it is not the direct object of hope ("eternal happiness with God") that is the same as the hoping subject, but the indirect object ("for me" / "ad se").

474 *ST* II-II.17.3.

475 "non licet sperare de aliquo homine, vel de aliqua creatura, sicut de prima causa movente in beatitudinem; licet autem sperare de aliquo homine, vel de aliqua creatura, sicut de agente secundario et instrumentali, per quod aliquis adiuvatur ad quaecumque bona consequenda in beatitudinem ordinata" (*ST* II-II.17.4).

476 "non licet sperare aliquod bonum praeter beatitudinem sicut ultimum finem, sed solum sicut id quod est ad finem beatitudinis ordinatum" (*ST* II-II.17.4).

477 *ST* II-II.17.5, ad 1.

478 *ST* II-II.17.5, obj. 1.

479 "quaecumque alia spes adipisci expectat, sperat in ordine ad Deum sicut ad ultimum finem et sicut ad primam causam efficientem, ut dictum est" (*ST* II-II.17.5, ad 1).

480 "spes habet rationem virtutis ex hoc quod attingit supermam regulam humanorum actuum; quam attingit et sicut primam causam efficientem, inquantum eius auxilio innititur; et sicut ultimam causam finalem, inquantum in eius fruitione beatitudinem expectat. Et sic patet quod spei, inquantum est virtus, principale obiectum est Deus" (*ST* II-II.17.5).

481 Unlike with faith, Aquinas does not define the act of hope in the *secunda pars* in a separate question or even at any length. Presumably this is because hope's act is less complex than faith's act, which involves both intellectual and volitional components. The act of hope was defined in the *prima pars* primarily with reference to the final cause aspect of hope: "actus spei est

expectare futuram beatitudinem a Deo" (*ST* I-II.65.4). Although this definition implies dependence on God ("a Deo"), it is only in the *secunda secundae* that this dependency is made explicity.

482 *ST* II-II.23.1, ad 1 characterizes this fellowship as imperfect *in via*, but perfect *in patria*. This paragraph summarizes this article. See also *ST* I-II.65.5: "societas hominis ad Deum, quae est quaedam familiaris conversatio cum ipso."

483 "non quilibet amor habet rationem amicitiae, sed amor qui est cum benevolentia, quando scilicet sic amamus *aliquem* ut *ei* bonum velimus. Si autem rebus amatis non bonum velimus, sed ipsum eorum bonum velimus *nobis*, sicut dicimur amare vinum aut equum aut *aliquid* huiusmodi, non est amor amicitiae, sed cuiusdam concupiscentiae, ridiculum enim est dicere quod aliquis habeat amicitiam ad vinum vel ad equum" (*ST* II-II.23.1, emphasis added).

484 And, obviously, charity differs from faith because it regards God under a volitional, not intellectual aspect: "sicuti fidei obiectum est prima veritas, ita caritas obiectum est summa bonitas" (*ST* II-II.26.1, obj. 2).

485 "caritate diligitur Deus propter seipsum. Unde una sola ratio diligendi principaliter attenditur a caritate, scilicet divina bonitas, quae est eius substantia" (*ST* II-II.23.5, ad 2).

486 See also *ST* I-II.65.5: "super amorem addit mutuam redamationem [i.e., act of returning love] cum quadam mutua communicatione, ut dicitur in VIII Ethic. Et quod hoc ad caritatem pertineat, patet per id quod dicitur I Ioan. IV, qui manet in caritate, in Deo manet, et Deus in eo."

487 "Cum igitur sit aliqua communicatio hominis ad Deum secundum quod nobis suam beatitudinem communicat, super hac communicatione oportet aliquam amicitiam fundari" (*ST* II-II.23.1).

488 "amicitia unionem quandam importat, dicit enim Dionysius quod amor est virtus unitiva" (*ST* II-II.25.4).

489 *ST* II-II.27.4, ad 3. And also, by making the believer worthy of that fellowship, charity "coniungit animam Deo iustificando ipsam" (*ST* II-II.23.2, ad 3).

490 Because, as mentioned, God is a rule of human acts by which they are judged good, as recalled in *ST* II-II.23.3, "Whether charity is a virtue?"

491 Charity "non fundatur principaliter super virtute humana, sed super bonitate divina" (*ST* II-II.23.3, ad 1).

492 Quoted in *ST* II-II.24.2, s.c.

493 *ST* II-II.24.2.

494 Jean-Pierre Torrell, *Aquinas*, 2:339.

495 "caritas importat unionem quandam ad Deum, non autem fides neque spes" (*ST* II-II.24.12, ad 5).

496 *ST* II-II.17.6.

497 "propter seipsum, mentem hominis uniens Deo per affectum amoris" (*ST* II-II.17.6).

498 *ST* II-II.23.6.

499 "bonum quod omnibus vult caritas, scilicet beatitudo aeterna" (*ST* II-II.26.7).

500 *ST* I-II.66.6, ad 2.
501 *ST* II-II.17.6, ad 3.
502 *ST* II-II.17.3: "Whether one may hope for another's eternal happiness?"
503 "idem bonum est obiectum caritatis et spei, sed caritas importat unionem ad illud bonum, spes autem distantiam quandam ab eo" (*ST* II-II.23.6, ad 3). As mentioned, charity is based on the communication of God's happiness to us.
504 "Hanc autem propinquitatem facit caritas, quia per ipsam mens Deo unitur" (*ST* II-II.24.4).
505 In *ST* I-II.64.4 and at the end of *secunda secundae*'s two questions on hope, *ST* II-II.18.4, ad 2.
506 "idem bonum est obiectum caritatis et spei, sed caritas importat unionem ad illud bonum, spes autem distantiam quandam ab eo. Et inde est quod caritas non respicit illud bonum ut arduum sicut spes, quod enim iam unitum est non habet rationem ardui" (*ST* II-II.23.6, ad 3).
507 Elsewhere, Aquinas states (without any argumentation) that charity is ruled by God's wisdom (*ST* II-II.24.1, ad 2). Perhaps this atypical characterization stems from the context of that discussion, which includes both a reminder of the fact that the will is part of the reason—since the will is the *rational* appetite—and also a comparison between the moral virtues (which are ruled by human reason) and the theological virtues (which are said to be ruled by God's wisdom, perhaps in order to parallel the rule of moral virtues). Another reason why wisdom is cited as the rule for charity may be that it is the gift that accompanies charity. Thus, it is analogous to claiming that faith is ruled by God's knowledge (since knowledge is a gift that accompanies faith).
508 *ST* II-II.24.12.
509 *ST* II-II.25.1. Our love for a neighbor, then, is not something extrinsic to that neighbor's nature, as if such love were merely following a precept that God, for some opaque reason, ordered us to follow. Rather, one should love one's neighbor because they were created through God's love and are the object of God's love.
510 "reprehensibile esset si quis proximum diligeret tanquam principalem finem, non autem si quis proximum diligat propter Deum, quod pertinet ad caritatem" (*ST* II-II.25.1, ad 3).
511 *ST* II-II.25.1, ad 2.
512 *ST* II-II.23.2, ad 1.
513 *ST* II-II.26.2, ad 1 and 1 John 4:10. Charity, of course, also involves love of self. In fact, that self-love forges the unity of the self, which is the condition for the possibility of union with another (*ST* II-II.25.4).
514 This example comes from *ST* II-II.24.8. It should be noted that charity cannot be considered perfect in this life on the part of the object loved. This love of the object could only be perfect if the object is loved as much as it is lovable, which only God could do. For further discussion of the degrees of charity, see *ST* II-II.24.9 on the three stages: beginner, proficient, and perfect. See also the general developmental distinctions made in the *prima secundae*. Charity "inchoatur quidem hic in praesenti per gratiam,

perficietur autem in futuro per gloriam, quorum utrumque fide et spe tenetur" (*ST* I-II.65.5).
515 "duplex est ordo, scilicet generationis, et perfectionis" (*ST* I-II.62.4). Again, "duplex est ordo. Unus quidem secundum viam generationis et materiae, secundum quem imperfectum prius est perfecto. Alius autem ordo est perfectionis et formae, secundum quem perfectum naturaliter prius est imperfecto" (*ST* II-II.17.8).
516 *ST* II-II.7.2, ad 1. In this case, the issue is purity of heart as an effect of faith. The same point is made, citing Aristotle, in *ST* II-II.8.4: "Voluntas autem non potest recte ordinari in bonum nisi praeexistente aliqua cognitione veritatis, quia obiectum voluntatis est bonum intellectum, ut dicitur in III de anima." And again in *ST* II.II.4.7, "Whether faith is the first of the virtues?": "voluntas non fertur in aliquid nisi prout est in intellectu apprehensum."
517 *ST* II-II.7.1.
518 "Sed contra est quod Matt. I, dicitur in Glossa quod fides generat spem, spes vero caritatem. Sed generens est prius generato" (*ST* I-II.65.4, s.c.).
519 *ST* II-II.7.1, ad 1.
520 "Non enim potest spes haberi de aeterna beatitudine nisi credatur possibile, quia impossibile non cadit sub spe" (*ST* II-II.4.7, ad 2). Again, "fides autem generat spem secundum quod facit nobis existimationem de praemiis quae Deus retribuit iustis" (*ST* II-II.7.1, ad 2). See also *ST* II-II.17.7, which states how modes of hope's object (eternal happiness and divine help) are proposed to us through faith: "nobis innotescit quod ad vitam aeternam possumus pervenire, et quod ad hoc paratum est nobis divinum auxilium, secundum illud Heb XI."
521 "homo aliquid amat, quod apprehendit illud ut bonum suum" (*ST* I-II.62.4).
522 "Per hoc autem quod homo ab aliquo sperat se bonum consequi posse, reputat ipsum in quo spem habet, quoddam bonum suum" (*ST* I-II.62.4).
523 "Unde ex hoc ipso quod homo sperat de aliquo, procedit ad amandum ipsum. Et sic, ordine generationis, secundum actus, spes praecedit caritatem" (*ST* I-II.62.4).
524 *ST* I-II.65.5.
525 *ST* I-II.66.6.
526 For a justification of this transposition of a term from physics to morals, see *ST* II-II.4.3: "Voluntary acts receive their species from the end, which is the object of the will. Now that from which something receives its species is related to the manner of a form in natural things. Therefore the form of any voluntary act is, in a certain measure, the end to which it is ordered, both because it receives its species from the end and because the mode of an action must correspond proportionally to the end." Cf. *De spe* 4: "Sicut autem forma in rebus naturalibus dat speciem, ita et in moralibus obiectum dat speciem actui, et per consequens habitui."
527 *ST* II-II.23.8.
528 "Ultimum quidem et principale bonum hominis est Dei fruition ... et ad hoc ordinatur homo per caritatem" (*ST* II-II.23.7).

529 "in moralibus id quod dat actui ordinem ad finem, det ei et formam. Manifestum est ... quod per caritatem ordinantur actus omnium aliarum virtutum ad ultimum finem" (*ST* II-II.23.8). Why? Because charity attains the ultimate goal to which all secondary goals must be ordered (*ST* II-II.23.7).

530 Eberhard Schockenfoff, "The Theological Virtue of Charity (IIa IIae, qq. 23–46)," trans. Grant Kaplan and Frederick G. Lawrence, in *The Ethics of Aquinas*, ed. Stephen J. Pope (Washington, DC: Georgetown University Press, 2002), 244–58, at 251, col. 1.

531 "caritas dicitur esse forma aliarum virtutum non quidem exemplariter aut essentialiter, sed magis effective, inquantum scilicet omnibus formam imponit secundum modum praedictum" (*ST* II-II.23.8, ad 1).

532 "caritas est radix omnium virtutem, secundum illud ad Ephes. 3, *in caritate radicati et fundati*" (*ST* I-II.62.4, obj. 1). See also *ST* I-II.65.5, ad 2: "caritas est radix fidei et spei, inquantum dat eis perfectionem virtutis. Sed fides et spes, secundum rationem propriam, praesupponuntur ad caritatem.... Et sic caritas sine eis esse non potest."

533 "Praeterea, Augustinus dicit, in I de Doct. Christ.... *Porro si credit et diligit, bene agendo eficit ut etiam speret*" (*ST* I-II.62.4, obj. 2), to which Aquinas replies: "Augustinus loquitur de spe qua quis sperat ex meritis iam habitis se ad beatitudinem perventurum, quod est spei formatae, quae sequitur caritatem."

534 *ST* I-II.65.4.

535 The Galatians text is mentioned, but without scriptural reference, in *ST* II-II.4.3, s.c.

536 On the difference between faith's imperfect and perfect acts, see *ST* I-II.65.4: "credere autem sit alicui propria voluntate assentire, si non debito modo velit, non erit fidei opus perfectum. Quod autem debito modo velit, hoc est per caritatem, quae perficit voluntatem, omnis enim rectus motus voluntatis ex recto amore procedit.... Sic igitur fides est quidem sine caritate, sed non perfecta virtus, sicut temperantia vel fortitudo sine prudentia." On hope's imperfect act: "Si autem hoc expectet ex meritis quae nondum habet, sed proponit in futurum acquirere, erit, actus imperfectus, et hoc potest esse sine caritate"; and on hope's perfect act: "si fiat ex meritis quae quis habet, quod non potest esse sine caritate."

537 Although he does not state it explicitly here, Aquinas means love of concupiscence. In a similar context dealing with the seeming priority of love to hope, he does mention this lower love explicitly. See *ST* I.II.66.6, ad 2: "Hope presupposes the love of what one hopes to obtain. This is the love of concupiscence, by which the one who desires a good loves himself more than something else. Charity, however, conveys the love of friendship, to which we are brought by hope, *as stated above (Q. 62, A4)*," i.e., the specific article considered here in these paragraphs (emphasis added).

538 And after this initial stage in which hope precedes love, love can then cause hope to grow. Aquinas summarizes this mutual interaction of hope and love as follows: "Per hoc enim quod aliquis reputat per aliquem se posse consequi aliquod bonum, incipit amare ipsum, et ex hoc ipso quod ipsum amat, postea fortius de eo sperat" (*ST* I-II.62.4, ad 3).

539 William J. Hill, "Appendix 6. Distinctive Nature of Hope: Its Relationships to Faith and Charity," in Thomas Aquinas, *Summa Theologiae*, vol. 33, *Hope, 2a-2ae, 17–22*, ed. William J. Hill (New York: Blackfriars and McGraw-Hill, 1966), 123–79, at 157.

540 N.B.: *aliquis* is used to refer to the object of perfect love, and not *aliquid*, which refers to the object of imperfect love. This usage reflects the fact that the perfect love of charity is truly personal and between friends, as opposed to hope's not-yet-fully personal relation.

541 Just as someone who fears punishment from God stops sinning and is led to love God.

542 For Aquinas's use of the image of a foundation to describe faith, see *ST* II-II.8.8, obj. 2: "faith is the foundation of the entire spiritual edifice." Faith is as basic to graced knowledge as the first principles are to natural knowledge (*ST* II-II.5.4, obj. 3). Consequently, its opposing sin, *infidelitas*, is "the greatest of sins because it undermines the foundation of the spiritual edifice" (*ST* II-II.20.3, obj. 1).

543 Hebrews 12:2

544 *De ver.* q. 28, a. 4: "haec tria computantur pro uno motu completo, in quantum unum includitur in alio."

545 Similarly, among the passions, hope is especially concerned with motion, as Gauthier notes: "Parce que l'espérance en a d'abord mesuré les possibilités, elle peut, et elle peut seule, commander l'action, elle est par excellence la passion motrice." *Magnanimité*, 332.

546 *ST* I-II.40.2.

547 *ST* II-II.27.4, which also references I.82.3, I.84.7, I.16.1, and II-II.26.1, ad 2. See also *De pot.* q. 6, a. 9, ad 3: "fides enim est perfectio intellectus, cuius operatio consistit in hoc quod res intellectae aliquo modo sunt in ipso; caritas autem est perfectio voluntatis, cuius operatio consistit in hoc quod voluntas in ipsam rem tendit. Unde per caritatem homo in Deo ponitur, et cum eo unum efficitur: per fidem autem ipsa divina ponuntur in nobis."

548 *ST* I-II.66.6, ad 1.

549 *In ad I Tim.* in *Opera Omnia*, Parma ed., 13:587. For examples already mentioned, see *ST* I-II.62.3, I-II.62.3 ad 3, et al.

550 *ST* II-II.18.1, ad 1.

551 *ST* I-II.67.4.

552 *ST* II-II.17.3.

553 *ST* I-II.25.4.

554 "Fides autem et spes attingunt quidem Deum secundum quod ex ipso provenit nobis vel cognitio veri vel adeptio boni, sed caritas attingit ipsum Deum ut in ipso sistat, non ut ex eo aliquid nobis proveniat" (*ST* II-II.23.6).

555 "idem bonum est obiectum caritatis et spei, sed caritas importat unionem ad illud bonum, spes autem distantiam quandam ab eo. Et inde est quod caritas non respicit illud bonum ut arduum sicut spes, quod enim iam unitum est non habet rationem ardui" (*ST* II-II.23.6, ad 3).

556 "ad appetitum duo pertinent, scilicet motus in finem; et conformatio ad finem per amorem. Et sic oportet quod in appetitu humano duae virtutes theologicae ponantur, scilicet spes et caritas" (*ST* I-II.62.3, ad 3).

557 At the conclusion to the *respondeo* to the question, "Whether charity increases indefinitely?" Aquinas states: "Unde relinquitur quod caritatis augmento nullus terminus praefigi possit in hac vita" (*ST* II-II.24.8).
558 See *ST* II-II.24.9: "Whether charity is rightly distinguished into three degrees: beginning, progress, perfection?" Also, see *ST* II-II.44.6: "Whether is it possible *in via* to fulfill this precept of love of God?" which distinguishes charity as perfect (i.e., when the end is reached), which is in heaven; and imperfect (i.e., when the end has not yet been reached, but the order to that end is not departed from), which is possible *in via*.
559 *ST* II-II.24.9.
560 *ST* II-II.24.4, ad 1.
561 For example, *ST* II-II.23.2, s.c., quoting Augustine: " 'caritatem voco motum animi ad fruendum Deo propter ipsum.' Sed motus animi est aliquid creatum in anima"; or *ST* II-II.18.1, ad 3: "motus spei et motus caritatis habent ordinem ad invicem, ut ex supradictis patet (*ST* II-II.17.8). Unde nihil prohibet utrumque motum simul esse unius potentiae. Sicut et intellectus potest simul multa intelligere ad invicem ordinata."
562 *ST* III.21.1, ad 3.
563 This is expressed as follows by a modern commentator on Aristotle: "In each moment of activity, potentiality is completely cancelled and transformed into actuality; in movement [however] the transformation is not complete till the movement is over. In other words movement differs from activity as the incomplete from the complete.... Movement ... is an actualisation, but one which implies its own incompleteness and the continued presence of potentiality." David Ross, *Aristotle* (London: Methuen, 1949), 83–84.
564 "Sed iste motus [i.e., sensing] est actus *perfecti* (est enim operatio sensus iam facti in actu per suam speciem, non enim sentire conuenit sensui nisi in actu existenti) et ideo est motus *simpliciter alter* a motu phisico. Et huiusmodi motus dicitur proprie *operatio* [emphasis added], ut sentire, intelligere et velle, et secundum hunc motum anima mouet se ipsam secundum Platonem, in quantum cognoscit et amat se ipsam." *Sentencia Libri De anima*, bk. 3, chap. 7, in *Sancti Thomae Aquinatis doctoris angelici Opera omnia iussu Leonis XIII. O. M.* (hereafter Leonine ed.) (Rome: 1882–), 45/1:230.
565 "Spes facit tendere in Deum sicut in quoddam bonum finale adipiscendum.... Sed caritas proprie facit tendere in Deum uniendo affectum hominis Deo" (*ST* II-II.17.6, ad 3).
566 *ST* II-II.27.2.
567 On charity as not arising from any lack, see *ST* I-II.66.6: "[Faith and hope] important in sui ratione quandam distantiam ab obiecto, est enim fides de non visis, spes autem de non habitis. Sed amor caritatis est de quo iam habetur, est enim amatum quodammodo in amante, et etiam amans per affectum trahitur ad unionem amati; propter quod dicitur I Ioan. IV, *qui manet in caritate, in Deo manet, et Deus in eo.*"
568 "caritas augetur per hoc quod intenditur in subiecto" (*ST* II-II.24.5). And see also *ST* II-II.24.5, ad 3: "Et hoc est quod facit Deus caritatem augendo,

scilicet quod magis insit, et quod perfectius similitudo spiritus sancti participetur in anima."
569 In *ST* II-II.24.6, ad 2. See also *ST* II-II.24.5: "caritas augetur solum per hoc quod subiectum magis ac magis participat caritatem, idest secundum quod magis reducitur in actum illius et magis subditur illi. Hic enim est modus augmenti proprius cuiuslibet formae quae intenditur, eo quod esse huiusmodi formae totaliter consistit in eo quod inhaeret susceptibili."
570 *De spe* 4, obj. 14: "in aedificio spirituali fides se habet ut fundamentum; spes autem quae erigit, se habet per modum parietis."
571 *In Epistolam ad Ephesios* (hereafter *In ad Eph.*), Prologus: "[The Ephesians are] erecti per spem: spes enim dirigit ad superna: unde significatur per columnam fumi, de qua dicitur Judic. 20:40 *Viderunt quasi columnam fumi de civitate ascendentem*. Spes enim, ad modum fumi, ex igne, idest ex caritate, provenit, in altum ascendit, in fine deficit, idest in gloria." *Opera Omnia*, Parma ed., 13:443.
572 *In Epistolam ad Hebraeos*: "Comparat enim spem ipsi anchorae, quae sicut in mari navem immobilitat, ita spes animam firmat in Deo in hoc mundo, qui est quasi quoddam mare." *Opera Omnia*, Parma ed., 13:720.
573 *In ad Eph.*, cap. 1, lect. 6: "Ad statum vero praesentem pertinet spes, quae est necessaria ad salutem ... [and which is] fortissima virtutum: Hebr. 6:18 'Fortissimum solatium habeamus, qui confugimus ad tenendam propositam spem; quam sicut anchoram habemus animae totam ac firmam.' " *Opera Omnia*, Parma ed., 13:452.
574 Throughout this section, it should be noted that the terms potency, motion, and act are used broadly and that it would be technically incorrect to argue that a virtue of the appetite can actualize a virtue of the intellect. The point is that the theological virtues are considered the potency, motion, and act *of* Christian humanism.
575 *ST* III.21.1, ad 3.
576 *Physics* 3.1, 201a10–11. McKeon, *Basic Works of Aristotle*, 254.
577 *Physics* 3.2, 201b31–202a37. McKeon, *Basic Works of Aristotle*, 255.
578 Using, with some minor adaptations, Aristotle's example in *Physics* 3.1, 201b9–201b15.
579 Ross, *Aristotle*, 83, drawing on Aristotle's example in *Physics* 3.1, 201b9–15: "The actuality of the buildable as buildable is the process of building. For the actuality of the buildable must be either this or that house. But when there is a house, the buildable is no longer buildable. On the other hand, it is the buildable which is *being* built. The process then of being built must be the kind of actuality required. But building is a kind of motion." McKeon, *Basic Works of Aristotle*, 255.
580 "motus est actus existentis in potencia, quia uidelicet recedens ab uno contrario, quandiu mouetur non attingit alterum contrarium quod est terminus motus, sed est in potencia ad ipsum, et quia omne quod est in potencia in quantum huiusmodi est imperfectum, ideo ille *motus* est *actus imperfecti*." Aquinas, *Sentencia Libri De anima*, bk. 3, chap. 7, in *Opera Omnia*, Leonine ed., 45/1:230. Aquinas is here contrasting motion proper,

as examined in the *Physics* (bk. 3, 200b12–202b29) with another kind of motion pertaining to the senses.
581 *ST* II-II.19.11, ad 3.
582 As argued by O'Connor, *Eternal Quest*, summarized in chapter 3 of this book.
583 This example is mentioned in Aristotle's refutation of the Megaric school, who denied the reality of motion. *Metaphysics* 9.3, 1046b28–1047b1.
584 *ST* II-II.7.2, obj. 3.
585 *ST* II-II.7.2, ad 3. Even the gift of understanding, which penetrates beyond the mere assent of faith to gain some perception of truth (*ST* II-II.8.5, ad 3), still falls short of the perfect understanding that knows the essence. Therefore, "ea quae directe cadunt sub fide intelligere non possumus, durante statu fidei" (*ST* II-II.8.2).
586 *SCG* III c. 40.
587 Romanus Cessario, *Christian Faith and the Theological Life* (Washington, DC: Catholic University of America Press, 1996), 101.
588 *ST* I-II.66.6, ad 1. See also *ST* I.82.3, "Whether the will is a higher power than the intellect?"
589 "Substantia enim solet dici prima inchoatio cuiuscumque rei, et maxime quando tota res sequens continetur virtute in primo principio, puta si dicamus quod prima principia indemonstrabilia sunt substantia scientiae, quia scilicet primum quod in nobis est de scientia sunt huiusmodi principia, et in eis virtute continetur tota scientia. Per hunc ergo modum dicitur fides esse substantia rerum sperandarum, quia scilicet prima inchoatio rerum sperandarum in nobis est per assensum fidei, quae virtute continet omnes res sperandas" (*ST* II-II.4.1).
590 *De ver.* q. 28, a. 4: "Et haec tria computantur pro uno motu completo, in quantum unum includitur in alio; denominatur tamen iste motus a fide, eo quod virtute continet in se illos motus, et in eis includitur."
591 This is the first set of translations listed in Deferrari's dictionary. The second set is "*first element, origin, principle, cause*, the *arche* of Aristotle ... synonym of *principium* and *causa.*"
592 It should be noted that Deferrari nowhere translates *virtute* as "virtually."
593 *Summa theologiae*, vol. 2, *Existence and Nature of God (Ia. 2–11)*, trans. Timothy McDermott (Blackfriars, in conjunction with McGraw-Hill: New York, 1964), 53.
594 *Expositio libri Posteriorum Analyticorum* (hereafter *In Post. Anal.*) book 1, lecture 3, Leonine ed., 1:146: "Principia autem se habent ad conclusiones in demonstrativis, sicut causae activae in naturalibus ad suos effectus (unde in II physicorum propositiones syllogismi ponuntur in genere causae efficientis). Effectus autem, antequam producatur in actu, praeexistit quidem in causis activis *virtute*, non autem actu, quod est simpliciter esse. Et similiter antequam ex principiis demonstrativis deducatur conclusio, in ipsis quidem principiis praecognitis praecognoscitur conclusio *virtute*, non autem actu: sic enim in eis praeexistit" (emphasis added).
595 *In Post. Anal.*, book 1, lecture 3, Leonine ed., 1:148: "sed erat notum *potentia sive virtute* in principiis praecognitis universalibus, ignotum autem

actu, secundum propriam cognitionem. Et hoc est addiscere, reduci de cognitione *potentiali, seu virtuali*, aut universali, in cognitionem propriam et actualem" (emphasis added.) This quotation is immediately preceded by the following reflections on how that which is generated from another is in some way already existing potentially in that other generating thing. "Quod autem generatur, ante generationem neque fuit omnino non ens neque omnino ens, sed quodammodo ens et quodammodo non ens: ens quidem in potentia, non ens vero actu: et hoc est generari, reduci de potentia in actum. Unde nec id quod quis addiscit erat omnino prius notum, ut Plato posuit, nec omnino ignotum, ut secundum solutionem supra improbatam ponebatur."

596 *ST* II-II.1.7. The full text reads: "Omnes articuli implicite continentur in aliquibus primis credibilibus, scilicet ut credatur Deus esse et providentiam habere circa hominum salutem, secundum illud ad Heb. XI, *accedentem ad Deum oportet credere quia est, et quod inquirentibus se remunerator sit.* In esse enim divino includuntur omnia quae credimus in Deo aeternaliter existere, in quibus nostra beatitudo consistit, in fide autem providentiae includuntur omnia quae temporaliter a Deo dispensantur ad hominum salutem, quae sunt via in beatitudinem."

597 *ST* II-II.17.7.

598 *Comp. theol.* II, 1. This connection between providence and hope is developed by Charles Bernard, *Théologie de l'espérance selon Saint Thomas d'Aquin* (Paris: J. Vrin, 1961), 63–69, who brings out the relationship between the personal and universal: "Certes, l'espérance est personnelle, mais la particularisation de son mouvement se situe entre deux plans universels: l'universalité du dessein de Dieu révélé à notre intelligence dans la foi, et l'universalité de son accomplissement où se meut déjà la charité" (68).

599 See also *ST* II-II.23.4, ad 2. Since the virtue that concerns the last end commands secondary virtues, and since charity has for its object the last end of human life, i.e., eternal happiness, "ideo extendit se ad actus totius humanae vitae per modum imperii, non quasi immediate eliciens omnes actus virtutum."

600 1 Timothy 1:5: "The end of the commandment is charity," as quoted in *ST* II-II.23.4, ad 3.

601 "caritas se extendit ad omnes actus humanos, secundum illud I ad Cor. ult., *omnia vestra in caritate fiant*" (*ST* II-II.24.1, s.c.).

602 On faith and hope as preambles or presuppositions of the law, see *ST* II-II.16.1 and II-II.22.1.

603 As for the first two theological virtues, faith and hope, "potest esse sine [caritate]." (And presumably faith can exist without hope, although Aquinas does not make this explicit.) It should be noted that this order refers only to the *acts* of the three theological virtues, since the virtues themselves, that is, *qua* habit, are infused simultaneously; see *ST* I-II.62.4. (Compare, however, *De spe* 3, ad 8, which states that "secundum quod [fides et spes] sunt informes, quandoque praecedunt caritatem tempore.")

604 *ST* I-II.65.4, referencing Aristotle, *Ethics* 2:6.

605 "Et ideo fides et spes possunt esse sine caritate, sed *sine caritate, proprie loquendo, virtutes non sunt*; nam ad rationem virtutis pertinet ut non solum secundum ipsam aliquod bonum operemur, sed etiam bene" (*ST* I-II.65.4).
606 "Ordine vero perfectionis, caritas praecedit fidem et spem, eo quod tam fides quam spes per caritatem formatur, et perfectionem virtutis acquirit. Sic enim caritas est mater omnium virtutum et radix, inquantum est omnium virtutum forma, ut infra dicetur [*ST* II-II.23.8]" (*ST* I-II.62.4).
607 Following Gal. 5:6 (summarized, for example, in *ST* II-II.4.3 s.c.) and James 2:20 (quoted in *ST* II-II.4.4, obj. 2) respectively.
608 On faith and hope as disposing one to charity, see *ST* II-II.24.2, ad 3, quoting the gloss on Matt. 1:2, "Faith engenders hope, and hope charity."
609 *ST* II-II.17.8, ad 2 on the movement of living hope: "qua scilicet aliquis sperat bonum a Deo ut ab amico."
610 "rursus in se quodam sancto circuitu refunduntur; quia scilicet, cum aliquis ex spe jam ad caritatem introductus fuerit, tunc etiam perfectius sperat, et castius timet, sicut etiam et firmius credit. Et ideo quod dicit quod ex caritate est spes, non loquitur quantum ad primam caritatis generationem, sed quantum ad secundam caritatis refusionem; secundum quod jam nobis indita, facit nos et perfectius sperare et credere" (*De spe* 3, ad 1).
611 *ST* II-II.17.3, "Whether one may hope for another's eternal happiness?"
612 *ST* II-II.27–33.
613 *ST* I-II.65.3.
614 *ST* II.II.17.6, ad 2.
615 Roger Haight, *Dynamics of Theology* (New York: Paulist, 1990), 21. See also 240–41, nn. 23–24.
616 Joseph Ratzinger, *Aus Christus Schauen: Einübung in Glaube, Hoffnung, Liebe* (Freiburg in Breisgau: Herder, 1989); English translation, *To Look on Christ*, trans. Robert Nowell (New York: Crossroad, 1991); republished as *The Yes of Jesus Christ: Spiritual Exercises in Faith, Hope, and Love* (New York: Crossroad, 2005), 69. References here are to the 2005 English edition.
617 Ratzinger, *Yes of Jesus Christ*, 70.
618 Bernard, *Théologie de l'espérance*, 105. See 105–26 for Bernard's elaboration of this "ensemble vivant" in the context not only of faith and charity, but also desire, confidence, providence, and the gift of fear.
619 *ST* II-II.23.8, ad 2.
620 *De spe* 1: "Sic igitur, sicut formale obiectum fidei est veritas prima, per quam sicut per quoddam medium assentit his quae creduntur, quae sunt materiale objectum fidei; ita etiam formale objectum spei est auxilium divinae potestatis et pietatis, propter quod tendit motus spei in bona sperata, quae sunt materiale obiectum spei."
621 As mentioned above in chapter 4, n. 88, Pinckaers attributes this change to the greater fittingness of efficient and final cause for a virtue of the will, in contrast to the cognitional terms of material and formal object, which are more suited to a virtue of the intellect. *Le renouveau de la morale*, 231–32.
622 For an overview of Aristotle transitioning, in the *Metaphysics*, from the distinction of form and matter to potentiality and actuality, see Ross, *Aristotle*, 175–78, esp. 176. Ross notes (p. 175) the use of the extrinsic

causes (which include what later became known as final cause and efficient cause) alongside the discussion of the formal and material causes, all of which ceded to the broader terms of potentiality and actuality that better captured the process Ross calls "the advance of things from a relatively unformed to a relatively formed condition" (p. 176).

623 *Spe salvi* §10: "Is the Christian faith also for us today a life-changing and life-sustaining hope? Is it performative for us—is it a message which shapes our life in a new way, or is it just 'information'?" All quotations from *Spe salvi* are from the official English translation on the Vatican website, http://www.vatican.va/holy_father/benedict_xvi/encyclicals/documents/hf_b en-xvi_enc_20071130_spe-salvi_en.html.

624 The centrality of Christ for any understanding of providence can be seen in Aquinas's use of the word "way" to describe both providence and Christ. Thus, the second aspect of faith's twofold *prima credibilia*—which are God's existence (the goal of happiness) and providence (the way to happiness)—receives a Christological cast in the second question of the treatise on faith. In the seventh article, "the way" is associated with Christ's humanity: "That through which the human person obtains happiness pertains, properly and in itself, to the object of faith. The way of coming to happiness for human persons, however, is the mystery of the Incarnation and passion of Christ" (*ST* II-II.2.7). Likewise, the humanity of Christ is described as "the way" in the prologue after the first question of the *Summa theologiae*, which maps out the basic structure of the three parts of the work: "Thirdly ... Christ, who, insofar as he is a human being, is the way for us to move to God" (Prologue immediately before *ST* I.2). Christ's humanity, then, is God's providentially arranged way through which the person moves to God.

625 Of course, the intimate union of divinity and humanity that Christ possesses by nature in the hypostatic union is something in which human persons will only participate by grace in the adoption of sonship (cf. Rom. 8:14–17).

626 *In Epistolam ad Romanos*, cap. 5, lect. 1, in *Opera Omnia*, Parma ed., 13:48.

627 *De spe* 1, ad 6: "Desiderium autem importat quidem motum in futurum, sed sine aliqua praesenti inhaesione vel spirituali contactu ipsius Dei."

628 These phrases are both Karl Rahner's. For "open upwards," see "Current Problems in Christology," *Theological Investigations*, vol. 1, trans. Cornelius Ernst (New York: Crossroad, 1982), 149–200, at 183: "Human being is rather a reality absolutely open upwards; a reality which reaches its highest (though indeed 'unexacted') perfection ... when in it the Logos himself becomes existent in the world." The phrase "fall into the abyss" is used in "Christology within an Evolutionary View of the World," *Theological Investigations*, vol. 5, trans. Karl-H. Kruger (New York: Crossroad, 1983), 157–92, at 192: "Every fall into the abyss of the unspeakable and incomprehensible in spirit and life means falling into the hands of the one whom the Son addressed as his Father, when in death he commended his soul into his hands."

629 Boyle, *Who Are We Now?* 251.

630 Henri de Lubac, *Catholicism: Christ and the Common Destiny of Man* (London: Burns and Oates, 1950), 209.

631 Murray, "The Construction of a Christian Culture," 118–23. I am grateful to Joseph Komonchak for sharing with me his transcription of the original lectures, which can be found in the Woodstock College Archives, Murray Papers, Box 6, File 422. Some of the force of this lecture has been blunted by the extensive editorial excisions in the published version presented in *Bridging the Sacred and Secular*. Among the many omitted passages is the following comment: Christ's "perfecting as man [happened] through the discipline of suffering," which indicates Murray's understanding of the role of the cross in "bridging" secular and sacred identities (Murray, *Loyola Lectures*, 27). For Komonchak's review of Hooper's edited volume, see "Murray's Mantle," *First Things* 65 (August/September 1996): 48–52.

632 Walter Kasper, "Christian Humanism," in *Proceedings of the Twenty-Seventh Annual Convention* (New York: Catholic Theological Society of America, 1972), 1–17, at 16.

633 John Henry Newman, *Parochial and Plain Sermons*, vol. 5, sermon 23, "Love, the One Thing Needful" (London: Longmans, Green and Co., 1907), 327–40, at 338.

634 Taylor, *Catholic Modernity?* 24l; and idem, "Inescapable Horizons," chap. 4 of *Ethics of Authenticity*.

635 Karl Rahner, "The Theology of Hope," *Theological Investigations*, vol. 10, trans. David Bourke (London: Darton, Longman and Todd, 1973), 242–59, at 255.

636 *ST* II-II.26.2, ad 1. Compare 1 John 4:20.

637 *ST* II-II.17.1, which argues that it is precisely the leaning upon God that constitutes hope's virtuousness.

638 *ST* I-II.40.6: "Utrum in iuvenibus et in ebriosis abundet spes?"

639 A theme richly explored by Josef Pieper, *On Hope*, trans. by Mary Frances McCarthy (San Francisco: Ignatius, 1986), especially in the opening chapter, "Reflections on the concept *status viatoris*," 11–21.

640 Murray, "Basket Weaving?" 185.

641 For example, see my comments on Rowan Greer in chapter 2 above. See also Stephen B. Bevans, *Models of Contextual Theology*, rev. ed. (Maryknoll, New York: Orbis, 2002), 21–22, which contrasts "creation-centered" and "redemption-centered" orientations as a key determining factor in the choice of one among the various models for contextual theology.

642 Zachary Hayes, *Visions of a Future: A Study of Christian Eschatology* (Collegeville, MN: Liturgical Press, 1989), 129–31.

643 Ratzinger, *Yes of Jesus Christ*, 134.

644 I use the terms "Augustinian" and "Thomist" as imprecise generalizations that name differing emphases in theologians who take their lead from Augustine or Thomas respectively. An Augustinian sensibility would insist on the sharp contrast between eschatological and secular hope, the deep and ineradicable nature of sin, and thus the limits—even tragic flaws—of all human projects. A good example of the roots of the less oppositional Thomistic sensibility can be seen in Aquinas's response to the question, "Whether any true virtue can exist without charity?" (*ST* II-II.23.7), in

which he qualifies Augustine by defending "true yet imperfect virtues" that intend temporal goods, such as "the preservation of the state."
Benedict's Augustinian sympathies, from his 1953 doctoral dissertation on Augustine to his 1996 self-description as "decidedly Augustinian," are well documented, for example, by Joseph Komonchak, "The Church in Crisis: Pope Benedict's Theological Vision," *Commonweal*, June 3, 2005, 11–14. They lie behind his ambivalence over *Gaudium et spes* (a document heavily influenced by the decidedly Thomist thinker, Marie-Dominique Chenu). In *Spe salvi*, Augustine is by far the most cited theologian in the encyclical (seven times). The use of the term "Augustinian," however, should not be taken to imply a bowdlerized account of Augustine's position. For example, in a telling discussion of Augustine of Hippo's episcopal responsibilities, which included liberating the oppressed and helping the needy, Benedict eschews any talk of "two cities." Instead, he states that it was precisely Augustine's hope that "enabled him to take part decisively and with all his strength in the task of building up the city … his city" (*Spe salvi* §29).

645 *Spe salvi* §1.
646 "id quod est futurum secundum rem, potest esse praesens in imaginatione" (*In III Sent*. d. 26, q. 1, a. 1, ad 5).
647 *ST* I-II.40.8.
648 *ST* I-II.21.4, ad 3.
649 "It commits the mistake of immanentizing the Christian Eschaton, i.e., of treating faith symbols as though they represented immanent reality rather than the transcendental reality of man's supernatural destiny." Ellis Sandoz, *The Voegelinian Revolution* (Baton Rouge: Louisiana State University, 1981), 109. Quoted by James V. Schall, S.J., "The Encyclical on Hope: On the 'De-immanentizing' of the Christian Eschaton," http://www.ignatiusinsight.com/features2007/schall_onspesalvi_dec07.asp (accessed December 3, 2007).
650 Christopher Dawson, *Religion and the Modern State* (New York: Sheed & Ward, 1938), 109–10. Quoted by Adam Schwartz, "Confronting the 'Totalitarian Antichrist': Christopher Dawson and Totalitarianism," *The Catholic Historical Review* 89, no. 3 (July 2003): 464–88, at 473.
651 Joseph Ratzinger, *Church, Ecumenism, and Politics*, trans. Robert Nowell (New York: Crossroads, 1988), 163, here in the context of the distinction between church and state.
652 Ratzinger, *Eschatology*, 59.
653 Ratzinger, *Eschatology*, 59.
654 *Spe salvi* §31.
655 *Spe salvi* §31.
656 Ratzinger, *Eschatology*, 26, emphasis added.
657 See the final sentence of *ST* II-II.20.1: "Et ideo sicut motus spei … est laudabili et virtuosus; ita oppositus motus desperationis … est vitiosus et peccatum."
658 Summarizing the *respondeo* to *ST* II-II.20.1.
659 *ST* II-II.20.2, obj. 2. The ad 2 clarifies that this denial is not of faith's or unbelief's universal estimate (that God's mercy is or is not infinite) but only

of hope's or despair's particular estimate (that for me in this state, on account of some particular disposition, there is or is not hope of divine mercy): "si quis in universali aestimaret misericordiam Dei non esse infinitam, esset infidelis. Hoc autem non existimat desperans: sed quod sibi in statu illo, propter aliquam particularem dispositionem, non sit de divina misericordia sperandum."

660 *ST* II-II.20.1, s.c.
661 *ST* II-II.20.3.
662 The quotation from the gloss on Prov. 24:10 that Aquinas includes in the *respondeo* of *ST* II-II.20.3 includes, significantly, both the theological and secular consequences of despair: " 'nihil est execrabilius desperatione, quam qui habet et in generalibus huius vitae laboribus, *et*, quod peius est, in fidei certamine constantiam perdit' " (emphasis added).
663 *ST* II-II.20.1, s.c.
664 In the final analysis, however, charity is the form of the virtues because it actually unites the person to the end and so orders all human acts to their ultimate finality. On charity as the form of all the virtues, see *ST* II-II.23.8, "Whether charity is the form of the virtues?" But see Ratzinger's comments on Eph. 2:12 and 1 Thess. 4:13: "According to these texts, hope is not just one virtue among others; it is the very definition of Christian existence." Joseph Ratzinger, "On Hope," *Communio: International Catholic Review* 12 (Spring 1985): 71–84, at 71.
665 "caritate diligitur Deus propter seipsum" (*ST* II-II.23.5, ad 2).
666 "spes, per quam tendat in illum finem sicut ad se pertinentem." *In Epistolam I ad Corinthios*, cap. 13, lect. 4, in *Opera omnia*, Parma ed., 13:265.
667 "spes praesupponit amorem eius quod quis adipisci se sperat, qui est amor concupiscentiae, quo quidem amore magis se amat qui concupiscit bonum, quam aliquid aliud. Caritas autem importat amorem amicitiae" (*ST* I-II.66.6, ad 2).
668 Ratzinger, "On Hope," 75.
669 *ST* II-II.20.3.
670 *ST* II-II.20.3. This question also compares despair with the vices opposing faith and charity insofar as they relate to God Godself: "unbelief and hatred of God are against God as God exists in Godself; despair, however, according as God's good is participated by us. Whence it is a greater sin, strictly speaking, not to believe God's truth or to hate God, than not to hope to obtain glory from God."
671 "praeceptorum quae in sacra Scriptura inveniuntur quaedam sunt de substantia legis; quaedam vero sunt praeambula ad legem. Praeambula quidem sunt ad legem illa quibus non existentibus lex locum habere non potest. Huiusmodi autem sunt praecepta de actu fidei et de actu spei" (*ST* II-II.22.1).
672 *ST* II-II.22.1.
673 *ST* II-II.22.1.
674 *ST* II-II.22.1.
675 Faith "praesupponitur ad legis susceptionem" (*ST* II-II.16.1, ad 1).

676 In his commentary on the *Sentences*, Aquinas expresses the distinct foundational nature of each theological virtue as follows: "spes est in homine principium omnium operationum quae ad bonum arduum ordinantur, sicut caritas omnium quae in bonum tendunt, et sicut fides omnium quae ad cognitionem pertinent" (*In III Sent.* d. 26, q. 2, a. 2, ad 2).
677 Daley, *Hope of the Early Church*, 218.
678 Responding to the criticisms of Jürgen Moltmann, Carl Peter develops the notion of participation, especially in terms of "participated eternity," to defend Aquinas's account of hope from the charge of temporal irrelevance. "Metaphysical Finalism or Christian Eschatology," *The Thomist* 38 (1974): 125–45, at 131. For a general account of Aquinas on the twofold nature of the good, see Denis Bradley, *Aquinas on the Twofold Human Good: Reason and Human Happiness in Aquinas's Moral Science* (Washington, DC: Catholic University of America, 1997).
679 *Spe salvi* §15.
680 *Spe salvi* §§16–23. Perhaps here one glimpses a certain nostalgia for pre-1960s Bavaria. According to Nicholas Boyle, Benedict stands in that not atypical stream of German intellectual life that lacks "any instinctive understanding of the commercial, industrial, and financial world, the circle of investment, employment, production, and consumption." Further, "no one who has their own memories of pre-industrial Catholicism (from Ireland perhaps) will fail to be moved by Ratzinger's recollections of the Corpus Christi processions of his childhood, the self-expression of a unified, God-directed community. But in the world to which Benedict has to minister," things have changed. Nicholas Boyle, "The New Spirit of Germany," *Tablet* 259.8587, May 7, 2005, 4–5, at 5.
681 To be fair, the section on Augustine as bishop (*Spe salvi*, §§28–29) indicates how his hope in God "enabled him to take part decisively and with all his strength in the task of building up the city" (*Spe salvi* §29). But Benedict's brief account of the connection between secular life and eschatological hope is framed in terms of love, not hope: "Love of God leads to participation in the justice and generosity of God towards others.... The love of God is revealed in responsibility for others. This same connection between love of God and responsibility for others can be seen in a striking way in the life of Saint Augustine" (*Spe salvi* §28).
682 *Spe salvi* §§35–40.
683 *Spe salvi* §30.
684 That is, the first section after the semantic and historical reflections, "Faith is hope" (*Spe salvi* §§2–3) and "The concept of faith-based hope in the New Testament and early Church" (*Spe salvi* §§4–9).
685 Other verses from Romans 8 are cited in *Spe salvi* §11 (Rom. 8:26) and §26 (Rom. 8:38-39), but they do not bear directly on the theme of rejoicing in hope. For Eph. 2:12, see *Spe salvi* §§2, 3, 23, 27, and 44.
686 *Spe salvi* §3, emphasis in original.
687 *Spe salvi* §23.
688 Ratzinger, *Eschatology*, 59.
689 N. T. Wright, *Christian Origins and the Question of God*, vol. 2, *Jesus and the Victory of God* (Minneapolis: Fortress, 1996), 310, emphasis in original.

Quoted in James Hanvey, "Charity Which Makes the Difference," in *Charity Which Makes the Difference*, Institute Series 7 (Heythrop College, London: Heythrop Institute for Religion, Ethics, and Public Life, 2008), 7–27, at 12. Hanvey's article offers an incisive account of eschatology's nonprogrammatic yet nonetheless profoundly political ramifications, e.g., in the parables' vision of the "great reversal."

690 See chapter 2 above.

691 *ST* II-II.17.4.

692 "non licet sperare de aliquo homine, vel de aliqua creatura, sicut de prima causa movente in beatitudinem; licet autem sperare de aliquo homine, vel de aliqua creatura, sicut de agente secundario et instrumentali, per quod aliquis adiuvatur ad quaecumque bona consequenda in beatitudinem ordinate" (*ST* II-II.17.4).

693 "non licet sperare aliquod bonum praeter beatitudinem sicut ultimum finem, sed solum sicut id quod est ad finem beatitudinis ordinatum" (*ST* II-II.17.4). Note that by acknowledging the critical role of secondary causation in hope, the mature Aquinas revised his earlier position that claimed hope was "only about eternal things" (*De pot.* q. 6, art. 9, ad 10): "spei non proprie attribuitur miracula facere; spes enim ordinatur ad aliquid consequendum, unde est solum de aeternis. Fides autem est de aeternis et temporalibus; unde potest se extendere ad facienda."

694 As mentioned, in the context of charity Aquinas gives the example of the "preservation of the state or anything of that kind" as an example of a true virtue that is imperfect unless it be referred to God (*ST* II-II.23.7).

695 *ST* II-II.17.1, emphasis added.

696 *ST* II-II.17.2, obj. 2. On the notion of prayer as emerging from hope, see also *De spe* 4, obj. 6: "oratio ex virtute spei procedit."

697 Thus, while an exegesis of Hebrews 10–11, with which *Spe salvi* begins, warrants the contrast between God (the enduring "hypostasis") and worldly possessions (the ephemeral "hyparchonta"), an exegesis of Jesus's teaching on prayer demands some account of their connection. Oppositional rhetoric that presents their difference must yield to a coherent explanation of how they relate. Something of that shift is seen at the end of Ratzinger's article "On Hope," which briefly discusses the Lord's prayer. But those comments are a concluding afterthought (occasioned by Ratzinger's rereading of the *Catechismus Romanus* while preparing the lecture) that sits uneasily with the earlier and far more elaborate comments on the difference between *hypostasis* and *hyparchonta*. Perhaps that is why Ratzinger said in the first, asterisked footnote to the article, "It seems to me that this [Franciscan] point of departure … remains to be completed" (p. 71). Benedict's section on prayer in *Spe salvi* briefly develops this trajectory when it states that through prayer "we become capable of the great hope and thus we become ministers of hope for others" (*Spe salvi* §34). For an illuminating account of Augustine himself moving from oppositional rhetoric to a more explanatory theological framework, see Khaled Anatolios, "Oppositional Pairs and Christological Synthesis: Rereading Augustine's *De Trinitate*," *Theological Studies* 68 (2007): 231–53.

698 In his commentary on Aristotle's *Ethics*, Aquinas writes that Aristotle "ponit ordinem habituum ad invicem…. [S]icut ars quae facit frena est sub

arte equitandi, quia ille qui debet equitare praecipit artifici qualiter faciat frenum et sic est architector, id est principalis artifex, respectu ipsius.... Equestris autem ulterius ordinatur sub militari.... Et per eundem modum aliae artes sub aliis." *Sententia Libri Ethicorum*, in *Opera Omnia*, Leonine ed., 47/1:6.
699 *ST* I-II.12.3.
700 So important is the notion of order for ethical inquiry that Aquinas begins his commentary on Aristotle's *Ethics* by citing the opening of Aristotle's *Metaphysics*: "Sicut Philosophus dicit in principio Metaphysicae, sapientis est ordinare. Cuius ratio est quia sapientia est potissima perfectio rationis, cuius proprium est cognoscere ordinem." *Sententia Libri Ethicorum*, in *Opera Omnia*, Leonine ed., 47/1:3.
701 *ST* I-II.21.4, ad 3. If this is the case, then it seems superfluous, at least for the purposes of my argument, to invoke (as Aquinas does in *ST* I-II.65.3) the infused virtues as distinct sources for moral action alongside natural virtues that have been supernaturally ordered. For if "all that a human person is, can do, and possesses" is ordered to God, then why are distinctively infused moral virtues needed alongside naturally acquired ones, which are presumably already transformed by the person's new ordering to God upon receiving faith, hope, and charity? But for a defense of the infused virtues, which includes references to the standard objections to Aquinas's account, see Bonnie Kent, "Habits and Virtues," in *Ethics of Aquinas*, 116–30, esp. 122–127.
702 In addition to the numerous instances where hope's act is described as tending towards something, see the specific reference to hope as "the motion of intention" in *ST* I-II.62.3: "voluntas ordinatur in illum finem et quantum ad motum intentionis, in ipsum tendentem sicut in id quod est possibile consequi, quod pertinet ad spem."
703 *ST* I-II.12.1, ad 4. The full quotation is as follows: "intentio est actus voluntatis respectu finis. Sed voluntas respicit finem tripliciter. Uno modo, absolute: et sic dicitur voluntas, prout absolute volumus vel sanitatem, vel si quid aliud est huiusmodi. Alio modo consideratur finis secundum quod in eo quiescitur: et hoc modo fruitio respicit finem. Tertio modo consideratur finis secundum quod est terminus alicuius quod in ipsum ordinatur, et sic intentio respicit finem. Non enim solum ex hoc intendere dicimur sanitatem, quia volumus eam, sed quia volumus ad eam per aliquid aliud pervenire."
704 "Motus autem voluntatis qui fertur in finem, *secundum quod acquiritur per ea quae sunt ad finem*, vocatur intentio" (*ST* I-II.12.4, ad 3; emphasis added in text).
705 I use the word "choose" deliberately because choice regards the means as ordered to the end, whereas intention regards the end as acquired through those means. See *ST* I-II.12.4, ad 3.
706 *ST* I-II.69.1.
707 *Spe salvi* §35.
708 *Spe salvi* §31.
709 Ratzinger, *Eschatology*, 101; translation slightly adapted. Original translation: "eschatology ... challenges us in most compelling fashion, to

dare to realize in our own lives that justice and truth whose claims upon us—along with those of love—are eschatology's very own content." Original German: "die Eschatologie die Ermutigung, ja die zwingende Herausforderung dazu ist, das Recht und die Wahrheit zu wagen; die Inanspruchnahme unseres Lebens für Wahrheit, Recht, Liebe ist geradezu der Gehalt der Eschatologie." *Eschatologie—Tod und ewiges Leben* (Regensburg: Friedrich Pustet, 1977), 89.

710 *Spe salvi* §35.
711 Similarly, in the context of suggesting that theological hope is a kind of supernatural magnanimity—because of the greatness to which it leads the human person—Gauthier speaks of the triumph of Aquinas's theology, which "du meme coup, assume, dans le chrétien, l'humain et explique, par l'humain, le chrétien." *Magnanimité*, 338.
712 Maritain, *Integral Humanism*, 102.
713 *Catechism of the Catholic Church* §1818.
714 "We become capable of the great hope, and thus we become ministers of hope for others" (*Spe salvi* §34).
715 Similarly, while it is indeed true that "my encounter with God awakens my conscience" (*Spe salvi* §33), it is also true that the encounter with my conscience, and the consequent hope to attain what my conscience prescribes, awakens my sense of God. As the *Catechism of the Catholic Church* asserts, "When he listens to his conscience, the prudent man can hear God speaking" (§1777).
716 "Filii, obedite parentibus vestris in Domino: hoc enim justum est. Honora patrem tuum et matrem tuam (quod est mandatum primum in promissione) ut bene sit tibi, et sis longaevus super terram." Eph. 6:1, cited from the Vulgate text used in *In ad Eph.*, cap. 6, lect. 1, in *Opera Omnia*, Parma ed., 13:498. The promise reads slightly differently in Exod. 20:12: "Honor your father and your mother, so that your days may be long in the land that the Lord your God is giving you." Deut. 5:16 is quoted above because Eph. 6:1–3, on which Aquinas comments, cites the Deuteronomic version of this commandment.
717 *ST* II-II.32.5, ad 4. The quotation continues: "Sic enim et apostolus interpretatur, I ad Tim. IV.8, dicens: Pietas ad omnia utilis est, promissionem habens vitae quae nunc est et futurae: quod dicit quia in praecepto de honoratione parentum additur promissio, ut sis longaevus super terram. Sub pietate autem comprehenditur omnis eleemosynarum largitio."
718 The biblical text that is cited in the *sed contra* of *ST* II-II.32.5 reads: "Then he will say to those at his left hand, 'You that are accursed, depart from me into the eternal fire prepared for the devil and his angels; for I was hungry and you gave me no food, I was thirsty and you gave me nothing to drink, I was a stranger and you did not welcome me, naked and you did not give me clothing, sick and in prison and you did not visit me.' "
719 Aquinas briefly touches on *amor mercenarius* in his treatise on hope during a discussion of "Whether servile fear is good?" (*ST* II-II.19.4, ad 3). Insofar as he understands it as the love of God *propter bona temporalia*, his discussion is of limited use to my discussion above, which concerns the

slightly different problem of doing good for the wrong reason, rather than loving God for the wrong reason.

720 Of course, merit and reward are always within the context of God's grace: "meritum hominis apud Deum esse non potest nisi secundum praesuppositionem divinae ordinationis: ita scilicet ut id homo consequatur a Deo per suam operationem quasi mercedem, ad quod Deus ei virtutem operandi deputavit" (*ST* I-II.114.1). But, since merit is the effect of cooperative grace, its operation is "non solum attribuitur Deo, sed etiam animae" (*ST* I-II.111.2).

721 "ne aliquis credat quod honoratio parentum non sit meritoria, quia naturalis est; ideo addit: *ut sit longaevus super terram.*" *In ad Eph.*, cap. 6, lect. 1, in *Opera Omnis*, Parma ed., 13:499.

722 "figurabantur magna bona, scilicet spiritualia." *In ad Eph.*, cap. 6, lect. 1, in *Opera Omnis*, Parma ed., 13:499.

723 "Nam qui gratus est in minoribus beneficiis, meretur majora recipere. Maxima autem beneficia habemus a parentibus; scilicet esse, nutrimentum et disciplinam. Quando ergo quis gratus est his, fit dignus ut majora recipiat: et ideo dicit: *ut bene sit tibi*: quia, ut dicitur I Timoth. 4, 8: 'Pietas ad omnia utilis est, promissionem habens vitae quae nunc est, et futurae,' " *In ad Eph.*, cap. 6, lect. 1, in *Opera Omnis*, Parma ed., 13:499.

724 "Vel potest referri ad sensum spiritualem: *Ut sis longaevus in terra* viventium. Psalm. 142, 10: 'Spiritus tuus bonus deducet me in terram rectam; propter nomen tuum, Domine, vivificabis me.' " *In ad Eph.*, cap. 6, lect. 1, in *Opera Omnis*, Parma ed., 13:499. That this reference from the Psalms refers to eternal life can be seen from another citation of the same text in *ST* I-II.68.2: "Sed in ordine ad finem ultimum supernaturalem, ad quem ratio movet secundum quod est aliqualiter et imperfecte formata per virtutes theologicas; non sufficit ipsa motio rationis, nisi desuper adsit instinctus et motio spiritus sancti; secundum illud Rom. 8:14,17, Qui Spiritu Dei aguntur, hi filii Dei sunt; et si filii, et haeredes, et in Psalmo 142:10, dicitur: Spiritus tuus bonus deducet me in terram rectam; quia scilicet in haereditatem illius terrae beatorum nullus potest pervenire, nisi moveatur et deducatur a spiritu sancto."

725 "quia Deus honorandus est sicut principium nostri esse, et quia parentes sunt etiam principium nostri esse ..., ideo conveniens est, ut post mandata ordinata ad Deum, primum esset ordinatum ad parentes." *In ad Eph.*, cap. 6, lec. 1, in *Opera Omnis*, Parma ed., 13:498.

726 "quia homines in aliis quae agunt quaerunt utilitatem propriam, et quia a parentibus iam senibus nullam expectant utilitatem, nisi a Deo provenientem." *In ad Eph.*, cap. 6, lect. 1, in *Opera Omnis*, Parma ed., 13:498–99.

727 *Gaudium et spes* §22 asserts that this participation in the paschal mystery is possible for non-Christians: "The Christian is certainly bound both by need and duty to struggle with evil through many afflictions and to suffer death; but, as one who has been made a partner in the paschal mystery, and as one who has been configured to the death of Christ, will go forward, strengthened by hope, to the resurrection. All this holds true not only for

Christians but also for all people of good will in whose hearts grace is active invisibly. For since Christ died for everyone, and since all are in fact called to one and the same destiny, which is divine, we must hold that the holy Spirit offers to all the possibility of being made partners, in a way known to God, in the paschal mystery." Flannery, ed., *Vatican Council II*, 186. Note Ratzinger's commentary on this paragraph, which recommends it above *Lumen Gentium* §16 because it more clearly shows the priority of God's agency. Herbert Vorgrimler, ed., *Commentary on the Documents of Vatican II*, vol. 5 (New York: Herder and Herder, 1969), 159–63.

728 *Spe salvi* §38.
729 From Seamus Heaney's poem "From the Republic of Conscience," in *The Haw Lantern* (London: Faber and Faber, 1987), 12–13.
730 *Spe salvi* §28, emphasis in original.
731 *ST* I-II.108.3.
732 "Quaestio sexagesimanona et septuagesima lectione frequenti, meditationeque iugi egent, non expositione." At the start of his commentary immediately after *ST* I-II.69.1 (Leonine ed., 6:456).
733 "beatitudines distinguuntur quidem a virtutibus et donis, non sicut habitus ab eis distincti, sed sicut actus distinguuntur ab habitibus" (*ST* I-II.69.1).
734 It should be noted, however, that the final two beatitudes actually refer to the reward, not the merit. "Et vero quae ad contemplativam vitam pertinent, vel sunt ipsa beatitudo finalis, vel aliqua inchoatio eius: et ideo non ponuntur in beatitudinibus tanquam merita, sed tanquam praemia" (*ST* I-II.69.3).
735 "beatitudines praesentis vitae, quae sunt spei" (*ST* I-II.70.2, obj. 2). The *Catechism* develops this ideas as follows: "Christian hope unfolds from the beginning of Jesus' preaching in the proclamation of the beatitudes. The beatitudes raise our hope toward heaven as the new Promised Land; they trace the path that leads through the trials that await the disciples of Jesus" (§1820).
736 This view reflects Aquinas's understanding of the difference between the old and new laws.
737 "Spes autem de fine consequendo insurgit ex hoc quod aliquis convenienter movetur ad finem, et appropinquat ad ipsum: quod quidem fit per aliquam actionem" (*ST* I-II.69.1).
738 "Beginning" if imperfect; "essence" if perfect. This paragraph summarizes *ST* I-II.69.3, "Whether the beatitudes are suitably enumerated?"
739 "Beatitudo vero activae vitae dispositiva est ad beatitudinem futuram" (*ST* I-II.69.3).
740 Interestingly, in his earlier commentary on Matthew's gospel, Aquinas parsed these three kinds of happiness (sensual, active, contemplative) not as (1) removing obstacles to, (2) disposing to, and (3) beginning future happiness, but instead as (1) removing from the bad, (2) doing good, and (3) disposing to the best. See *Lectura super Evangelium S. Matthaei* (Rome: Marietti, 1951), 69 (lecture on chapter 5, part II, §433). By describing the acts intending active happiness as not simply doing good but disposing to future happiness, and by describing the acts intending contemplation as the

beginning of future happiness and not only disposing to it, Aquinas's later account in the *Summa theologiae* conveys a deeper sense of the participation of secular acts in the eschatological goal.

741 *ST* I-II.69.4, ad 1.

742 *ST* I-II.69.4.

743 "Discedunt etiam aliqui ab operibus misericordiae, ne se immisceant miseriis alienis. Et ideo dominus misericordibus repromittit misericordiam, per quam ab omni miseria liberentur" (*ST* I-II.69.4). The partial definition of mercy as "entering another's chaos" is from James Keenan, *The Works of Mercy: The Heart of Catholicism* (Lanham, MD: Rowman and Littlefield, 2005).

744 Ratzinger similarly discusses the beatitudes in the context of hope in his *Yes of Jesus Christ*, 56–64, but focuses on their Christological basis, their paradoxical structure, and their status as more than "moralism." Ratzinger discusses in detail only the second beatitude ("Blessed are those who mourn, for they shall be comforted"), and his primary purpose is to illustrate the beatitude's paradoxical nature; thus he paraphrases it, in a not entirely clarifying manner, as "Happy are those who are not happy" (ibid., 56).

745 *In Epistolam ad Romanos*, cap. 6, lect 1, *Opera omnia*, Parma ed., 13:60: "Christus enim postquam fuit mortuus, resurrexit: unde conveniens est ut illi qui conformantur Christo quantum ad mortem in baptismo, conformentur etiam resurrectioni ejus per innocentiam vitae. Et hoc est quod dicit *si enim complantati facti sumus similitudini mortis eius*, id est, si in nobis assumamus similitudinem mortis eius, ut ei incorporemur sicut ramus qui inseritur plantae: ut quasi nos in ipsa passione Christi inseramur, *simul et resurrectionis erimus*, scilicet, similitudini eius complantati, ut scilicet in praesenti innocenter vivamus, et in futuro ad similem gloriam perveniamus."

746 *Dei verbum* §18.

747 *ST* I-II.106.1.

748 *ST* II-II.8.7.

749 *ST* I-II.66.6, ad 3.

750 For a specific discussion of the non-mercenary nature of theological hope, see J. le Tilly, *Somme théologique. L'espérance. 2a-2ae, questions 17–22* (Paris: Desclée, 1950), 226–29.

751 For a creative extension and more communal account of Aquinas's view of the beatific vision, see Germain Grisez, "The True Ultimate End of Human Beings: The Kingdom, Not God Alone," *Theological Studies* 69 (2008): 38–61. For a specific examination of the social nature of Christian hope, as modeled on Christ, see Pierre Charles, "*Spes Christi* II: Equisse de l'histoire d'une doctrine," *Nouvelle Revue Theologique* 10 (1937): 1057–75.

752 The reverse applies as well, in that bad acts carry the seeds of their own punishment. Thus, if one misplaces one's desire for the infinite in something finite, then "punishment" inevitably follows, in the form of sadness stemming from a twofold recognition that (1) finite things, as the name suggests, come to an end and so by themselves cannot satisfy eternal longings; and (2) one has forgone a deeper participation in God's love by

exclusively focusing on worldly goods. On the proportionality between punishment and the two basic kinds of sin (turning from God and turning inordinately to mutable goods), see *ST* I-II.87.4, whose *respondeo* begins "poena proportionatur peccato."

753 As John Bowlin suggests in the conclusion of *Contingency and Fortune in Aquinas's Ethics* (Cambridge: Cambridge University Press, 1999), 220. No doubt Christian hope shares some affinities with Stoicism in the sense that they both hold that fortune cannot ultimately erode happiness. Nonetheless, a less truncated account of Aquinas's doctrine of hope, which places it within the breadth of Aquinas's theological vision, undercuts this suggestion. For a stronger contrast between Stoicism and Christianity, see Taylor, *Sources*, 219.

754 Specifically, as hope moves one to charity and its accompanying effect of mercy. See *ST* II-II.30.

755 This comment was made in a lecture at Boston College in 2001, and is recalled from memory.

756 *Spe salvi* §37.

757 *Spe salvi* §36.

758 *Spe salvi* §36.

759 E.g., *Spe salvi* §38.

760 Ratzinger has written eloquently on the power of this witness in the second section of "On Hope," entitled "The dimensions of hope: its Franciscan element," 78–80.

761 *Deus caritas est* §10.

762 *Deus caritas est* §12.

763 See Lonergan, *Insight*, 710–51.

764 Merkt touches briefly and very generally on this idea in the following suggestion of a parallel between efficient/final cause in hope and *exitus/reditus* movement in creation: "Thomas's theology of hope ... which is built upon the concepts of efficient and final causality, certainly seems to express beautifully the *exitus-reditus* schema." *Sacra Doctrina and Christian Eschatology*, 334. But because Merkt's suggestion remains at the level of hope's general causal terms and does not treat the specific divine attributes under which hope approaches God, it cannot give much substance to the argument I am advancing here.

765 *ST* I-II.113.9: "Whether the justification of the impious is God's greatest work?"

766 "The wonder of all wonders: that beings are." Martin Heidegger, *Was ist Metaphysik?* 10th ed. (Frankfurt am Main: Vittorio Klostermann, 1969), 46–47.

767 I am indebted to Robert Sokolowski's reflections in *Christian Faith and Human Understanding* (Washington, DC: Catholic University of America Press, 2006), especially his essay "Phenomenology and Eucharist," on the relationship between creation and resurrection, which I have applied here to hope.

768 "omnis collatio boni supra debitum eius cui confertur, ad misericordiam pertineat" (*ST* I.23.1, ad 3).

769 *ST* I.21.4, ad 4.
770 *ST* I.21.4.
771 "Patri appropriator potentia, quae maxime manifestatur in creatione" (*ST* I.45.6, ad 2). See also the framing of the issue of creation from nothing in terms of power, *ST* I.45.5, ad 2 and ad 3.
772 *ST* I-II.110.2, ad 3.
773 Bouyer, *Christian Humanism*, 101–2.
774 See Aquinas's commentary on Ps. 20:5 (*Opera omnia*, Vivès ed., 18:340): "tria sunt quae debent movere ad sperandum in Domino. Primo divina *providentia*. Homo non consuevit sperare in illis ad quos sui cura non pertinet. Ad Deum autem pertinet cura nostra; ideo dicit, sperat in Domino, cujus est gubernare. Secundum est *misericordia*: Luc. 1, 50: Misericordia ejus a progenie in progenies. Tertium est *potestas*; et ideo dicit, Altissimi: Ps, xc, 1: Qui habitat in adjutorio Altissimi" (emphasis added).
775 These qualities of confidence, trust, joy, and so forth are explored richly in the second part of Bernard's *Theologie de l'Esperance*, "La vie de l'espérance."
776 Adapting Joseph Komonchak's formulation, "What distinguishes the Church from the world is precisely what relates the Church to the world," in "The Church and Redemptive Community," in *Foundations in Ecclesiology*, supplementary issue of the journal *Lonergan Workshop*, vol. 11 (Boston: Boston College, 1995), 167–189, at 186.
777 Tracey Rowland, *Culture and the Thomist Tradition: After Vatican II* (New York: Routledge, 2003), 80–82. The correlations of the other two theological virtues echo Aquinas more closely: faith is correlated to intellect and truth, and charity to will and the good.
778 See, for example, her contrast between the "Aristocratic Liberal" or "neo-pagan" version of self-cultivation (e.g., von Humboldt and Nietzsche), in which "antagonism was necessary for human achievement and progress" and the "Christian notion of original peace." Rowland, *Culture and Thomist Tradition*, 74. Contrast St. Paul: "Suffering produces endurance, and endurance produces character, and character produces hope" (Rom. 5:3–4).
779 Rowland, *Culture and Thomist Tradition*, 78, quoting Russell Hittinger, "Theology and Natural Law Theory," *Communio* 17 (Fall 1990): 402–9, at 403.
780 John O'Malley, "Vatican II: Did Anything Happen?" *Theological Studies* 67 (2006): 3–33.
781 O'Malley, *Four Cultures*, 174.
782 Stephen Schloesser, "Against Forgetting: Memory, History, Vatican II," *Theological Studies* 67 (2006): 275–319, esp. the section "Context: The Challenge of Late-Modern Humanisms," 304–15.
783 Schloesser, "Against Forgetting," 279.
784 Pieper, *On Hope*, 21.
785 Schloesser, "Against Forgetting," 306.
786 "The Transition from a Classicist World-View to Historical-Mindedness," an address delivered at a meeting of the Canon Law Society of America in

1966, in Bernard Lonergan, *A Second Collection: Papers* (Toronto: University of Toronto Press, 1996), 1–9. Schloesser cites this article in "Against Forgetting," 307–8; O'Malley cites it in "Vatican II," 16 n. 27.
787 Boyle, *Who Are We Now?* 5.
788 " 'Message to Humanity': issued at the beginning of the Second Vatican Council by its Fathers, with the endorsement of the Supreme Pontiff," in Walter M. Abbott, ed., *The Documents of Vatican II* (New York: Guild Press, 1966), 3–7, at 5–6.
789 On the humanist concern for the common good, see O'Malley, *Four Cultures*, especially the chapter on humanism: "Culture Three: Poetry, Rhetoric, and the Common Good," 127–77.
790 "Message to Humanity," in Abbott, ed., *Documents of Vatican II*, 6, 7.
791 Avery Dulles, *The Assurance of Things Hoped For: A Theology of Christian Faith* (New York: Oxford University Press, 1994). Dulles also entitled his study of John Paul II *The Splendor of Faith: The Theological Vision of Pope John Paul II* (New York: Crossroad, 2003).
792 Quoted in O'Malley, "Vatican II," 32.
793 That is, on externally observable and legally enforceable acts. On these different styles, see O'Malley, "Vatican II," 18–31.
794 For a history of this issue, see Francis Sullivan, *Salvation Outside the Church?* (New York, Paulist, 1992).
795 *ST* I-II.40.8, ad 1.
796 David Tracy, *On Naming the Present: Reflections on God, Hermeneutics, and Church* (Maryknoll, NY: Orbis, 1994), 11–15. Samuel Eisenstadt, *Fundamentalism, Sectarianism, and Revolution: The Jacobin Dimension of Modernity* (Cambridge: Cambridge University Press, 1999). See also Boyle, *Who Are We Now?* 54–56.
797 See Martin Marty and R. Scott Appleby, *Accounting for Fundamentalisms: The Dynamic Character of Movements* (Chicago: University of Chicago Press, 1994).
798 For recent illustrative examples, see Sam Harris, *Letter to a Christian Nation* (New York: Knopf, 2006); and idem, *The End of Faith: Religion, Terror, and the Future of Reason* (New York: W. W. Norton & Co.), 2004.

Index

act
    charity as, 107–8
analogy of being, 51–52
Aquinas, Thomas
    on Beatitudes, 137–40
    on charity, 88–91, 91–94, 97–100, 107–8
    on creation, 49–56, 123
    on desire, 56–61
    on despair, 124–25
    on faith, 31–32, 37, 62–64, 80–81, 82–85, 91–94, 97–100, 102–7
    on Fourth Commandment, 134–36
    on grace, 61–66, 72–74, 76–79
    on Incarnation, 31–32
    Maritain on, 10
    Moltmann on, 45–46, 70, 142
    on motion, 97–99, 101–2
    on nature/grace relation, 61–66, 76–79
    on virtues, 72–74, 80–94
    Wolterstorff on, 46–47, 129
Aristotle, 58, 76, 93, 99, 101
Art and Scholasticism (Maritain), 10
Augustine, 41, 58, 93
Beatitudes
    Aquinas on, 137–40
Benedict XVI
    on charity, 116, 128–29
    on eschatology, 122–23, 123–24
    on hope, 109, 112, 116, 119, 120, 127–29, 132, 141
Bouyer, Louis, 143–44
Boyle, Nicholas, 8–9, 13
    Christian humanism of, 15, 18–23, 25–27, 38–39
    on human good, 15, 19–21, 114
    on nature and grace, 26
    on transcendence, 15
Buckley, Michael, 37–38
Catechism of the Catholic Church, 133
Catholicism (de Lubac), 114
charity
    as act, 107–8
    Aquinas on, 88–91, 91–94, 97–100, 107–8
    Benedict XVI on, 116, 128–29
    and faith, 89–90
    and hope, 89–90, 91–94, 97–100, 107–12

and participation, 88–89
and theological virtues, 91–94, 107–8
Christian Hope and Christian Life (Greer), 41–43
Christian humanism. *See* humanism, Christian
Clarke, W. Norris, 4, 50–51
Commentary on Boethius's "De Trinitate" (Aquinas), 64
Commentary on Posterior Analytics (Aquinas), 105
Compendium theologiae (Aquinas), 72
creation
 Aquinas on, 49–56, 123
 and God, 49–56, 142–44
 and hope, 142–44
cross, hope and, 113–17, 121–22, 136, 138–40
Culture and the Thomist Tradition (Rowland), 146–47
Daley, Brian, 127
Dawson, Christopher, 6–7, 13, 122
de Lubac, Henri, 114
despair
 Aquinas on, 124–25
 and hope, 124–25
De Spe (Aquinas), 110–11, 114
Deus Caritas Est (Benedict XVI), 116, 128–29, 142
Dickinson, Emily, 18
Donne, John, 41, 42
Duffy, Eamon, 13
Dulles, Avery, 150
eschatology
 Benedict XVI on, 122–23, 123–24
 hope and, 115–18, 121–22
Eschatology (Benedict XVI), 122–23, 123–24
Ephesians, 128, 134
Erasmus, 5
faith
 Aquinas on, 31–32, 37, 62–64, 80–81, 82–85, 91–94, 97–100, 102–7
 and charity, 89–90
 and hope, 86, 91–94, 97–100, 104–5, 106–7, 108–12
 objects of, 82–85
 as potency, 102–7, 108–12
 and transcendence, 97–98
1 John, 61
1 Timothy, 135
Fourth Commandment, Aquinas on, 134–37
"From the Republic of Conscience" (Heaney), 25–26
fundamentalism, 152–53
Gadamer, Hans-Georg, 4
Gaudium et Spes (Vatican II), 2, 6
Girard, René, 30

God
- charity and, 88–91
- and creation, 49–56, 142–44
- as Creator, 49–56
- desire for, 56–61, 77–79
- as efficient cause, 40–41, 42, 50–54
- as final cause, 40–41, 42, 54–56, 85–87
- and hope, 40–41, 42, 85–88
- human as image of, 5, 58–59
- immanence of, 52–54
- as object of faith, 82–85
- as object of hope, 86–87, 116
- participation in, 50–53, 66–69, 88–89, 125
- Taylor on, 14
- and theological virtues, 77–79
- transcendence of, 51–52, 65

good, human
- Boyle on, 15, 19–21, 26–27, 114
- Taylor on, 14, 17, 30–31
- and hope, 120–44
- and transcendence, 26–27, 30–31, 55–56

grace
- Aquinas on, 61–66, 72–74, 76–79
- Boyle on, 26
- and nature, 26, 61–66, 76–79
- and virtue, 72–74

Gregory of Nyssa, 41
Greer, Rowan, 41–43
Haight, Roger, 109
Hauerwas, Stanley, 13, 60
Haw Lantern, The (Heaney), 25–26
Hayes, Zachary, 118
Heaney, Seamus, 25–26, 34
Hebrews, 83, 84, 104, 106
Hill, William, 94
Hittinger, Russell, 28

hope
- Benedict XVI on, 109, 112, 116, 119, 120, 127–29, 132, 141
- and charity, 89–90, 91–94, 97–100, 107–12
- and Christian humanism, 38–41, 112–18, 145–47, 152–53
- and creation, 142–44
- as cruciform, 113–17, 121–22, 136, 138–40
- and despair, 124–25
- and eschatology, 115–18, 121–22
- and faith, 86, 97–100, 104–5, 106–7, 108–12
- and God, 40–41, 42, 85–88, 91–94, 116
- and human good, 120–44

    and Incarnation, 113–15
    Kaufman on, 43–45
    Moltmann on, 45–46
    as motion, 97–112, 148–51
    Murray on, 36–37
    passion of, 74–76
    and pilgrimage, 40, 43, 112–13, 140
    and transcendence, 100, 108–9, 112–17
    as virtue, 76–80
    Wolterstorff on, 46–47
hopes, secular, 120–44
Hopkins, Gerard Manley, 25
humanism, Christian
    of Boyle, 15, 18–23, 25–27, 38–39
    definitions of, 4–5
    history of, 6–12
    and hope, 38–41, 112–18, 145–47, 152–53
    and Incarnation, 31–37, 39
    of Maritain, 9, 11, 12, 32–35
    of Murray, 7–8, 35–37
    of Taylor, 13–14, 15–18, 22–23, 27–31, 38–39
    and Vatican II, 148–51
"Humanism of the Cross, The" (Murray), 36
humanism, secular, 1–2, 5, 17–18, 34
human person
    as image of God, 5, 58–59
    as pilgrim, 40, 43, 112–13, 140
image of God, human as, 5, 58–59
In Face of Mystery (Kaufman), 43–45
identity
    Boyle on, 18–22
    Taylor on, 15–18
Incarnation
    Aquinas on, 31–32
    Christian humanism and, 31–37, 39
    and hope, 113–15
Integral Humanism (Maritain), 9, 11, 12, 32–35
Irenaeus, 5, 35
"Is It Basket Weaving?" (Murray), 35
John of the Cross, 4
Kasper, Walter, 114–15
Kaufman, Gordon, 43–45
Kerr, Fergus, 13, 28
Lash, Nicholas, 13
Le-Bao-Tinh, Paul, 141
Lonergan, Bernard, 149
love, charity and, 88–91, 94. *See also* charity

Man and State (Maritain), 11–12
Maritain, Jacques, 9–12, 14, 22–23, 32–35, 133
Martin, David, 12
Marty, Martin, 152
Massa, Mark, 8
Modern Social Imaginaries (Taylor), 30
Moltmann, Jürgen, 45–46, 70, 142
motion
    Aquinas on, 97–99, 101–2
    hope as, 97–112, 148–51
Murray, John Courtney, 7–8, 35–37, 114
nature/grace relation
    Aquinas on, 61–66, 76–79
    Boyle on, 26
Newman, John Henry, 115
Nichols, Aiden, 16
Niebuhr, Reinhold, 16
O'Connor, William, 59–60
O'Malley, John, 148–51
participation
    in Aquinas, 50–53, 66–69, 88–89, 125
    and charity, 88–89
    in God, 50–53, 66–69, 88–89, 125
passions, 74–76, 79, 94
Paul VI, 38, 145
Philippians, 69
Pieper, Josef, 76–77
pilgrimage, hope and, 40, 43, 112–13, 140
Pius IX, 10
Pius XII, 35
potency, faith as, 102–7, 108–12
Putnam, Hilary, 13
Quaestiones disputatae De veritate (Aquinas), 97
Radcliffe, Timothy, 21
Rahner, Karl, 4, 67, 115
Ratzinger, Joseph. *See* Benedict XVI
Religion and the Rise of Western Culture (Dawson), 7
Romans, 88, 128, 132
Rorty, Richard, 12
Rowland, Tracey, 146–47
Schloesser, Stephen, 10, 148–51
2 Peter, 66
Secular Age, A (Taylor), 12, 14, 16, 29–31
secularization, Taylor on, 17–18, 27–31
Sources of the Self (Taylor), 14, 15–16, 18, 27, 28, 30
Spe salvi (Benedict XVI), 112, 116, 119, 120, 123, 127–29, 132, 141
Taylor, Charles, 9, 12–13

Christian humanism of, 13–14, 15–18, 22–23, 27–31, 38–39
on human good, 14, 17
on transcendence, 14, 17–18, 27–31
Taylor, Jeremy, 41
Torrell, Jean-Pierre, 63, 70, 89
Tracy, David, 140, 152
transcendence
Boyle on, 15
as cruciform, 113–17
as eschatological, 115–18
and faith, 97–98
of God, 51–52, 65
hope and, 100, 108–9, 112–17
and human good, 26–27, 30–31
Taylor on, 14, 17–18, 27–31
Understanding Europe (Dawson), 7
Vatican Council II, interpretation of, 148–51
virtue
Aquinas on, 72–74, 80–94
charity and, 91–94, 107–8
and grace, 72–74
hope as, 76–80, 85–88
and passions, 74–76, 79, 94
theological, 76–80, 80–94
See also charity; faith; hope
Voegelin, Eric, 122
Who Are We Now? (Boyle), 13, 15, 16, 25
Williams, Bernard, 28
Williams, Rowan, 13
Wolfe, Alan, 12
Wolterstorff, Nicholas, 46–47, 129
Wright, N.T., 129

Herder & Herder is proud to present books that celebrate what is distinctive about Catholic theology. Each of these books offers a greater appreciation for the enduring value and urgency of Catholic intellectual life in our new millennium.

Anna Bonta Moreland
KNOWN BY NATURE
Thomas Aquinas on Natural Knowledge of God

In recent decades, Thomas Aquinas has been recruited as an ally by theologians, including post-liberal scholars, who suggest that without proper Christian faith, no person can know God. In this groundbreaking book, Anna Moreland offers a fundamentally different account of Aquinas's vision. Aquinas, she demonstrates, clearly articulates a widespread Catholic view that has recently come under suspicion by both Protestant and Catholic theologians—that God can be known in some way by all persons.

This book is an indispensable resource for everyone interested in major contemporary theological debates, including natural theology and interreligious dialogue.

"A serene contribution to an ongoing debate, yielding further evidence of Aquinas's abiding intellectual valence."—David Burrell, C.S.C. Hesburgh Professor Emeritus in Philosophy and Theology, University of Notre Dame, author of *Aquinas: God and Action*

"*Known by Nature* is a most impressive piece of work, drawing on Anna Moreland's comprehensive command of the relevant texts and her subtle, historically sophisticated interpretations."—Jean Porter, John A. O'Brien Professor of Theology, Univ. of Notre Dame, author of *Nature as Reason: A Thomistic Theory of the Natural Law*

978-0-8245-2481-4 (pbk.)

Of Related Interest

Francis Cardinal George, OMI
THE DIFFERENCE GOD MAKES
A Catholic Vision of Faith, Communion, and Culture

"A scholarly and spiritual collection of essays on the role of the Catholic faith in the modern world, from one of the most thoughtful men in the American hierarchy."

—*Publishers Weekly*

In contemporary American society, it can seem as though there is little room left for religious faith. Is there any need for belief today? Does God make any difference in our lives?

In this wide-ranging vision of Catholic faith, Cardinal George, Archbishop of Chicago, calls us to reflect on how God, revealed in Jesus Christ, makes a difference in everything we do and all that we are. In the light of the risen Christ, Catholics are united to each other, to other Christians, and to people of other religions and no religion at all. By recognizing our identity in communion, we learn that we are not individuals — we can discover our identities only in and through others. Our relations, whether personal or public, make us who are.

To invite use to enter more deeply into this vision, Cardinal George draws from the great voices of Catholic faith, from Cyril of Alexandria, Maximus the Confessor, and St. Francis of Assisi to Popes John Paul II and Benedict XVI. He also weaves in his own experiences of faith — from a moving encounter with a non-Christian in Zambia to the remarkable pilgrimage of young people who observed Pope John Paul II's visit to Mexico City.

978-0-8245-2582-8 (cloth)

Of Related Interest

Grant Kaplan
ANSWERING THE ENLIGHTENMENT
The Catholic Recovery of Historical Revelation

Revelation is one of the most important concepts in Western religious thought. Since the Enlightenment, however, traditional notions of revelation have come under critique, even to the point of being wholly abandoned. In this book Grant Kaplan examines some of the well-known and lesser-known figures in the Enlightenment and post-Enlightenment, showing that a Catholic retrieval of revelation is possible and even preferable to alternative paths.

Major figures and topics include: Lessing • Kant • Fichte • Schelling • Johannes Kuhn • The philosophy of history • German idealism • The Catholic Tübingen School • The genealogy of modernity • Faith and reason

978-0-8245-2364-0 (pbk.)

Of Related Interest

Robert Barron
THOMAS AQUINAS
Spiritual Master

Catholic Press Award Winner!

Thomas Aquinas is widely considered the greatest and most influential of Catholic theologians. Yet too often his insights into the nature of God and the meaning of life are seen as somehow cold, impersonal, and divorced from spirituality. In this award-winning book, Robert Barron shows how Aquinas's profound understanding of the Christian mystical life animates and helps explain his writings on Jesus Christ, creation, God's "strange" nature, and the human call to ecstasy.

978-0-8245-2496-8 (pbk.)

Check your local bookstore for availability.
To order directly from the publisher,
please call 1-800-888-4741 for Customer Service
or visit our website at *www.CrossroadPublishing.com*.

ABOUT THE AUTHOR

Dominic Doyle is an assistant professor of theology at Boston College's School of Theology and Ministry. A graduate of the University of Cambridge and Harvard Divinity School, he received his doctorate in systematic theology from Boston College. His writing has appeared in *Theological Studies, Gregorianum, Irish Theological Quarterly,* and *Studies in Spirituality.* His theological interests include theology of culture, doctrine of God, and theological anthropology.

Dominic has received a number of awards, including a John Templeton Award for Theological Promise, the Catholic Theological Society of America's Catherine LaCugna Award to New Scholars, and an Analytic Theology Course Award from the University of Notre Dame's Center for Philosophy and Religion. He has also participated in the Institute for Advanced Catholic Studies' Generation in Dialogue Program with Bernard McGinn and in a Wabash Center Workshop on Teaching and Learning. He is presently working on a book on the relationship between positive psychology and the theological virtues. A native of the United Kingdom, he lives in Boston with his wife, Tracy.